THE
COPPOLAS

THE
COPPOLAS

A MOVIE DYNASTY

IAN NATHAN

PALAZZO

First published in 2021 by Palazzo Editions Ltd
15 Church Road
London, SW13 9HE
www.palazzoeditions.com

A CIP catalogue record for this book is available
from the British Library.

Hardback ISBN 978-1-78675-122-5
eBook ISBN 978-1-78675-043-3

Bound and printed in the UK
10 9 8 7 6 5 4 3 2 1

"The measure of a work of art is from how deep a life does it spring."
James Joyce

"The whole family has got that virus."
Bill Murray

CONTENTS

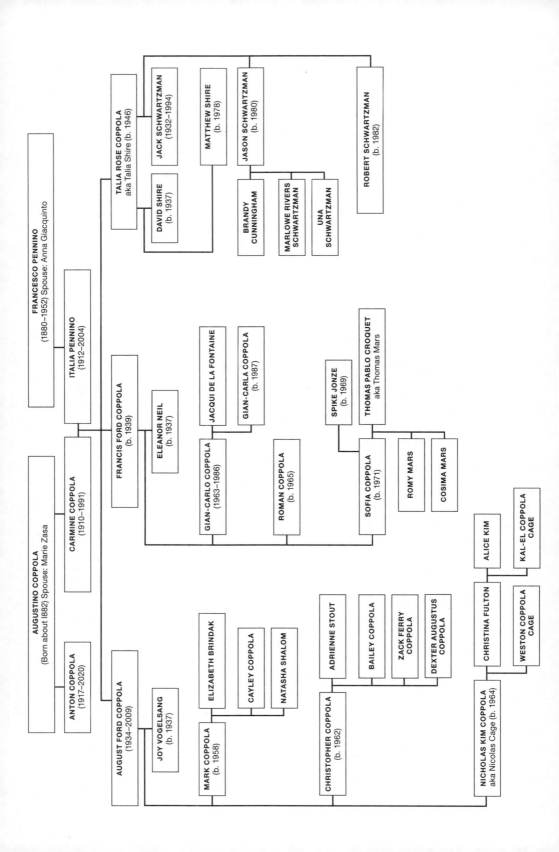

PROLOGUE

The storm only grows in intensity. Outside in the dimming light, the roads are becoming flooded. Soon all they can see is rainfall as if a veil has been lowered over the world. Water is leaking in through the walls, spilling from room to room, and lifting the carpet. People are rolling up their trousers and wading in and out of the kitchen, shifting perishables upstairs. Spirits remain high. They open bottles of Italian wine and grab for the boxes of pasta, shipped in by the brilliant cinematographer Vittorio Storaro and his crew direct from Rome.

At last, Francis Ford Coppola arrives, soaked through. The director's car has been stuck at an intersection for an hour-and-a-half. He had to get out and push. No one has a chance of making it home, he announces, and does a head count. They had fourteen for dinner, including the editors, who had been there all day preparing a clip reel for potential buyers in Cannes.

So the world's most feted director makes pasta.

We have Eleanor Coppola's perspicacious diary with which to chart a course through these strange times. The intimate details she provides of life during the making of *Apocalypse Now*. Life, you might say, during wartime.

The children are unfazed by calamity: Gio and Roman are playing poker, and Sofia, only five years old, is dashing around the backyard in her raincoat, chasing frogs. Mud is streaming into the swimming pool. *La bohème* soars from the stereo that had been sent from San Francisco at the director's request. But opera struggles in vain against the endless percussive rain: censure from the gods in the form of a typhoon sweeping in from the South China Sea. They have to shout to be heard.

It is a fine dinner. How Coppola loves to cook. It is an act of creation with instant rewards and an appreciative audience. Cooking eases his burdened mind. Halfway through the meal, the electricity goes down. They have dessert by candlelight, gathered around the long table. He sees how wonderful their faces look in the orange glow. Catching the flickering light, casting shadows on the wall.

He wishes movies could be this perfect.

When the rain eases, they try and sleep. But at 4 a.m. the electricity is revived and *La bohème* starts up again, and the espresso machine begins to steam.

PART I
FRANCIS

CHAPTER 1

WILL POWER

The Early Years, Dementia 13 (1963)

Francis Ford Coppola is unafraid as the ambulance argues its way through the streets of Queens. He can hear his parents weeping. He knows this is a family crisis. But it is as if this drama is happening to someone else, another pale boy, and he is writing the story as it unfolds. Outside a blur of burgeoning New York prosperity is left in their wake: supermarkets rivalling family stores, the latest boast of movie marquees, rusting trams overtaken by curvaceous Fords, Buicks, Pontiacs, maybe the occasional Cadillac Coupe de Ville. Given the chance, he would have taken note of it all – the bright textures of post-war America.

His mother blames that overnight campout with the Cub Scouts, one of the extracurricular offers provided by Brooklyn's New York City School – the latest slab of public education in which he is proving an unremarkable student. Italia and Carmine Coppola are regularly called in to discuss their son's academic shortcomings.

The camping expedition had fallen victim to terrible weather. Not quite the biblical whirlwinds that await Coppola and the Philippines in an unforeseeable future. It had nevertheless rained non-stop, turning the campsite into a prophetic quagmire. The boys were sleeping in dirty water. On his return, Francis complained of a stiff neck. His unimpressed father packed him off to school. With the stiffness spreading through his limbs, the school nurse didn't hesitate.

Before he knew it, his parents had been telephoned, thrown into anguish by the sudden diagnosis, and he is bound for Jamaica Hospital, the red brick edifice on 89th Avenue crowned with an American flag. Inside is a mesmerising tableau. We picture it with the hungry lens of one of those celebrated montages. There are kids everywhere, stashed in bathrooms, piled high on racks, and out in the hallways. Polio is rife in the city. As night falls, it is the cries of the other children that finally frighten him.

The year is 1949, and a nine-year-old boy calls out for his mother in the dark. Is it significant that this is the age when Vito Corleone sets off for America in *The Godfather Part II*?

Coppola recalled his childhood trauma with practised art, the memories as sharp as sunlight. How the next morning he had climbed out of bed and collapsed to the floor. He couldn't lift himself up. His left arm, left leg, and back were completely paralysed. They kept him in hospital for a week, before Carmine brought him home to their 212th Street apartment. His parents were distraught as they pinned him beneath the cold bed sheets to make sure he wouldn't fall out.

They took him to a French doctor, a family connection, who spoke in measured tones. He needed to understand he would never walk again.

So began the year that never was. Struck down with polio, Coppola was bedbound and mostly alone. He was a pariah, unclean, too contagious for neighbouring children to be allowed to visit. The only company of anyone close to his own age was his devoted older brother, August, and occasionally his younger sister Talia.

There was a day when Italia carefully lowered him into the bathtub and then the doorbell had rung. He remembered slipping inexorably down the smooth porcelain. The hot water had reached his nose when his mother burst back into the room. In *The Conversation*, Gene Hackman's unravelling wiretapper Harry Caul extracts an identical story from a childhood afflicted with illness.

Salvation came from the bonds of family.

Carmine chose to ignore the doctor's dire forecast. With financial help from the March of the Dimes – set up by Roosevelt to stem the tide of polio – he sought out a physiotherapist. Inch by inch, Coppola, scarecrow-thin as a boy, was taught to move his bony limbs. Through the ministrations of his therapist and parents, he willed himself into recovery, first his arms, then his legs. It was like being reborn.

Adversity changes you. Maybe even defines you. Physically, polio left him with a slight limp. Somehow, he joked, it was most pronounced when he had an arm round a girl. He would never be athletic, but he grew robust. Those limbs would never fail him again. But on some psychological or spiritual level he knew that you are never the same person. "Generally, I feel that people who have been traumatised tend to develop levels and wrinkles that really add something to them."

Adversity certainly wasn't done with him yet. But if he hadn't come close to death, he would never have lived. Truly lived, that is. The adventure that unfolded across the following seven decades is unparalleled.

Coppola was not idle in his solitude. And this is key. He allowed his imagination to roam where his body couldn't. He was glued to the black-and-white Motorola television his father had brought home when he was seven – a rare luxury in their neighbourhood. There were cowboy movies, and the science-fiction serial *Captain Video and His Video Rangers* on the DuMont Television Network. Even before his illness, Coppola loved *The Floor Show* on NBC, especially ventriloquist and inventor Paul Winchell, who traded lines with his uppity puppet Jerry Mahoney. Coppola had an autographed picture of Winchell above his bed, and a replica dummy of Jerry sitting on a nearby chair. He taught himself to do routines, entire conversations with his replica friend. He mounted elaborate shows, selling tickets to his family. Telling them stories.

Almost forty years later, in *The Rainmaker*, a jazzy legal thriller stalking the injustices of America's medical insurance system, Johnny Whitworth's leukaemia victim has a ventriloquist's dummy at his bedside.

On Sunday mornings was Coppola's favourite: the Horn & Hardart's *Children's Hour*, a variety show cast entirely with children. As sponsored by the self-service Philly restaurant chain, whose trademark vending machine fad is satirised in his zaniest film, *You're a Big Boy Now*.

"The most gorgeous little girls in the world sang and danced," he reminisced. The spirit of collaboration among the kids moved him. Long before he ever thought of becoming a director, he began dreaming up a studio. A place, he said, where like-minded people could work together like children, "with music, puppets, scenery, lights, dramatic action, whatever we wanted to do."

The great collective promise of American Zoetrope was born in the haze of convalescence as he surrounded himself with imaginary collaborators.

Relatives came bearing gifts. Alongside precious access to the household television, his father provided a radio, record player, and reel-to-reel tape recorder. They shared a love of gadgets and innovation, the fine wiring of the great entrepreneurial American spirit. These were the poles of the Coppola soul: science and storytelling, technology and theatre.

His maternal grandfather and namesake, flamboyant Francesco Pennino, arrived one day with the wondrous offering of a 16mm projector. Coppola began to experiment. Using his father's tape recorder, he made up soundtracks, talking like Mickey Mouse, which he strained to synch to the old family movies clicking through the projector. "I could never quite get it," he said, still frustrated. He began to edit the scenes of family life with scissors, trying to give them pace and drama. "I'd make myself the hero," he said.

Out of adversity comes art.

Francesco Pennino had a thing for the movies. Landing in New York in 1905 – in view of Lady Liberty – he passed through the vaulted halls of the immigration centre on Ellis Island in search of a land of opportunity. Behind him was a penniless youth in Naples. An Italian songwriter and musician, he had come to the New World to make his fortune. And so he did. Serving as pianist to the great operatic tenor Enrico Caruso, with his cleft chin and heavy-lidded eyes, later the victim of extortion by émigré Sicilian gangsters known as the Black Hand. Pennino's songs leaned more toward the Neapolitan tradition: grand stories of the heart filled with tragic turns and lost loves. He ran a Brooklyn theatre, composed and performed, but movies stole him away.

He delighted in the embryonic art form. So ripe with melodrama, they were songs made of light. He became acquainted with one of the partners in what became Paramount Pictures, the studio that was to have such a dramatic part to play in the fortunes of his grandson. Family legend – every Italian family carefully curated and embellished a tapestry of colourful stories – has it that Pennino's firm, The Paramount Music-roll Company, is the source of the studio's grandiose name. Furthermore, Paramount offered him the chance to compose scores for its swelling slate of silent films, but with an innate distrust for these emerging Hollywood types he chose to go it alone. That instinct would run in the blood.

Another family legend, mostly put about by his son-in-law Carmine, has it that Pennino was known to enjoy the company of breathtaking beauty Pearl White, star of *The Perils of Pauline* serial.

Spying a ready immigrant market for imported Italian silents, by 1931 Pennino ran a string of movie theatres across the New York boroughs, periodically returning to the old country to acquire titles. His daughter, Coppola's mother Italia, a real beauty, was reputedly courted by European studios to become an actress. Pennino was appalled by the notion. Such were the double standards of Italian patriarchs.

Movies and music, invention and guile: this heady turn-of-the-century elixir poured down both sides of the family. In this new country you were free to invent yourself.

Coppola's paternal grandfather cut a more humble figure. Augustino Coppola was a tool-and-die maker, but a talented man. He would help invent and build the first Vitaphone sound-on-disc system for Warner Bros. "The machine that made movies talk," enthused his grandson.

With the new century, Augustino had likewise taken ship for a promised land. Behind him were the untamed Southern hills of Apulia on the shores of the Gulf of Taranto. The Coppolas were peasant stock, and Augustino lavished that same grandson with stories of crime and punishment in the arid heights above the villages, an extensive family mythology of internecine skirmishes and scurrilous banditry. Blood feuds that crossed years, unyielding honour codes. These were not, perhaps, the fabled vengeances of the Cosa Nostra in Sicily, but there were nonetheless gangsters lurking in the gene pool.

There are legends too of Augustino taking money from local New York hoods to oil their guns. But he was a decent man intent on raising the horizons of his seven children. He loved culture, especially music, and pushed his offspring to pursue an instrument. Carmine and his brother Anton proved talented enough to pursue careers as musicians and composers. Shy, stuttering, left-handed Carmine, the wide-eyed boy who had watched those gangsters loiter in his father's workshop, spoke through his flute. He was a virtuoso, but the instrument would become his burden as well as his joy.

Look about: the 20th Century is waking up. The great melting pot of America is the new hope. This immigrant nation made up of a patchwork of tight-knit communities, such as the Italians who poured into New York. Families crammed into the tobacco-brown tenements of a bustling city, where gossip is shared, and stories born. If their children grow up speaking English on the streets, it is Italian at the dinner table. Traditions are upheld – church and family. However, in Little Italy, on the Lower East Side, or Brooklyn, or Queens – throbbing with people on the sidewalks and among the market stalls – electric lights, automobiles, trams, musical halls, and cinemas declare the future is on its way.

Are these not the headwaters of those magnificent contradictions in Coppola's films? The instinct for nostalgia; that caress of period detail. And the press of the avant-garde. Tradition wrestles with change. Silent cinema gives way to sound.

This is the New York both his grandfathers knew as young men. The infant city that Coppola would authenticate with poetry, splendour and violence in perhaps the most perfect passages in all his filmmaking – the Little Italy sequences from *The Godfather Part II* where the slender Vito Corleone, bearing Robert De Niro's dark eyes, begins his ruthless climb toward power.

Backstage at the Radio City Music Hall was like stepping into the *Arabian Nights*. The impressions are vivid: long thighs and high heels, the surging crescendos of the orchestra, a sweet scent of sawdust and sweat. By 1951, Carmine had taken up a full-time role at the glittering Sixth Avenue landmark, and once a month Coppola and his brother were given leave to visit their father's place of work. Carmine arranged the music for the Rockettes, the world-famous high-kicking chorus line. Coppola was transfixed by the lighting console that could alter the entire mood or shine a spotlight to fix the audience's gaze on a single performer.

Carmine's musical gifts had lifted him free of the hardships of childhood. His beloved older brother, Archimedes, who had encouraged him to play, had died at seventeen. Carmine brought his flute to the hospital, promising to make good on his talent.

He gained a scholarship to Juilliard, New York's vaunted arts conservatory. Too young to know better, Coppola had been convinced his father was a "magician". Then he learned it was "musician". But it was still magic. The soft, airy voice of the flute would forever bring back memories of his father, whose practice filled their home with music.

A friend at Juilliard introduced Carmine to Italia Pennino, this quiet treasure born above her father's Brooklyn theatre, and they were soon married.

Italia was a proud mother radiating calm and affection to her children, but in the antiquated tradition of Italian families dutifully fixed in the part of homemaker. Her life hung upon her husband's needs. We can see her delicate cheekbones and amber-brown eyes in the striking features she gave to her daughter Talia, who became an actress. "Mammarella" bequeathed to her second child a love of cooking. Her speciality was calzone with braciole, rolls of beef stuffed with breadcrumbs and cheese. Family meals were vivid rituals and social occasions. Coppola would commemorate his mother's talents in a line of Mammarella pasta and sauces, putting her photo on the label – the smiling Italia, aged seventeen.

"In a family of artists," he said, "she brought magic to our creativity."

It was Italia who kindled the art in her children with games of make-believe, slipping money to a teenage Coppola for the theatre matinees his father didn't take seriously.

After Juilliard, Carmine followed the opportunities that came his way. He had a young family to feed. In the early 1940s that meant the Detroit Symphony Orchestra, but by 1946, when Talia was born, they were back in New York, floating between apartments in the suburbs on Long Island. Carmine became first-chair flautist for acclaimed conductor Arturo Toscanini and the NBC Symphony Orchestra. After that came the opportunity at Radio City, where his brother Anton served as conductor.

They may not have been wealthy, but jolted from apartment to apartment, school to school, the children never lacked for middle-class comforts. Coppola remembered his pre-polio years as a blessed time. All the toys and gifts their doting father bestowed on them, assuaging his guilt at the disruption his career had wrought.

"The family was a living presence," said August: aunts, uncles, and cousins flowed in and out of their lives. They were raised as Americans, but constantly reminded of their heritage. Evenings were filled with folktales and games. And music, of course. Always music. There were family outings to see Broadway musicals. They were raised with a sense of time and technique. "We took life note by note," said August.

It was another gift from their father: to spend their lives searching for a perfect melody.

Carmine brought so much to his children, but Coppola came to understand his father was a disappointed man. Carmine aspired to compose: serious works, songs, perhaps even musicals. He yearned for recognition that never came – to be known in his own right, as befitted his talents. Being a soloist for Toscanini was never enough.

Carmine believed in America. A first-generation son of immigrants, he knew that fame and fortune were the arbiters of one's worth. And talent was the key that unlocked the door to success. This was what made him restless and bitter.

"Talent was a big commodity in our family," recalled Coppola, not long after his father's death in 1991. "My father was very tough on whether you had the gift of talent or not." Lurking in the early biographies is the frank retort that his father "was a frustrated man who hated anybody who was successful."

There was no room in the family for another artist.

Are certain boys destined to become their fathers like Michael Corleone and the Don? Carmine bequeathed to his son that insatiable hunger. "What inspired my father's career," Coppola once said, "was his vanity and his desire to be appreciated."

At night, as Carmine's three children said their prayers, they would always finish by asking God to "give Daddy a break."

To fix the moment in time, Francis Ford Coppola was born in the Henry Ford Hospital in Detroit, Michigan on April 7, 1939. He always hated his name, despite its grand provenance: that of his successful grandfather Francesco, with the distinctive "Ford" in honour of automobile magnate

Henry Ford. This was to commemorate both the hospital of his birth and the fact that at the time of Coppola's birth, Carmine's tempestuous career had blown him to the *Ford Sunday Evening Hour*. Hence the family had relocated to Motor City.

Coppola thought his name was too close to the feminine Frances. At school, his classmates deliberately mistook it for a girl's name. It hardly helped that his mother called him "Francie". Italia had a disheartening habit of comparing her children. August – "Augie" – as tall and handsome as a prince, as well as a model pupil, was the "brilliant one". Talia – "Tally" – was the "beautiful one" and her father's favourite. Francie was the "affectionate one".

For the record, and both siblings have their significant part to play in the Coppola story, August was born on February 16, 1934 in Hartford, Connecticut, and Talia on April 25, 1946 in Lake Success, New York.

With his beatific childhood swept away by polio, he awoke to an awkward body and restless mind. Picture a teenage Coppola, consumed with self-loathing: skinny still, as he would be until his twenties, with horn-rimmed glasses over myopic eyes, conscious of what he thought was an oversized lower lip, cleft chin, and unruly jet-black hair. He thought he looked like Ichabod Crane. Constantly changing schools – he counted twenty-three in total – he found it hard to make friends. He was an outsider, drifting to the library or theatre department as a refuge.

Francis was nothing like his confident brother. Yet there was no jealousy – August was his beacon.

Despite the five-year age gap, they had a special bond. "Like Corsican brothers," said Coppola. They would cut school and take the subway to Manhattan to admire the toys in F.A.O. Schwartz and A.C. Gilbert. It was the chemistry sets that caught Coppola's eye. He saved up the $50 for the A.C. Gilbert Atomic Energy Laboratory, which included a Geiger counter, uranium samples, and a cloud chamber with radioactive needle. Since designated one of the top ten most dangerous toys of all time.

It was August who introduced his brother to the cinema: movie matinees at the Center Theater on Queens Boulevard, near 45th Street, across from the White Castle burger stand. Together they took in special effects driven marvels like *War of the Worlds* and *The Shape of Things to*

Come. Coppola vividly remembered the "psychedelic" *Snow White*. A swashbuckling Errol Flynn, Bela Lugosi, Abbott and Costello: these are the first ingredients to shape the director to come.

However, it was the lavish films of Hungarian producer Alexander Korda that spoke to him. As richly coloured as a jewel box, *The Thief of Bagdad* is his "all-time favourite movie". The adventures of its urchin hero Abu transported him into realms just as he had pictured them in fairy tales. What power, what magic.

Coppola simply wanted to be like his older brother. Grave and worldly, August aspired to be a writer. He knew which books to read, what to say about politics and philosophy. It was August who educated his brother on how to talk to girls; Augie who fired his imagination and widened his horizons.

Weak eyes fiercely focused through beer-bottle glasses, Coppola was, in his own words, a child "of scientific leaning". He took delight in the latest gadgets his father brought home from the shops on New York's "Radio Row". Like the Presto acetate tape recorder Coppola had put to use during his illness, or the record player that gave voice to operas and symphonies.

Coppola experimented and invented. Kids nicknamed him "Science" at school, a cachet he liked. He figured out how to remotely let off bombs in nearby gardens like premonitions of films to come. Still editing those family movies, he got into the exhibition business by charging his friends to watch, running his "own little movie company" out of 212th Street.

He read up on the great scientific dreamers and inventors, the Andrew Carnegies, Thomas Edisons, and Henry Fords, who wanted to make a better world. Ingenuity was what set America apart. What gave you a chance. There was a failed attempt to build his very own television set, and fanciful plans for remote controls, and the introduction of colour, like the candy store of movie screens. Coppola reached for a future beyond his grasp.

Television was like a genie, offering wishes to those who listened close enough. As the schedules swelled through the 1950s into a first Golden Age, he was beguiled. It was television that convinced him he could write plays. "This was a period known for its live, televised dramas," he explained: vivid, socially attuned work by writers like Paddy Chayefsky and Rod Serling, and fast-rising directors like Arthur Penn, Sidney Lumet, and John Frankenheimer. Even though many were filmed live, he could see the "cinematic expression" at work.

Aged fourteen, Coppola is in the kitchen with August fooling around. They re-enact scenes from a romantic movie they've seen. The younger brother begins to look through his fingers, framing the older sibling, imagining he is operating a camera – directing the scene.

Running away from military school sounds like the beginning of a movie. The distinction between life and celluloid begins to blur. At Carmine's insistence, he was enrolled into the prestigious New York Military Academy in Cornwall-on-Hudson thanks to a musical scholarship playing the tuba – the Coppola genes had donated a significant parcel of musical talent, and a love of marching bands orientated him toward the ungainly instrument. We can hear the rousing clamour of brass bands throughout his films.

More than ever, he was a bookish misfit. This was a sporting school where physical prowess dictated social station. Weakened by his polio, Coppola felt isolated and depressed. During football games, he would sit at the back of the bleachers perusing a tattered copy of *Ulysses*, shaping himself into the archetype of the misunderstood hero, or writing love letters for older students at a dollar a page, with the sweetheart's picture provided for inspiration.

Breaking point came when the faculty rewrote his lyrics for the school musical, and Coppola fled to the Manhattan playground he had frequented with August. Carmine and Italia were away touring with a production of *Kismet*. So for three days their son wandered the streets, stumbling into the cinemas and the peep shows on 42nd Street, sleeping in doorways, drifting where the mood took him. The sudden sense of liberation was almost unnerving, and the bright, neon, half-threatening impressions will be channelled into *You're a Big Boy Now*.

August again took pity on his young brother. He was studying literature at the University of California, Los Angeles – forever "UCLA" – and invited Coppola to spend the following summer with him. Laidback, sun-kissed, cultural California suits his younger brother. At ease among the students, he joined in their earnest discussions; learning the latest things to read, the newest things to say; telling the girls, so much older than him, that one day he'll be famous, and when he is he'll buy them a sports car.

Carmine worried that each of his children were showing signs of an artistic temperament. How would they ever earn a living? Was this the American way? Playing the patriarch, he decreed that his offspring take up reliable, no-nonsense vocations. As Talia said, "the biggest thing for Italians was to be a doctor, a lawyer, an engineer, get married." He wanted the best for them, but there was always that subtext. I am the artist.

August, as the eldest, will be a doctor. Francis, so good with technology, will be the family's engineer. Pretty Talia will one day get married and have children.

Hofstra had never seen the like of it. *Inertia* was the first production to be written, produced, and directed by students. In truth, the driving force was a single, unstoppable student. Only Coppola, still in his junior year, had the chutzpah and self-belief to adapt the H. G. Wells story "The Man Who Could Work Miracles", write the lyrics, and direct. Only Coppola could convince the faculty to let him do it. Given the taxing number of set changes, and the complex production numbers, it was testament to the young visionary that it went so well. Belying its title, *Inertia* was a huge success, and Coppola the recipient of his first Dan H. Laurence Award.

"I had the talent to get the show on," he said.

Hofstra University, with its Dutch trees and rare tulips, arboretum and Shakespeare festival, has a bohemian air and Coppola is infected. Seven miles from home, this extension of the New York University in Hempstead, Long Island, mixed law and medicine with the arts. August had attended before going on to UCLA, recommending its liberated attitude to his younger brother, who enrolled in 1955 to major in theatre arts and ignore his father.

"I was a child of the nineteen fifties," he gushed. "Everything was theater."

Tennessee Williams! Elia Kazan! Marlon Brando! These were now his great influences – bottling the lightning of life. There is even a Hofstra production of *A Streetcar Named Desire* to Coppola's name.

He thrilled to the mechanics of theatre, being backstage in the "engine room", accompanied by memories of Radio City. He learned the secrets of scenery, lighting, props, and costumes, and the knack of sewing, rope knots, cooking up animal glue, and coiling cable.

"I was always up a ladder hanging a light, watching the professors work with the actors," he said. That was the next stage, dealing with actors, blocking scenes, and finding the drama. He found he loved the company of actors (there were a number of Coppola performances, but no lightning bolt), and how the soul of the text was found in rehearsal. To all those aspiring movie directors who come begging for wisdom, his advice is begin in theatre. Get the experience of working with actors without the "obligation of the camera".

Enclosed in Hofstra's embrace, the forgotten son would win an unprecedented three Dan H. Laurence Awards for theatrical direction and production, and a Beckerman Award for outstanding services to the Theatre Department (the $200 prize was equally welcome), which he had single-handedly transformed. Even in his element, he plotted revolution.

Coppola was the natural leader, born to it − a young man with a vision. "He doesn't know what he's doing half the time," remembered Joel Oliansky, a Hofstra peer who would follow Coppola to Hollywood, "and the other half of the time he's brilliant." His popularity soared − enough to be elected president of the drama society, The Green Wig, and the musical organisation, The Kaleidoscopians. So he rolled them together as The Spectrum Players, with a manifesto of one show every Wednesday. To do so he took control of the money. The budgets, he realised, came from extracurricular funding, for which the students paid a fee. Yet it was the faculty who always directed the theatre productions.

"We began producing the shows," he delighted. "I made myself director of all of them." Coppola productions became famed for their scope and complexity, and a determination to throw off convention. Attendance boomed.

History will record that the Coppola regime would only last a year. After which the faculty pushed back, introducing a rule that restricted any student to no more than two shows a year. But a mutinous spirit was born. With a young man's idealism, he was enthralled by the Marxist promise of working as a collective. And with an artist's pretension, he longed to be at the centre of everything.

One afternoon on a solemn fall day, Coppola glimpsed a poster on a university noticeboard and in that glance his life was transformed. The poster announced a forthcoming screening of *October: Ten Days That Shook the World,* the silent epic directed by Soviet genius Sergei Eisenstein. "I had never heard of Eisenstein," confessed Coppola.

There were only three people sitting there as the film whirred through the projector, cutting across the church-like hush, and Coppola had never seen anything like it. "I had never seen a film that worked liked that," he said. "On that day I knew I wanted to be a filmmaker."

He saw the film on a Monday, Coppola liked to tell interviewers prospecting for epiphanies. By Tuesday morning he was a director.

Flush with the possibility of storytelling with a camera and the language of the edit, those things he had begun as a stricken boy, Coppola made haste to the library to read up on Eisenstein.

Born in Riga in 1898, the son of a civil engineer-architect and devoted father, Eisenstein ran the gamut of languages, architecture, caricature, and theatrical design before he found his calling. Experimental theatre had filled his head with the Picasso-like possibility of deliberate incongruities. Coppola recognised a kindred soul. Eisenstein likewise admitted that, "he fell into cinema." This strange-looking man, staring out of old photos with an intense, slightly amused gaze, and the domed head of a cartoon scientist, will be his first cinematic guide.

Utilising oblique angles, close-ups, the play of light on seething bodies, and the great flurry of montage, Eisenstein's third film – following *Strike* and *Battleship Potemkin* – was a state funded celebration of the Soviet ideal. It portrayed the tumult of events of the Russian Revolution in 1917 as pure propaganda, but with such cinematic beauty.

Remember this: it is the surging narrative and visual potential that electrifies Coppola. Technology entwined with art. An obsession breaks out in him as strong as polio – his imagination leaps. He takes regular sorties to the Museum of Modern Art, soaks up the greats, drawn to the experimentalists. Another Soviet pioneer, Lev Kuleshov, Eisenstein's tutor, famously juxtaposed images of the actor Ivan Mosjoukine, his face neutral, and shots of a bowl of soup, a child laid out in a coffin, and a woman sprawled on a divan.

The combination of the identical expression with a different image changed the meaning: viewers inferred that the actor was expressing hunger or sorrow or desire. They are reputed to have raved about Mosjoukine's performance.

The innermost power of editing was revealed – the emotional response of the audience could be manipulated by association. A "collision" of images, according to Eisenstein's theory of relativity. It was entirely possible to make an audience feel sympathy for gangsters.

A philosophy was born: Coppola wanted to fuse the immediacy of theatre with film's thrilling dynamism. To bring film closer to a living thing. He sold his car, bought a 16mm camera, and encouraged his theatrically minded peers to help him direct a short film pivoting on Kuleshovian daring. Having taken her children on an outing to the countryside, a woman falls asleep. When she awakens, they are gone. As she frantically searches for her children, what was once an idyllic setting grows threatening. It was never finished.

Besides Eisenstein, we can spy another significant artist who sprang from theatre into film, determined to write his own rules and set himself apart: a large, outspoken yet sensitive personality who would come to incense the Bürgermeisters of Hollywood.

He was named Orson Welles.

Born in Kenosha in 1915, Welles was the son of an inventor and musician, an unhappy man unsuccessful at both. The cherub-like softness and insolent smile contrasting with that cello-deep voice, Welles rose faster and to greater heights than any other, only to fly too close to the Hollywood sun. In New York, barely twenty-two, he launched his repertory company, Mercury Theatre, and set about turning Broadway on its ear. The lighting! The radical staging! The clash of politics and melodrama! He tried to do much the same with Hollywood, a shining light with his band of devoted followers. In *Citizen Kane*, he too made an American masterpiece about a lost soul.

The kinship with Coppola is obvious. Though Coppola has taken greater risks, gained the heat of adulation in his own time, and achieved his version of *Heart of Darkness*.

Lest we forget, Kazan made that leap too, from Broadway triumph to the movie screen, and took Brando with him. He was a first-generation Greek immigrant, born in Constantinople in 1909, and brought to New York when he was eight. Forever the outsider. He tried out acting and stage management and communism, before directing the greatest theatre of his generation. On the West Coast, among the sleepy palms, Kazan pioneered Method, a new reality for the movies.

For now, as 1960 dawned, Coppola knew his path to be true. Graduating Hofstra, he chose UCLA, once again following in August's footsteps, and enrolled in their film school. Crossing a continent to find himself.

Before we depart Hofstra for Southern California, a warning shot from the future. There was such a thing as too much ambition. *A Delicate Touch* was planned to rival Broadway with a thirty-piece orchestra, dizzyingly elaborate musical numbers, and the book and lyrics by Francis Ford Coppola. Beset by technical problems it was abandoned, including a set façade toppling toward the front rows. Disaster was narrowly averted by a quick-thinking stagehand grabbing hold of the tottering scenery.

"If you love something," preached Coppola, many years later, "you'll bring so much of yourself to it that it will create your future." Beneath everything, the many highs and lows that will define his career, runs a passion as deep as the ocean. "My films are my life," he said. And his life will be his films. As he had willed himself to walk again as a boy, he willed his career into existence with everything he had. And a lot that he didn't.

When Coppola arrived on UCLA's Trousdale Parkway campus he was, as with most things, at the head of a wave. In a few short years, a proliferation of like-minded but fiercely individualistic talent would spill out of the film schools to transform an industry: not only UCLA, but its great rival USC (the University of Southern California), and, back East, the halls of NYU. A generation of directors would become household names: Coppola, Martin Scorsese, Brian De Palma, George Lucas, John Carpenter, Oliver Stone, and Robert Zemeckis. Orbiting their world, but never as film students, were friends, adversaries and revolutionaries like Steven Spielberg, Peter Bogdanovich, William Friedkin, Robert Altman, Dennis Hopper, and Paul Schrader. These names will figure highly in the years and pages to come. But we are not there yet. There are only hairline cracks in the dam. Old Hollywood clings on.

In 1960, as Coppola walked into the old Quonset huts from World War II that housed the film department in a woody enclave behind the main buildings, he was met by a hidebound institution. Film wasn't a serious major. As sound designer and future collaborator Walter Murch noted, "it was also this bubble of refuge from being drafted." The Vietnam War was now a factor.

Upon arrival, students were given the disheartening news that only ten percent of them were even going to stay in the film programme. "Our mildest hope was to make an industrial film," said Coppola. Hollywood was an apparition. No one from UCLA had ever directed a feature film.

Immediately, the sunless corridors of the film department felt like a step backwards. Coppola returned to being a loner. There was none of the collective thrill of theatrical productions. Not yet. It was so full of talk. And no girls at all. The core of fellow students who endured cultivated a holier-than-thou negativity, putting down the lazy Hollywood system, thinking they were the next Kurosawa, but always preferring to debate theory rather than getting out there and shooting something.

Among the students was a young Jim Morrison. Among the tutors was an ageing, disenchanted Jean Renoir, who told his stories, and Dorothy Arzner, once the only female director working in Hollywood. Always stand by the camera, she impressed upon Coppola, so that the actors can see your face. The course was sold as a mix of film history and practice, but there was scant opportunity to lay hands on the sparse quota of equipment or time on one of the three ageing Moviolas in order to edit what you had. The 8mm and 16mm cameras were kept under lock and key. The one sound stage was barely a closet. It often seemed as if the one thing you couldn't do at UCLA film school was make a film. That was before Coppola.

Carroll Ballard, who would one day direct *The Black Stallion*, recalled that after a year as a student he had little to show for himself. Yet here he was, roped into being a grip on a film being directed by this effusive, domineering Italian guy who had been there a matter of weeks.

Fired up from his glorified exploits at Hofstra, Coppola schemed his way around prevailing attitudes to make two student films. Revealingly, both contemplated matters of the ego. *The Two Christophers* portrayed a cold-blooded boy who plots to murder a rival with the same name. His next, *Aymonn the Terrible*, was about a narcissistic sculptor who only made statues of himself. The latter demonstrated not only Coppola's growing sophistication as a screenwriter, but the extent of his natural gumption.

Imagining the protagonist framed beside Michelangelo's David, Coppola remembers that the Forest Lawn Cemetery has a full-sized replica of the statue. So what if filmmaking was strictly forbidden on cemetery grounds? He appeals to their better natures. Who could refuse a poor student and his modest crew? Next he calls upon the Chapman Company, purveyors of camera cranes to the movie industry. On the promise he provides a photograph of a Chapman crane beside the statue of David, he negotiates the loan of their largest model, gratis. To the dismay of the groundkeepers, this humble student filmmaker arrives at Forest Lawn with a sixty-man crew, including Ballard, and a crane as tall as a Ferris Wheel.

The other students held him in awe. What you might consider a love-hate attitude. Coppola had become a cypher for an entire generation's hopes and dreams and managed to have the whole department running to the beat of his drum. He had this irrepressible, almost manic-depressive energy like a ringmaster and clown rolled into one. They began to ask themselves – is this what it took to be a filmmaker?

Coppola wasn't stopping to second guess his methods. "I had this overwhelming urge to make films; not to read about them or see them, just to make them."

The advert from Roger Corman was on the noticeboard. The notorious producer was in need of an assistant, and film students, he knew, made for eager and cost-effective employees. So he went fishing at UCLA, and Coppola took the bait. He was well aware of Corman's reputation, his repertoire, and the opportunity he presented.

Producer, director, impresario, and miserly mogul, Corman made his fortune on the margins of Hollywood. He mixed a combustible temper with a dealmaker's cunning. Considerations of art or taste did not waylay Corman as his factory churned out B-movies as fast and cheap and sensationally as possible. The titles tell you all you need to know: *Machine*

Gun Kelly, Attack of the Crab Monsters, The Little Shop of Horrors, et al. American International Pictures, his distributor, epitomised a subculture of cinema's democratic promise outside of the studios' grasp.

Corman got blood out of stones, semi-clad ingénues, and willing students. Cut away the huckster veneer, and you will find one of the great independent spirits in film history, and that ingenuity rubs off. There was no better film school in Hollywood. Corman's feisty underworld birthed an astonishing array of future talent: Scorsese, Peter Bogdanovich, Ron Howard, John Sayles, and on to the likes of Joe Dante and James Cameron.

The one thing you were guaranteed was hands-on experience. If you were nearby you joined in.

Arzner put in a good word – this kid doesn't stop. Coppola was in an increasingly tight spot. He was barely living off his father's $10 cheques. On the day Corman's people were due to call back about an interview, his phone was about to be cut off. "So, I'm sitting by the phone saying, 'Please, please don't cut it off!'" The phone rang. He had the job. Two hours later the line went dead. Such are the fine margins in the Coppola legacy.

There were zero airs and graces. Coppola washed Corman's car and moved "the sod" on his lawn, while serving as script doctor, production assistant, and second-unit director. In its clammy way it was akin to Hofstra. You knew a glue pot and paint brush, but you also got to serve as dialogue director on the *Tower of London* with Vincent Price. That was exhilarating.

Verifying Coppola's first feature film isn't easy. Even before his exploits with Corman, there are forays into the underworld. His early days are a little foggy, creatively and morally. Definitions blur. Though, he remained candid about it all.

So what if he made two nudie pictures? They may not be Eisenstein, but this was work with a camera for which he was being paid. We are hardly talking pornography. After Russ Meyer had escaped obscenity charges and made a pot of money out of the x-ray vision comedy *The Immoral Mr. Teas*, investment flooded into ultra-low-budget exploitation flicks. As with Corman, less principled film students provided cheap labour behind the camera.

So Coppola wrote and directed *The Peeper*, a short about the comic escapades of a Peeping Tom. *Tom and Jerry* stuff according to the director, and shooting the nudity made him uncomfortable. His mother's stern warnings to treat women with respect rang in his sensitive ears. "Some people saw it, and offered to buy, but they themselves had already shot a vast amount of footage of Western nudie, about a drunken cowboy who hits his head and sees naked girls instead of cows."

Coppola was set the task of intercutting the two films under the title *Tonight for Sure* – squaring up the narrative by adding scenes of the two protagonists meeting up to tell their stories. Most of it isn't really his film at all, but there for the first time in the credits it says, "Directed by Francis Ford Coppola."

That was something.

Next thing he knew, he was shooting twelve 3D minutes of *Playboy* model Jane Wilkinson to be edited into a black-and-white German nudie. With this cocktail, entitled *The Bellboy and the Playgirls*, Coppola contrived another light-hearted tale of would-be voyeurism with a bellhop spying on lingerie models.

His first official duty for Corman was re-editing a Russian science-fiction import called *Battle Beyond the Sun* for a princely $250. The producer had picked up the reels for next to nothing, and Coppola persuaded his boss that he could speak Russian. Find a story that makes sense for an American audience, he was instructed.

"Monsters play well at the drive-in," Corman made clear. "Communism does not."

Unable to decipher the Soviet plot, Coppola invented the entire storyline and dubbed dialogue. He then headed to his bathtub with latex to stage a fight between two monsters, a male and female per Corman's directive, one perhaps a little like a penis, the other maybe resembling a vagina.

It was Corman who taught him to be self-reliant.

Observe Coppola in his frenzy: still UCLA's brightest, attending lectures, screenings, seminars, stirring up revolution; every spare hour spent at Corman's beck and call; and now, by night, at his typewriter, wired on pots of coffee, churning out an original screenplay in one marathon session.

The next morning he is due to take a physical for the draft. Vietnam looms like a storm cloud. The loose, crazy plan is that his exhaustion will cause him to flunk the examination (his polio hasn't proven an issue).

Somehow he passes; eight hours later back in his rooms he passes out. Somehow he is never drafted.

Such is the duality of these formative days that the screenplay in question, *Pilma, Pilma* – a reconfiguration of *The Two Christophers* by way of Tennessee Williams (he never aimed small) – won the prestigious Samuel Goldwyn Award. This was a rare victory for a screenwriter over a novelist. The kind of thing studios paid attention to.

This pattern of fevered struggle would become a habit: a way of drawing the best from himself, demon nights at the typewriter. Chaos suits him.

Upon receiving his $2,000 prize, Coppola went straight out and bought himself an Alfa Romeo sports car. He would drive through LA and feel as if he had made it. That became a habit too – a taste for the good things in life.

Dementia 13 is the debut movie that tends to stick. The one deemed official by polite filmographies, and a treatment he drafted in one night. In early 1962, Coppola was crisscrossing Europe in a Volkswagen minibus outfitted for the buoyant crew of Corman's *The Young Racers*, a Grand Prix epic that saved on mounting expensive races by shooting actual Grand Prix.

"You know anyone who can do sound recording?" Corman had asked a few weeks earlier. Anyone cheap.

"I can," volunteered Coppola, before heading home to read the manual. Once they were shooting in Monte Carlo, France, Belgium, and England, Coppola was doubling up as second-unit cameraman, recklessly spread-eagled by the trackside clutching a handheld camera. Has he ever found filmmaking quite as thrilling again?

On wrapping the film in Liverpool, Corman had to rush home to direct *The Raven*, with Vincent Price, Boris Karloff and Peter Lorre waiting. "A wonderful picture," reminisced Coppola. Edgar Allan Poe brought out the flamboyant in his chief and presented his assistant with an opportunity. Corman's hasty departure had curtailed the usual policy of squeezing two movies out of any cast and crew if he could.

Coppola seized his moment, producing the treatment he had written, bent over his typewriter on the floor of his hotel room.

His title was *Dementia*, and in truth he had little more than a strange scene with which to entice the producer. "A man removes his clothes and dives to the bottom of a murky pond," he explains, "in his hand is a set of dolls that have been tied together…"

"Change the man to a woman, and you can do it," responded Corman, offering a threadbare budget of $20,000. The producer also added the unlucky "13" to the title – so they could persuade theatres to play the movie every 13th.

Left to his own devices, Coppola is gripped by a new energy, and that old guile. He doubles his budget by selling the British distribution rights to producer Raymond Stross, and hops across the Irish Sea to shoot out of Ardmore Studios in Ireland, close to a ready supply of English-speaking actors in Dublin. For exteriors, the gothic sprawl of Howth Castle provides a suitable supply of crenulations, crosses, arches, and gravestones, plus a reed-banked pond. During the unending slog of *Apocalypse Now*, stretching like purgatory across years, he must have thought back to his debut, shot in nine days flat.

His thinking was commercial. "*Psycho* was a big hit and William Castle had just made *Homicidal*, and Roger always makes pictures that are like other pictures. So it was meant to be a horror film with a lot of people getting killed with axes and so forth."

So what do we have? Written in a feverish rush, it is fussily plotted – shrill, venal blonde Louise Haloran (Luana Anders) comes in search of an inheritance to her in-law's lonely mansion, staying quiet about her husband's sudden death in the prologue. It is Anders who plunges to the bottom of the pond in her underwear with a handful of dolls, fake evidence of a ghostly child with which to rattle the matriarch's fragile heart. Surfacing, she will be met with a swooping axe.

The early death of the leading lady was an idea nakedly borrowed from *Psycho*. It's the best scene.

British actor Patrick Magee, kept on after *The Young Racers*, launches into long speeches with showboating relish as the family doctor determined to unravel the mystery. The Halorans have a stew of secrets, including an axe murderer in their company.

Corman would call. Add more sex and violence, no artsy psychological stuff. Nevertheless, there is a literary gleam to its atmospheric setting, supernatural ambiguity, and the old yarn of a family curse – the pedigree of *Rebecca*, *Laura*, and *Jane Eyre*. Coppola mounts a compelling air of menace, with cinematographer Charles Hannawalt doing a sterling job with the angular black-and-white visuals, especially given the director had stolen his girlfriend.

In its own heated way, *Dementia 13* is the first of Coppola's family dramas.

Viewing the work of his debutant, Corman decreed it fair, but it needed at least another beheading, and an explanatory introduction – the film had come in too short and too confusing. Jack Hill was dispatched to make up the short fall, adding the death of a chattering poacher, a fake head bouncing down the woodland path.

In retrospect, Coppola can admire his handiwork. The narrative shortcomings, which are sizeable, are offset by visual range. He had the freedom to consider every shot. "An extremely impressive first effort," if he does say so himself.

The box office returns were enough to earn Coppola some much-needed money. What reviews he received tended to be mixed. "The photography's better than the plot," sniffed *The New York Times* in a critique that would lead to a longstanding family joke when Coppola thought he had read praise for the "solid direction".

August had to put him right. "No, dope, it says 'stolid', not 'solid'."

Before we move on – we must return briefly to the production of *Dementia 13* to record a momentous meeting.

Overdressed in a fur-collared coat, naively thinking that all movie sets were glamorous affairs, Eleanor Neil climbs to the third floor of the old house, where the production office is housed. She is slender and porcelain pale; with her long dark hair parted in the middle you might think Ali MacGraw or a young Natalie Wood. Her first view of her future husband is of a bearded man sitting shirtless in his pyjama bottoms. He is furiously typing, and she catches a scent suggesting that he'd been up all night, grinding out a screenplay on mimeograph pages.

"You had the feeling he was a risk taker," she said. Little could she know how often she would watch her husband in just such a pose: willing his film into existence. From the very beginning he was a runaway train, you either leapt on or got blown aside. Eleanor – "Ellie" – was the only one who ever truly managed to apply the brakes.

We should take a good look at Eleanor in 1962, because she is so vital to this story. She will be Coppola's greatest collaborator, his most enduring supporter, his wife, an artist and filmmaker in her own right, and through her luminous diaries the most lucid biographer we have of her driven husband. Reading the frank and moving *Notes*, her account of the making of *Apocalypse Now*, she is extraordinarily perceptive (and often very funny) about the nature of art and filmmaking, and a woman badly buffeted by the currents of her husband's passions. She will also be confidante, mentor, and mother to Gio, Roman, and Sofia, of course, their three children.

She is pretty and assured, three years his senior, with a cultivated bohemian air displayed in Eisenhower jackets and billowing skirts in a bold mix of colours.

Born in Los Angeles on May 4, 1934, she grew up in Sunset Beach. Her father was a political cartoonist who died when she was only ten, while her mother struggled with the prescribed 1950s model of the pristine homemaking wife. "She was considered eccentric and fought depression," recalled Eleanor, who longed for the father she never knew. He had gone to art school in France, travelled in Mexico. She had his wanderlust and courage, dropping out of college to travel in Europe and South America.

Eleanor is both opposite and a reflection of Coppola – Kay to Michael Corleone, though she hates that – waspy, reserved, shrewd, and deeply empathetic. She is the voice of reason amid the three-ring circus; an observer at heart. But there is otherworldliness. She goes in for I Ching and Zen meditation. Throughout an extraordinary life, she found her spirit torn between her desire to be a good wife and mother, the homemaker, and her desire to paint, design, write, and shoot.

In 1963, she was studying for her masters in applied design at UCLA, where she specialised in tapestries. After travelling to Mexico and Peru, and hitchhiking around Europe, she had come over to join her then boyfriend, Hannawalt. She had to pay her own way and was offered $100 a week to help out the art department.

She began spending more and more time with Coppola. He had such determination and natural authority, but he was exotic too. Intense. She had never known an Italian-American before – someone who could be so emotionally expressive. They became inseparable.

"In my naïve and romantic young mind I imagined Francis would continue to make small independent films and I would work with him."

The wedding was a surprisingly small affair. Eleanor had a job in Las Vegas, hanging one of her tapestries in McCarran Airport. She hadn't even met his parents yet.

On February 2, 1963, with ten family members, they found a chapel, tied the knot, and stayed at the Dunes. The next day her mother treated the couple to a helicopter ride – which might have been an omen. That was it. No *tarantella*, no cash in white envelopes.

A week earlier, when Eleanor had learned she was pregnant, Coppola had been away working on a Corman movie. She considered her options. Abortion was illegal in 1963, and she hadn't the nerve to research illegal means. So she could either give the baby up for adoption, or get married. Her voice was calm as she told Coppola, not wanting him to feel any pressure. She watched as joy filled his eyes and voice.

"I've always wanted a family."

CHAPTER 2

MOVIE BRAT

You're a Big Boy Now (1966), Finian's Rainbow (1968),
The Rain People (1969)

The USC boys would pile into their beat-up cars and dare the freeways to Burbank, where he had an office on the Warner Bros. lot. By 1967, Francis Ford Coppola was already a legend. He alone had pulled open the door and let in a crack of light – the possibility that a rumpled nobody with horn-rimmed glasses, fresh out of film school, could make movies on the studio dollar. Buddha-like, he would preside over discussions as his acolytes shared their plans to reshape Hollywood and dream projects they longed to get off the ground.

It was thrilling to be within the four walls of the legendary Warner backlot. However much they wanted to upset this shiny apple cart, they were still titillated by the history of their surroundings. Outside the window, the famous water tower stood sentinel over the rows of soundstages – the factory floor of the golden era.

Among their number was skinny, bespectacled, director-in-waiting George Lucas from Modesto, California; New York born Walter Murch, a real intellectual destined to become one of the industry's defining sound designers; and John Milius, a big man with a big personality from St. Louis, Missouri, who will prove to be a great writer, sometime director, and full-time agitator.

There was an irony in the appointment of Coppola as scout leader. After all, he was an alumnus of UCLA, the great rival. "We saw them as drug–crazed narcissists," laughed Murch. "They saw us as soulless technocrats." In simpler terms, USC put the emphasis on the technical disciplines: cinematography, editing, sound, etc., whereas UCLA leaned into storytelling. Students would attend one another's screenings and throw fruit at the screen.

This union of schools, a ragged, unlikely bunch to be sure, was at the forefront of a revolution.

It's a rose-tinted view. And a highly mythologised one. Books have been written to encapsulate the shift in power that took place in the oncoming 1970s: all these joyous creative freedoms granted to young (male) filmmakers. Depictions of the inmates running wild on the asylum lawns in Peter Biskind's dark and detailed set text, *Easy Riders, Raging Bulls*, and Mark Harris's *Scenes from a Revolution*.

To be precise, Coppola is not a Movie Brat. He was among the first wave of New Hollywood, three films down as it crashed on the Californian shore. Which dates him alongside William Friedkin, Peter Bogdanovich, Dennis Hopper, Mike Nichols, Bob Fosse, and Woody Allen. But it seems like a churlish technicality not to include him in the second wave. The ones designated as the Movie Brats. These were his friends and followers, the film students made good, who he led out of the wilderness, Moses with a light meter: Lucas, Milius, Murch, Carroll Ballard, Caleb Deschanel, and Willard Huyck, their number bolstered by Martin Scorsese and Brian De Palma, heading West from New York, and an eager upstart who had already worked in television named Steven Spielberg.

All of them had their eyes glued to the international scene, where cinema had broken the shackles of tradition. Not only with the French New Wave, but arthouse darlings like Ingmar Bergman, Akira Kurosawa, Milos Forman, Roman Polanski, and the Italian neo-realists, who along with their lion-taming compatriot Federico Fellini were dispensing with plot and flowing on emotional impulse.

The Movie Brats were enamoured with auteur theory. Invented by French critics, swooning over Hitchcock and Ford, it declared the director to be the sole author of a film. But here lay a paradox: filmmaking by definition is a collective process made up of cast and crew, producers and executives. At its best, they form a surrogate family enterprise. It is one of the things that drew Coppola to the light. As his ambitions grew, he gathered bigger and bigger families around him. Yet as the French said, this was an era defined by individualistic directors fighting for their vision against the age-long conformity of the studios.

They had things to say – more than they knew.

"We were running too fast for anyone to stop us," said Coppola, sharing a stage with Scorsese, both grey-haired and pot-bellied in later life, but the old sparkle is undimmed. There was none of the middle management they have now, he added. The director could still be the acknowledged author.

This friction – auteur versus team, moneylender versus artist, collective aspiration versus singular mind – ran through the heart of New Hollywood. One that would be manifested most dramatically in the fortunes of Coppola – arguably, and it is a very good argument, the foremost filmmaker of the era.

According to Biskind, New Hollywood spans from 1967, with *Bonnie and Clyde*, to 1980, with the groans of *Heaven's Gate*. Within those bounds lie Coppola's crowning achievements: two *Godfathers*, *The Conversation*, and *Apocalypse Now*. But hindsight is easy. For Coppola, such freedoms were never freely given. He had to fight for all of his films. Moreover, beyond the glorious 1970s, lie many more fascinating expressions of his talent.

What is undeniable is that Coppola was the one who took the chances, gambling his savings, homes, and reputation on the next dream. He forged the path that others followed.

"He was the one who made us hope," said Lucas.

"He always said we were the Trojan horse, but that wasn't quite true, because he was inside opening the gate," proclaimed Milius, whose knack for a rhetorical flourish would be invested into *Apocalypse Now*. "None of those other guys – Lucas, Spielberg, all of them – could have existed without Francis's help. And his was a much more interesting influence than theirs. Francis was going to become the emperor of the new order, but it wasn't going to be like the old order. It was going to be the rule of the artist."

But we are getting ahead of ourselves. The year is still 1963, and Coppola's early experiences of the old order will be a succession of hard lessons.

Married, with a young son, he could no longer indulge the low pay and extended hours of Roger Corman's workshop. The last assignment of his B-movie apprenticeship was finishing *The Terror* in Big Sur, a sub-Poe Napoleonic-era muddle of mysterious barons, missing girls, and inevitable crypts, with a fading Boris Karloff and rising Jack Nicholson. Given four days to wrap things up, Coppola took twelve, looking for shots, and forcing Nicholson to brave the surf in full Napoleonic raiment. The fledgling superstar claimed he nearly drowned; Coppola only remembered the grousing. Returning from the Pacific coast, he said farewell to Corman, with no hard feelings. Another protégé was off to make his way in the big leagues. Homage to his early mentor would be paid in asking the mogul (and show-off) to cameo during the senate hearings in *The Godfather Part II*.

More serious work now lay ahead of him. His Samuel Goldwyn screenwriting prize was opening doors. Within a week of returning from his wedding, Coppola was offered the chance to adapt Carson McCullers's *Reflections in a Golden Eye* – melodramatic entanglements on a military base in the American South – for literary-leaning production company Seven Arts. He was a cheap option, he was well aware of that. "Some shlump," he said. But compared to Corman, $375 a week for a six-week stretch was life-changing money.

Led by the mercurial former theatrical agent Ray Stark, Seven Arts blew a lot of hot air in his direction after he delivered his script. Who is this genius? Surely, it was Dalton Trumbo writing under another pseudonym. "They gave me all that junk," he recalled. A much more ready reward was a three-year contract to join the writing staff. This meant dropping out of UCLA finally, which didn't require much soul searching. His extracurricular exploits were generating snide remarks from his purist peers, obsessing over Godard.

The day after he got his first job as a screenwriter, he found a sign on the bulletin board denouncing him as a "Sell-out!" There was an open resentment that he was out there making money. The truth was he was breaking down antiquated barriers between the film schools and studios – he had found employment! The idea he had somehow compromised his values was like a thorn pressed into his mind. Would art always have to wrestle with mammon?

"The position of the screenwriter is an absurd, ridiculous one," growled Coppola. His time at Seven Arts was a sharp lesson in the circumlocutions of Hollywood. After the manic freedoms of Corman, where everything ended up on the screen, now all his effort was for little to no end.

When *Reflections of a Golden Eye* finally got made, with Marlon Brando and Elizabeth Taylor, director John Huston used an entirely different script. Not one of the eleven screenplays Coppola wrote during his tenure in the Seven Arts writing room ever got to the screen as he wrote them. He was obviously talented, with a knack for tricky adaptations, which would be passed along to other writers to be reworked and reworked again. It was Kafkaesque: a production line where you created something good enough to be turned into something else. Personal expression was glossed into product.

He thought of the playwrights he so revered, for whom the text was sacrosanct. Catching up on the films filtering in from the French New Wave – Godard! – he saw auteurs at work, whose work seemed to burst spontaneously from their Galois-streaked fingertips.

Ironically enough, his next thorny task was to adapt Tennessee Williams's one-act play *This Property Is Condemned* (which he knew well, having directed a version at Hofstra). Stark was under the illusion he was an expert in the American South. Coppola worked on that for months. It was due to be directed by Richard Burton, but he departed, along with Elizabeth Taylor, after clashes with Seven Arts over casting.

Coppola did at least get to meet Williams. He delivered the script for his idol's approval straight to his hotel room. Williams answered the door in his bathrobe, took the script, and then closed it again without introductions. Years later, Williams visited the Coppola winery and shook his hand.

"By the way," he croaked, "could you cash a hundred-dollar check for me?"

Coppola still has that check framed in his library.

Cynicism set in. The failings of this antiquated system were so obvious to him. Left behind at Seven Arts is some of Coppola's finest work. *The Disenchanted*, about another tormented American icon in F. Scott

Fitzgerald – and another who toiled at the Hollywood coalface – is said to be close to his best writing.

Ever the prophet, while at Seven Arts, Coppola suggested to a fellow screenwriter that someone should adapt the comic book *Batman*. This was before even the 1960s television show. He had been hung up on comics as a kid. Decades hence, with the industry dominated by the superhero genre, such early enthusiasm is forgotten. Speaking to the author in 2009, the conversation turned to recent hit *The Dark Knight*, which he accepted was well made. "But in the end," he sighed, "it is just a man in a silly suit."

The next bitter lesson: in 1963, a chasm yawned between screenwriter and director. However vital to the process, writers were a lower caste. Coppola pressed Stark for an opportunity to direct, but it was increasingly clear they had no intention of elevating him to the big chair.

What kept him going was the money. By now, he was on $1,000 a week. The family moved into a stylish A-frame in Mandeville Canyon, and Coppola exchanged his Alfa Romeo for a Jaguar. Cars were emblems of success. As, true to his roots, was family. His first child, Gian-Carlo – "Gio" – was born on September 17, 1963 in Los Angeles. Corman was made godfather.

But the desire to direct was like the pull of a drug. "I would have done anything," he confessed. Even fund his own film. He began to save money. Buying equipment and reels of film when he could. However, it is not in Coppola's nature to wait on providence, and he gambles on a quick fix, risking all his savings, every cent, on the stock market. Scopitone had patented a jukebox that played short films, but there were no takers. He lost it all.

The cycle of boom and bust had begun.

Falling back on Seven Arts, he was dispatched to Paris on a rescue mission. The latest in a final tally of ten writers who failed to find a film in *Is Paris Burning?*, Rene Clement's lumbering World War II epic about the liberation of the French capital. One of its briar-patch of plot-strands follows Gert Frobe's departing General von Choltitz being talked out of Hitler's diktat to burn the city by a bored Orson Welles as the Swedish ambassador. Coppola's predecessor had died on the job, and his impassioned replacement immediately frayed against what he saw as political censorship. For the use of Paris locations, President de Gaulle insisted the screenplay play down any communist presence in the uprising. In fact, Coppola was not allowed to use the word "communist" at all. "It was traumatic," is about all he could muster about the experience. He was a puppet, a functionary, and soon replaced by the more sanguine novelist Gore Vidal. They are the only credited screenwriters, not that either take any pride in a film that manages to be both drab and hectic.

Paris did at least offer the chance to sample French New Wave films fresh out of the oven (making a mockery of the sludge he was wading through). And Paris was where his second child, Roman, was born on April 22, 1965. And to keep his head, it is in Paris Coppola began a semi-autobiographical screenplay, infused with the freedoms preached by Francois Truffaut and Jean-Luc Godard. What will at last take shape as his second film as director, *You're a Big Boy Now*.

Meanwhile, Hollywood began to reshuffle the deck. In need of financial resuscitation, Warner merged with the boisterous Seven Arts, sending a breath of air through the musty old studio, and in more immediate terms landing Coppola an office on the lot. Every day he walked past soundstages and prop shops. Caught the scent of sawdust in the air. This close to the action, he began to scheme his way toward directing three films in quick succession.

But first Coppola wins an Oscar. Well, to get this straight, he writes a screenplay for which he will eventually win his first Oscar. This is Hollywood thinking circa 1966: Fox plan a biopic of the controversial American General George S. Patton and need a screenwriter. Coppola, who knew next to nothing about Patton, had just (about) written *Is Paris Burning?* so is automatically classified as a "war writer". He gives his agent a withering glance, but the fee is $50,000. He goes deep, researching the vainglorious World War II general, and decides Patton is "nuts". His only answer is to strike a course between the poles of the man: brilliant tactician and narcissistic warmonger.

The screenplay for *Patton* took six months, was shelved, revived, and partly rewritten by Edmund North. Out of Franklin J. Schaffner's longwinded 1970 movie, with a stunning central performance by George C. Scott (evidence of what a great actor might contribute of himself to the words), it is Coppola's oddities that still land. Especially the film's meta-opening, which has Patton pontificating his hawk-like philosophy before a gigantic American flag. He had fought for that idea. Another valuable lesson: the things that get you into trouble are usually the things for which you are remembered.

You're a Big Boy Now is Coppola's fizzing cocktail. A heady, ultra-modern mix of everything going: the narrative looseness of the French New Wave, the pop-realism of Richard Lester's *A Hard Day's Night*, *Peanuts*, Disney, sitcoms, and a grab-bag of autobiographical detail, with the familiar streets of New York serving as the playground for its rites-of-passage mania.

How did he leap the chasm? Coppola simply figured out that the best way to get what you want from the studios is to play them at their own game – the deal. The small print in his Seven Arts contract pointed out that *anything* he wrote belonged to them – which meant his new script. So he merged what he had with an adaptation of the similarly themed novel by David Benedictus called *You're a Big Boy Now*. For which Coppola had slyly bought a $1,000 option. QED: the studio couldn't proceed with a film, because he owned the rights. Of course, he had a compromise ready: why don't they let him direct his own screenplay?

He was given a budget of $800,000, and twenty-nine days in New York. Which marked a historic breakthrough. An inexperienced kid who turned up to meetings in jeans and a grin was directing a mainstream film.

The plot is slight. Klutzy Bernard Chanticleer (Peter Kastner) is "dying to grow up", which translates to finding love, sex, and purpose in the big city. As tradition dictates, he is caught between two women: devoted if unassuming librarian Amy (Karen Black) and merciless go-go dancer Barbara Darling (Elizabeth Hartman). But his biggest challenge comes in the shape of his domineering and self-absorbed father I.H. (Rip Torn) and operatically overbearing mother Margery (Geraldine Page).

Something else that attracted Warner Bros.-Seven Arts was Coppola's plan to save money by having unknown leads, keeping the bigger names like Torn and Page for secondary roles.

Can we see a self-portrait in the beaming, bewildered Bernard? He wears thick-rimmed glasses, and eagerly confronts the world with a big heart, only to be frequently crushed by its indifference. He also repeats a variation on Coppola's runaway pilgrimage to Manhattan's sex shops and adult bookstores. Can we read a heightened version of Coppola's parents in the make-up of Bernard's mother and father? Or that Black's slender, reasonable, pretty Amy carries hints of Eleanor? In a highly self-reflexive move, Coppola beams images from *Dementia 13* onto the wall of a psychedelic nightclub.

Before they have shot a scene, Coppola would ride up on his motorcycle to the Manhattan rehearsal space, where he encouraged the actors to develop their characters. At times, it was like therapy. He had this theory – characters should become the actors. But on the first day of shooting he was terrified. He paced the set, fumbling his lines, as the crew awaited instruction. He had to go outside, draw a breath, and compose himself. Then he plunged.

Let off the leash, Coppola is cavalier and extravagant, as if nothing can stop him. The film's theme is freedom, and its style follows. The frantic, screwball storytelling mode may lack discipline, and is only sporadically funny, but it breaks new psychological ground. Note that Coppola's hip bildungsroman predates *The Graduate*.

The director's powers of persuasion proved vital. Here was a sharp lesson – New York doesn't welcome movies, and much of it was shot freewheeling about a real city. Coppola had to win locations by guile or charm. When the Public Library refused him a permit, he appealed to the mayor and got his way. May's Department Store allowed him to shoot a chase scene, but without interrupting its lunchtime rush. Only the crew knew what was going on, with cameras hidden in shopping bags. "It started a riot," delighted Coppola. Poor Kastner got pulled into a fight by a passer-by.

Dowsing for the future, we can see something of its improvisational mania in *Apocalypse Now*. Traces of its surreal zip are found in *One from the Heart* and *Rumble Fish*. The brio of Lovin' Spoonful's contributions to the score would resurface in Coppola's use of The Doors or Tom Waits or Stewart Copeland. Its high spirits are there in *Peggy Sue Got Married*. The run-and-gun shooting style prepared the way for *The Rain People*.

The feel for location is true of nearly all of Coppola's work, and the final ecstatic images of a young couple in love dashing along the streets of New York could have spilled out of *Breathless* or *Bande à part*. Or Sofia Coppola's *Lost in Translation*.

Here, maybe louder than anywhere, is the breath of Coppola's always-make-it-personal approach; the first clue that all his films will come from the heart. And he could charm a performance from an actor – Page would be Oscar nominated for Best Supporting Actress: Hartman for a Golden Globe as Best Actress.

Stranded way ahead of its time, *You're a Big Boy Now* didn't trouble the box office greatly. But it gained entry into the Cannes Film Festival competition, receiving a nomination for the Palme d'Or and establishing a lifelong bond with the French film community.

Critics were measured in their appreciation. The *Los Angeles Times* caught glimpses of "an auteur film." *Newsweek* got ahead of itself and Coppola's career by comparing this young American to Welles and Kubrick. *Life*, however, was only tired out by its "self-admiring brattiness."

That's the one that Coppola remembered.

In a typically outrageous, Wellesian manoeuvre, he also submitted *You're a Big Boy Now* as his master's thesis at UCLA. Which gained him his degree (mostly in absentia). And allowed him the last laugh. The sell-out was prospering.

Times were changing. Albeit slowly. Coppola had gained entry into a waning, cultural power – a business in decline. Once the great engine for a nation's entertainment, by the mid-1960s the studios were these old, white whales; the thrusting moguls dead or dying. Of the legendary names, only Sam Goldwyn and Jack Warner were clinging on – Coppola had met the latter in his early days in Burbank: a handshake, a suspicious glance, no more. The thinking was still antediluvian: musicals and epics with which to defy the monopoly of television. In 1967, *The Sound of Music* became the biggest film of all time, more an indictment of the arthritic age than a success worth celebrating.

Reflexively, Hollywood opted for more of the same.

Funny Girl, *Doctor Dolittle*, and *Star!* rattled into production. Warner Bros.-Seven Arts decided to follow their wheezy (and expensive) Arthurian spectacular *Camelot* with *Finian's Rainbow*, a Broadway oddity from 1947. Written by E.Y. Harburg (who had contributed lyrics to *The Wizard of Oz*), the tone was whimsical toppling into blarney – with a patina of social consciousness. This was an immigrant fable. In this case, the Irish: the recent arrival of Finian and his fragrant daughter Sharon to a sharecropping community in deepest "Missitucky" (a fictional Kentucky) along with a "borrowed" pot of leprechaun gold, able to dispense wishes. On their trail is the leprechaun in question, one Og, with dire warnings about the misuses of magical gold. Power and money can so easily corrupt.

At which point, Coppola's phone rang.

"Listen, we're looking for some director to do *Finian's Rainbow*, with Fred Astaire and Petula Clark," producer Joe Landon barked down the line. "Do you have any ideas?"

Which was a roundabout way of offering him the job. On the general assumption that he had brought heart, zest and evidence of technical verve to *You're a Big Boy Now*, was young and therefore inexpensive, and had written a handful of screenplays camped in the American South. "They wanted to zip it up," he guessed.

Weighing up the offer, Coppola knew there were many cons. Wary of another pricy pageant in the shape of *Camelot*, the studio's commitment ran to $3.5 million and a twelve-week studio-based schedule, far short of the scope and financial backing usually afforded a mainstream musical. They could economise by using the old *Camelot* sets. And this was creaky, patronising, cockamamie stuff. "A lot of liberal people were going to feel it was old pap," saw Coppola, wincing at how the hackneyed portrayal of black farm workers might be received by a burgeoning civil rights movement. And a woefully cockeyed thread in which Keenan Wynn's racist senator has been turned black.

You couldn't get much further from the jazzy bites of life he had designated as his "exceptional" house style. He would be breaking the promise he had made to himself.

But as Coppola contemplated his immediate future, the pros were all too evident. This was a musical – a genre close to his heart. Remember those ambitious productions at Hofstra. And Astaire was a prince of the golden age, a dancer and choreographer beyond compare. *Top Hat, Swing*

Time, The Band Wagon. Only Gene Kelly came close. So what if he was now sixty-eight, there was all that iconic baggage, and a grace still there in his limbs. Pop sensation Clark was providing glamour and creamy vocals for heroine Sharon, with beaming, one-note British hoofer Tommy Steele as the human incarnation of Og, and Canadian lounge singer Don Francks providing luckless local farmer Woody Mahoney with the expressive range of a barn door.

An early draft had proposed a contemporary rethink populated with hippies and folksingers from San Francisco. Coppola hastily reinstated the original period setting, where its unreliable politics could be obscured in the dusty backdrop. He saw it along the lines of *The Wizard of Oz*. A Midwestern fairy tale.

"I thought there was something warm about it," he insisted. "And I thought that maybe if I could do it right, that if I could find the balance, I could make it timeless. It'd be like *Snow White*."

There was also a more personal motivation. "I thought, frankly, that my father would be impressed," he said.

Now we get to the root of it. *Finian's Rainbow*, light and jolly as an Irish jig, was a chance to assuage a pocket of guilt. Back in his teenage years there lay a prank that went wrong, a misjudgment that had left his father crushed.

Coppola had meant well. He could see how heartbroken his father was over his faltering career. So a fourteen-year-old boy, working over the summer for Western Union, hatches a foolish plan to make his father laugh. He fabricates a telegram from the musical director of Paramount Studios, inviting Carmine to come to Hollywood and write the score for the forthcoming movie *Jet Star*. He sends it to the family address. Arriving home, the son sees his father triumphantly waving the telegram in the air. "It's my break! It's my break!" Confessing to the joke, Coppola watches the happiness drain from his father's eyes.

With uncanny presentiment, when Coppola called, Carmine was on the road conducting a production of *Half a Sixpence* (which Steele had headlined both on stage and film). He invited his father to come to Hollywood to help with the orchestration – a genuine offer. Carmine and Talia would make their stay in Hollywood permanent.

Whatever the underlying sentiment, Coppola was also being pragmatic. A three-script contract with Seven Arts, one of which he was now deigned experienced enough to direct, had dissolved with the Warner merger. Early pages of *The Conversation* and *The Rain People* lay stacked beside his typewriter. *Finian's Rainbow* was a chance to get back behind a camera, and maybe provide a pot of gold to fund those small films on his own.

The old refrain.

Moreover, he convinced himself he could bring some fresh thinking to the genre. Shake things up from the inside. Including the immediate proposition that they take the entire production on location to Kentucky and lean into the portrayal of immigrant life. Lighten the whimsy, maybe. In hindsight he could laugh. "That's when I found out they had very specific ideas about how they wanted to make it." Ideas that weren't up for debate.

He was granted leave for three weeks of rehearsal. With his head briefly back among the tulips and DIY fervour of Hofstra, Coppola requisitioned a small building on the lot, brought in an audience, had Carmine play his flute along with a pianist and a drummer, and ran through the entire script with Astaire and the cast like a live performance. Then on June 26, 1967, production began.

"I tried to lay low," said Coppola. He wanted to make it timeless, affectionate, true to its Broadway roots. But he bristled at the memories. Resources were so stretched he found his plans slipping away. By the second week, he was "faking it". Choreographing the numbers became a nightmare. It was all so awful. Veteran choreographer Hermes Pan, an old Astaire sidekick stuck in his ways, had to be fired. This left Coppola to devise his own dance routines. He could picture the essence of a scene, the camera closing in on a hillside and Clark hanging up sheets, say. But the precise steps were beyond him. He had no time to figure things out. There are miscues and jump cuts that don't match. Steele fell back on familiar crutches, shamelessly mugging his way to the inevitable happy ending.

Finian's Rainbow has dated more than any other Coppola film. Even *Dementia 13* retains a woozy, cult appeal. His third film is a studio trinket, a late entry into a spent genre lolloping along on bogus folklore. Left to gather dust for a year, when it finally gained a release in October 1968, even with some spirited studio backing, audiences were unmoved. The young crowd was wowed by a different mood: the self-conscious sensations of *Bonnie and Clyde, The Graduate*, and *Rosemary's Baby*. New Hollywood.

The reviews were wildly mixed (something he got used to). "Enchanting," sang the *Chicago Sun-Times*. "Stunning," said *Sight and Sound*. "Always appealing," offered The *Saturday Review*. "A shuffling relic," groaned *Newsweek*. "Ham-handed," pouted *Time*.

Within the limitations of time and money and expectation, this is Coppola's film. But it never felt personal. The next lesson was imparted -- a taste of life on the studio conveyor belt. And yet, there is something here. We get glimpses of a talent reaching for style within a by-the-numbers studio template.

Coppola squeezed eight days of location shooting out of the harried studio, and headed up the coast to Monterey, Carmel, Modesto, and San Francisco. A bucolic, quasi-Mediterranean landscape that held the desert at bay with temperate North Pacific winds, with a bohemian Emerald City perched on a rocky peninsula. This is the first glimpse of a new home.

He makes a striking feature of beginning the musical numbers with wide, arable vistas, shot from a helicopter's vantage, almost enough to fool the watcher into believing the film had been made on location. In fact, the cast had to negotiate clumps of earth and grass laid down on soundstage floors.

Coppola brings lightness to an old routine. He begins to value close-ups. He even stirs some minor-chord socialist rabble-rousing. And handles Astaire with care. In his final musical, the old charmer is still charismatic, even sprightly.

Potty, patchy, crowd-pleasing *Finian's Rainbow* wasn't entirely divorced from the grand dreams of the Brats either: UCLA compatriot Carroll Ballard shot the lyrical title sequence, and a day came when Coppola spied an odd figure lolling by the edge of the set as if waiting to be noticed. A scrawny kid, dressed in a white T-shirt, black chinos, and sneakers, not talking to anyone. This it transpired was George Lucas.

It is worth pausing to examine a momentous occasion in film history — these two punks first fixing eyes on one another.

Lucas was a real bright spark at USC, and winner of the Samuel Warner Memorial Scholarship, which came with a six-month internship at the studio – basically, the chance to wander the backlot and observe a working studio. With the downturn in Warner's fortunes, that currently amounted to *Finian's Rainbow*. Nevertheless, he heard a lot of talk about Coppola, and was curious to see the *wunderkind* at the forge.

Close enough to the same age (Lucas is six years younger) they immediately hit it off. Everyone else on the production must have been over fifty. All these grey-haired lifers who had watched the stars parade by. Coppola liked the fact this kid began by telling him exactly what he was doing wrong. He promised Lucas he could hang around as long as he "came up with one good idea every day."

This young man would one day offer Hollywood a lucrative route back to the old genres, but not before establishing himself as a fellow buccaneer and Coppola's closest friend. History will always celebrate the bond between Spielberg and Lucas, with all their populist hi-jinks, but it was Coppola and Lucas who changed things.

They were so very different. Coppola would speak; Lucas would listen. Coppola was a sunflower, Lucas a shrinking violet. Coppola spent the money, while Lucas saved it. Coppola loved working with actors; Lucas coveted design. Lucas used to describe his friend as building pyramids from the top down, whereas he would always start at the bottom.

There was something symbiotic in the relationship.

Without Coppola, Lucas may never have had the guts to become a director, and never made *THX-1138*, *American Graffiti*, and *Star Wars*, redefining popular entertainment (so Coppola has a hand in that). Without Lucas, with his trusted advice and good sense (especially in a crisis), Coppola may never have found his way into his great work: certainly *The Godfather* and *Apocalypse Now*.

They have stayed friends, but things would cool. Pulled in different directions as the Zoetrope dream faded. Coppola envied the money Lucas earned, and the self-sufficiency. He felt abandoned. Lucas resented the control Coppola exerted, and all the critical acclaim he gained.

But this meeting of minds, surrounded by the old sticks of a moribund system, is the most significant partnership in American culture in the last one hundred years.

In 1967, they were the only two people at the studio with beards.

He found Shirley Knight crying at a party in Cannes. Someone had been rude, and she could be sensitive. This was 1967, Coppola had flown to the festival with *You're a Big Boy Now*, and he knew the striking blonde actress from her two Academy Award nominations: *The Dark at the Top of the Stairs* in 1960, and *Sweet Bird of Youth* in 1962. Born in Kansas, Method trained at New York's Actors Studio, and seasoned on stage, Knight radiated an unusual mix of vulnerability and defiance. Her sharp features were highly expressive, and she gravitated toward the kind of strung-out roles that warded off stardom. Cannes would present her with an acting award for her alarmingly amoral sex-bomb in the interracial drama *Dutchman*.

"Don't cry," said Coppola, "I'll write you a movie."

Thinking about his consoling words later, he realised he meant it. The idea appealed to what he called his "romantic preconceptions" of cinema. The way that Michelangelo Antonioni wrote scripts for the shimmering Monica Vitti. And Knight was exactly the kind of off-centre talent he could imagine as a muse.

This was a growing habit – self-analysis, self-mythologising. Writing a biography in interviews and public pronouncements. He also had a script in mind.

Where *Finian's Rainbow* had acknowledged his father, *The Rain People* paid tribute to his mother. Following a fierce quarrel with Carmine, Italia had once fled the family home, and was missing for two days. Having cleared her head, she returned, informing her husband and children she had stayed in a motel. Which wasn't true, she had been at her sister's house. Yet Coppola couldn't shake the image of his mother alone in a cheap motel room.

A family drama became fiction. First as an unsatisfactory short story called "The Old Gray Station Wagon", written for a creative writing class at UCLA. In that variation, there were three women who have fled their marriages: a young, newly married housewife; a middle-aged woman with children; and an older woman, flying from a lifelong partnership. With Knight in mind, Coppola tightened the screenplay's viewpoint to one – a Long Island newlywed named Natalie, who is overwhelmed by the news she is pregnant and hits the open road in a Ford station wagon with no destination in mind. We will never see her caring husband (voiced by Robert Modica), only hear his plaintive voice on the telephone.

The story takes dramatic shape around the character of Jimmie "Killer" Kilgannon, a hitchhiker Natalie picks up on a whim. As convincingly conveyed by a young James Caan, a college football injury has left Killer brain damaged. He is a child in a man's body, and will stir complex, unwanted maternal feelings within the heroine. "It's like a woman sitting next to the kid she is going to have," explained Coppola.

While still on the studio lot as Jack Warner's fading regime scrambled for survival, Coppola knew he was unorthodox. He wanted to express himself as a director. The do-thy-bidding studio model was oppressive. Discovering a forgotten closet in the producer's building, he even began stockpiling stolen film.

Coppola craved a mix of his Hofstra and Corman days, working with next to nothing, moving quickly, improvising scenes as they went. "Everything I wanted to do, but wasn't permitted on *Finian's Rainbow*," he said. He conceived of the anti-studio film, hustling across the USA like a travelling show. The very process of storytelling would inform the story. *The Rain People* was the first experiment in the new filmmaking bohemia he and his followers had foretold. Lean, cost-effective productions, liberated from commercial imperatives. Personal stories told with those quixotic European values.

Only right now, still under contract, Coppola needed the backing of the studio. And with *Finian's Rainbow* not yet released, and its director having no great confidence in the results, he didn't have much time for negotiation before his credit ran out. So again, he called the studio's bluff. Feeding the in-house rumour mill with the idea that he was developing a secret project, one that he had already begun to shoot. His office was empty for days. In fact, he, Lucas, Caan, and a bare-bones crew, had made a sortie to Hofstra to shoot rough footage of a football game. Material they could use for flashbacks – shards of impressionistic backstory. Using $80,000 of his earnings from *Finian's Rainbow*, he began to outfit a mobile filmmaking road trip.

Poker-faced before the studio inquisition, he fed them a dose of Finian's blarney. "I'm starting to shoot on Monday, and I need some money and if you don't give it to me, I'll get it from somebody else." There were no potential investors; he didn't even know what his budget amounted to.

They offered him $750,000.

So in April 1968, they lit out for America with a half-formed script, a convoy of filmmakers in search of a story. Communicating by two-way radios, the seven vehicles crossed eighteen states in 105 days, from Long Island, where Italia had made her brief exodus, to pancake-flat Nebraska. With money tight, they lived out of roadside motels, grabbing shots where the impulse took the director – art and life in steady communion.

One of the motorhomes was equipped as a mobile edit suite. It also included wardrobe, make-up, and film stock. The minimal crew included Lucas, cinematographer Bill Butler (who would go on to shoot *The Conversation* and *Jaws*), art director Leon Erickson, and editor Barry Malkin. They were, declared Coppola, "a sort of self-contained movie studio." Once they were in post in San Francisco, the impish, brilliant sound designer Walter Murch would join their merry band.

Eleanor followed in a Volkswagen van with Gio and Roman and took an uncredited cameo as the ex-wife of Robert Duvall's traffic cop, glimpsed in flashback. Duvall was a late addition. He was sharing a flat with Caan at the time, who recommended him after Rip Torn had dropped out.

The next lesson: however free you might think you are, trouble will find you. That's filmmaking. Production would always be emotionally draining.

Aside from the logistical challenges of shooting on the hoof (the whims of negotiating locations and permits from state to state), Coppola's relationship with Knight became strained. Used to some structure, she struggled with the uncertainty of Coppola's methods, the wilful chaos, and the lousy motels. The script was no more than a blueprint, and all the improvising was changing the nature of her character. The way the crew hung on Coppola's word as if he was Orson Welles really began to rankle. So they fought. The set became increasingly tense. But her agitation was also fuel for an intuitive performance: brittle, naïve, and jaggedly human. Natalie is not supposed to be likeable so much as plausible. It is an astute depiction of manic depression, veering between wild excitement and despair.

As Natalie and Killer's journey goes on, the film builds into psychic and physical violence, and finally tragedy. The breezy humour of his previous films is traded for a brooding intensity, a state of mind the director will inhabit across his finest films.

There are extraordinary scenes: a cruel visit to the wealthy Virginia family of an ex-girlfriend, who wants only to be rid of this forlorn boy; the vivid image of Killer freeing hundreds of hapless chicks from a Nebraska animal farm.

Coppola was staking his claim on New Hollywood. The writer Roger Ebert saw the mirror image of Hopper's era-defining *Easy Rider* – instead of hippy rebels you have the odyssey of a desperate middle-class housewife partnered with an oversized kid. Coppola observes the vicissitudes of the American landscape through the sullen gaze of a woman who cannot escape herself. From widely different perspectives, both films home in on a peculiar form of American anxiety.

For all the handheld European energy, Coppola also imbues his vérité images with the classical. The gravitational pull of the grandiose makes him distinctive. Even if *The Rain People* is his most intensely realistic piece of storytelling, there are allusions to *Of Mice and Men* and Huckleberry Finn yearning for where the river might take him. Huck's spirit is in Coppola too – always looking for the next horizon. Life alone isn't enough to hold him.

The title provides a note of elusive lyricism, with Killer describing "Rain People" who disappear when they cry. "They look like ordinary people," he says. Asked to explain himself, Coppola alluded to "sad people who cry a lot over marriages that don't work."

In 1968, the idea of a woman who gets up and leaves her husband was a radical proposition. But for Coppola – and this is telling – the film is attempting to both understand why she desires freedom and affirm his belief in the primacy of the family.

His mother returned.

Where *Easy Rider* caught a nerve, *The Rain People* went ignored, another box office flop. Renowned painter and critic Manny Farber appreciated the "grotesque-sad mood of the turnpike life." There is a disenchanted quality that speaks to its times, but dissuaded audiences. It has no love story, admitted Coppola, and no sex. Many reviewers regretted its shortcomings (insubstantial plot, downcast atmosphere, contrived ending), but divined hope from the artistry. "It's the sort of failure that has interesting implications for the future of American films," predicted *The Washington Post*.

The Rain People marks a significant juncture. It stirs up possibility. The chance to break free of Hollywood, and that convoy of pioneers would keep on past Burbank and up to San Francisco to settle a new frontier. It also begins to fix a Coppola palate: penetrating close-ups and authentic, scene-setting wides. Deep psychological enquiry matched by dense visual texture. A style is being forged that will be fulfilled in very different worlds. The leap to the masterworks is not so distant. The director returned to California in confident mood.

The hubris of the endeavour even ran to Coppola finding the money to fulfil Lucas's idea of shooting a making-of documentary, which he ostentatiously christened *Filmmaker*. Lucas captures all the idealism and the despondency – those Coppola rhythms. There is a telling moment of the director midway through a furious phone call with a perplexed studio. "The system will fall by its own weight!" he shouts, bearing his soul like a biblical prophet.

There are other auguries from those mercurial days. Production assistant Mona Skager remembered Lucas held in a trance by the old *Flash Gordon* serial playing on a hotel lobby television. He began to talk about a movie he would make one day filled with holograms and spaceships. He meant *Star Wars*.

"The zoetrope was an early device to create the illusion of a motion picture." Coppola would take his time, scholastic by nature. Enjoying the words. "In the 1860s, it was a popular toy – a revolving cylindrical box with slits in it, making pictures appear to move – but I'm sure it was used much earlier."

In Greek, he would say, "zoe" means "life," and "trope" means "turn" or "movement." So what the word really meant was "life movement". Over the many years of Coppola's career, American Zoetrope has taken many shapes, riding the highs and lows of an entrepreneur's fortunes. With every bankruptcy, the dream has endured. For all the wild ambition, and lunacy, that have gone into the embodiment of Coppola's grand filmmaking enterprise, that logo heralds some of the greatest films ever made.

Try: *American Graffiti, The Godfather, The Conversation, The Godfather Part II, Apocalypse Now, The Black Stallion,* and *Lost in Translation.* This is quite apart from fostering late work from sleeping giants. Try: Jean-Luc Godard, Wim Wenders, and Akira Kurosawa.

But more than that was the philosophy. What defined a zoetrope, what made it work, was the concept of revolution. And that is what these young filmmakers wanted – to find a new way.

The idea finally took shape while rumbling from town to town on *The Rain People.* It was the natural thing to do. Take the risk to set up a new filmmaking community – the community element was important. Francis, said Eleanor, "dreamed of this group of poets, filmmakers, and writers who would drink espresso in North Beach and talk of their work, and it would be good."

"We began to feel like Robin Hood and his band," enthused Coppola. They would have the filmmaking machine in their own hands. It could be anywhere, and they headed north, up the Pacific Coast Highway, the ocean glittering beneath the cliffs.

San Francisco was important too. It was arty, liberated, the countercultural capital, and refuge for the Beat Poets. And it was beautiful – a citadel overlooking the sea. They could simply implant themselves there as a filmmaking community, and still be close enough to LA to be able to draw from the pool of talent spread around the studio walls. Filmmaking was too deep-rooted in LA. It was an industry town, stuck in its ways. Union membership was restrictive. The chance to simply make a film was remote for most of them.

Key was the creation of a hub in which they could build a technical infrastructure of sound systems and edit suites. Coppola was still the scientist. He would build a filmmaking centre beyond the grasp of the studios. "I thought we had the potential to have a company that could change the system," he explained. "The holy grail, balanced between art and commerce."

This is when Coppola goes to Denmark with Eleanor and sees paradise. She has old friends in Copenhagen, and someone mentions the idealistic filmmaker Mogens Skot-Hansen, who runs his own film company (commercials, features, soft-porn). Intrigued, Coppola gets hold of an address – an elegant mansion in Klampenborg, down near the sea, and stays for three weeks. Laterna Studios is everything he dreams of. Edit suites, sound facilities, pretty blonde girls, communal lunches, and a room set aside for Skot-Hansen's collection of antique filmmaking devices and zoetropes.

Coppola and Lucas searched for their own mansion. But equipment was already ordered and on its way. "I wasn't keeping track of the money," shrugged Coppola, who had dashed through the European tech-conventions buying up state-of-the-art editing machines and modular mixing studios like the chemistry sets from his boyhood. Out of urgency, they moved into an old recording studio at 827 Folsom Street. With a headquarters, they were a company. American Zoetrope: Coppola as owner, Lucas as vice president, and Skager as treasurer and secretary.

The doors to Folsom Street officially opened on December 13, 1969. There was a huge party to celebrate, a thousand strong, swarming with filmmakers, artists, rock stars, and dealers from the San Francisco scene. Studio heads had flown up to stand nervously at the edge of the throng staring into Hollywood's manic future. The three-storey loft cut a strikingly different style to the mock-Tudor offices on the studio lots. The walls were hung with bold Finnish Marimekko fabrics (chosen by Eleanor), and a silver espresso machine steamed up the hallway. The seven edit suites and optical facilities were stood at the centre, encircled by rooms for props, wardrobe, and design, along with refrigerators for film storage. Coppola had a corner office.

"It was all part of what we saw as the beginnings of the technical democratisation of the filmmaking process," said Murch. Coppola immediately ordered the latest $40,000 Mitchell camera.

At heart, he was being nostalgic. Zoetrope was, he said, to be "a synthesis of my wonderful experiences at Hofstra, then applied it to this wonderful group of USC students." They would have a family atmosphere, where his door was always open to ideas. "I wanted *La bohème*, the Beat Poets, pretty girls — the bohemian life." Every Thursday night they screened new or classic movies, with Chinese food.

Like a queen bee, the hive began to gather around Coppola: Milius, Ballard, Murch, Caleb Deschanel, Robert Dalva, Willard Huyck, Matthew Robbins and more. They ranged from radical Marxists to commercial directors, and all were eager to make their mark.

Budgets would be kept low, decreed Coppola, with each film costing $777,777 (seven was his lucky number), but with their expertise and lack of overheads, they would look as if they had cost millions. The old studio paradigm was falling into decay. They had learned with *The Rain People*, you could be light on your feet. "It freed up the process," said Lucas.

As the 1970s dawned, Folsom Street was filled with the scent of possibility. Partying, talking, writing, figuring things out: they were like Warhol's Factory, or Mercury Theatre, or the pioneers of the silent era who didn't yet know the rules. There was plenty of dope to go round, but Coppola and Lucas never partook. Filmmaking was the better drug.

Calls came in from Stanley Kubrick, Mike Nichols, and John Schlesinger. What could Zoetrope offer them? One day, it was actually Orson Welles on the line, proposing a 16mm production.

There is a splendid photo taken on the Folsom Street roof on the completion of photography on *THX-1138*. The original Zoetrope gang dressed as bandits, clutching film cameras and lighting stands, a wild bunch armed to the teeth. Among them, Lucas hides at the back; Milius wears a sombrero and gun-belt; Coppola, the alpha-dog, is in a black Stetson holding the zoetrope, presented to him by Skot-Hansen.

The only problem was money.

Zoetrope not only needed budgets, but access to a distribution network. They couldn't yet cut the studio umbilical. So Coppola did what he did best and massaged a deal. Having been acquired by the Kinney National Company in 1969, Warner Bros.-Seven Arts was now simply Warner Bros. Inc. again, and under new management. Coppola convinced new CEO, Ted Ashley, to buy into his out-of-town project with the lure of seven core Zoetrope projects, most of which had already been rejected by the previous regime. They weren't to know, he figured.

Four are now lost to time: *Vesuvia*, *The Naked Gypsies*, *Have We Seen the Elephants?*, and *Santa Rita*. But Coppola was still intent on his surveillance thriller *The Conversation*, and Lucas was pursuing an exploration of the ongoing war in Vietnam from a script by Milius called *Apocalypse Now*. With familiar chicanery, Coppola claimed to Warner that Lucas had already started on an ambitious science-fiction thriller called *THX-1138*.

All the studios had nervously witnessed the out-there vibe of *Easy Rider* capture the youth market. To Warner's thinking, this unruly San Francisco troupe was a potential supply line to the precious, unpredictable baby boomers, with Coppola as the parental figure.

Zoetrope were granted $2,500 a week seed money, with the prospect of the individual budgets being met.

The first film to be ready was indeed Lucas's $777,000 debut, the Orwellian *THX-1138*, shot in part on San Francisco's BART subway, and starring Robert Duvall. Coppola served as executive producer and left his friend to it. Drawing on Fritz Lang's *Metropolis*, Kubrick's *2001: A Space Odyssey*, and NASA's space programme, it is a formally brilliant but distant love story set against a sterile 25th-century futurescape of drug-induced docility and robotic guards. Names and emotions have been outlawed. It is a fascinating irony how Zoetrope's earliest films – *THX-1138* and *The Conversation* – were so concerned with the perils of technology, even as the filmmakers revelled in the possibilities it afforded.

New Hollywood of the 1970s had found its most advance party, but there was naivety too. Egalitarianism and the movie business are not a natural fit. Everyone was off doing their thing, wanting a slice of the rewards. Coppola was herding auteurs.

On seeing a few reels of *THX-1138*, he was taken aback. "This is either going to be a masterpiece or masturbation."

One Sunday afternoon in the spring of 1969, Coppola was thumbing through *The New York Times* when a small ad in the bottom corner of the page caught his eye.

"The ad showed a black book with a puppeteer's hand, and it said *The Godfather* by Mario Puzo." This Puzo must be some Italian intellectual, he mused, and his book some treatise on power and Machiavelli. Maybe this was an avant-garde novel in the Robbe-Grillet style – the stuff he liked. The logo appealed to him. "It implied power," he said.

He could have no idea how that book would change his life. Or how wrong and right he was about the subject matter.

The day's coincidences were not yet done. Two producers from Paramount paid a visit. Al Ruddy and Gray Frederickson were in San Francisco shooting the Robert Redford biker picture *Little Faust and Big*

Halsy – next in a line of flops dogging the studio. They didn't know it yet, but Ruddy and Frederickson would soon be assigned the exhausting task of producing an adaptation of Puzo's not quite so intellectual novel. While they were swapping gossip at Coppola's house, the phone rang.

Eleanor came in, a little flustered. He really needed to take the call. Marlon Brando was on the line.

"It was the first time I had ever spoken to him in my life," said Coppola. Brando had called to turn down the role of Harry Caul in *The Conversation*, even though, as Coppola had implied in his letter, the part had been written with him in mind.

Coppola is not inclined toward notions of destiny; he merely considered the convergence of these events to be "odd". A few weeks later Paramount called.

CHAPTER 3

LEAVE THE GUN. TAKE THE CANNOLI

The Godfather (1972)

They take Mulholland Drive to the crest of the hill in search of a hidden mansion. Bougainvillea enchanted walls and Indian Laurel bushes as tall as Palm Trees resisted prying eyes. Jack Nicholson has an ocean view nearby – he had been considered for Michael Corleone or maybe Tom Hagen. It depended on whom you asked. Beside him in the car, Francis Ford Coppola has a slender crew: Japanese documentary photographer Hiro Narita, and a solemn Italian barber named Salvatore Corsitto, earmarked for the part of the undertaker Bonasera – already freshly dressed in a black suit.

"No loud noises," Coppola instructs his companions. He had heard that Marlon Brando hated loud noises, and often wore earplugs on set. Like ninjas, he says again. No one was to refer to this as a screen test. Brando didn't do screen tests.

His palms are sweating.

When the assistant finally lures Brando from his bedroom, Coppola's stomach clenches.

Paramount had squirmed at the idea of Brando as Don Vito Corleone. They had done their utmost to dissuade him, including simply ordering him not to cast the actor. He was way out on a limb here. The rewrite guy turned director. The footage needed to convince his bosses of a grand Italian patriarch, a man in his sixties, armoured in quiet authority. Coppola pictured a mythical presence: "An actor of such magnetism, such charisma, just walking into a room had to be an event." Which was why his thoughts turned so emphatically to America's greatest exponent, however jaded he had become. However much that light had dimmed.

Brando's hair is blond and long enough to be tied in a ponytail. He wears a Japanese kimono and an unhappy expression. He is heavyset. But still a ravaged beauty, Kazan's man: star of *A Streetcar Named Desire*, *On the Waterfront*, and *Viva Zapata!*.

So canny with actors, Coppola has brought plates of Italian sausage and cheese, cigars and espresso, to appeal to Brando's senses, and watches him nibble at the offerings. He suggests they run a few lines. Record the moment. Wait, the actor responds, and a tin of boot polish is retrieved, which he runs through his hair, slicking it back. He rolls some Kleenex into two small balls and pads his gums.

"I want to be like a bulldog."

Stood before a mirror, his face grows jowly and aged. He adds shadows beneath his eyes with stage make-up.

"You t'ink I need a moustache?" his voice is changing, it has become husky and remote, drawn from deep inside – a consequence, the actor had decided, of the Don having been shot in the throat at some point.

"Oh yeah," replies Coppola, anxious to comply, "my Uncle Louis had a moustache."

Talking to himself, mumbling, improvising lines, Brando starts to relax. When the phone rings, he greets the caller without breaking character. "*Yeeeerrrsssss?*"

The voice would be refined before shooting: Brando practising in the bath with tapes of mob traitor Joseph Valachi testifying before Robert Kennedy's government hearings in 1963. That was the first time the outside world had ever heard talk of the Five New York Families, known collectively as the Cosa Nostra – the Sicilian Mafia.

Coppola takes his chance. He brings in his undertaker, who strolls up to Brando and urgently begins the speech that would pass into legend. "I believe in America. America has made my fortune..." Maybe it wasn't yet so perfect. Startled, Brando listens and then responds, joining in.

"It was a miraculous transformation," said Coppola, who could foresee his film to come, tilted into laconic magnificence. A forty-seven-year-old actor – that is how old Brando was – had become an ageing Mafia chief. All of it caught on a borrowed 16mm video camera. Then they were gone. Cast out of Eden.

Coppola showed the tape to Charlie Bluhdorn on the thirty-third floor of the Gulf & Western Building, a lean skyscraper on Columbus Circle in New York that was apt to sway in high winds. The manufacturing conglomerate was Paramount's new owner, and Bluhdorn the volatile chairman. An Austrian émigré made good, his manner tended to be as blunt as his English. He would have the final say.

"That's incredible!" started Bluhdorn, eyes fixed on the screen. "Who's dat man? Who's dat man? Dat man's the Godfather. Gotta get him!"

He had no idea it was Brando.

"People are shocked to hear I think of *The Godfather* series with sadness," reflected Coppola, a stony eye fixed on the most momentous events of his career. "I see those films almost as a personal failure."

Well might we cry out and clutch our brows. The irony! The irony! These were the films that made his reputation, earned him his first fortune, assured his place in the Hollywood firmament, and transformed American cinema. Let us not quibble; with *The Godfather* alone, Coppola created one of the enduring monuments of American culture.

We were left thunderstruck.

Bathed in Goyaesque shadows, great wells of sepia and inky black, or washed in spacious sunlight, the images come to us like our own memories. Proud Bonasera making his entreaties to the lamp-lit Don, a cat purring in Brando's affectionate grasp – maybe, as Coppola claimed, a stray that had wandered onto the set. The director learned it was much easier to give Brando props than notes. Or the severed head of a thoroughbred pooling blood, a concoction of Karo syrup and food colouring, onto silk sheets – a genuine horse's head, obtained from a slaughterhouse in New Jersey, not that it stopped the animal rights people climbing on Coppola's back. Or Luca Brasi extruding a tongue the size of a rump steak, his face turning puce as the garrotte bites into his throat – there was no need for make-up, former wrestler Lenny Montana could hold his breath until the blood vessels in his face nearly burst. Or Sonny slaughtered at the tollbooth, which took three days, 400 squibs, and $100,000 to outdo *Bonnie and Clyde*. Or the final shot of a door closing in Kay's face – the wife excluded from the inner sanctum.

Pauline Kael, the ice queen of *The New Yorker*, knew that the director had "pushed himself farther than he may realize."

With *The Godfather*, wrote critic Michael Sragow, assaying the film on its 25th anniversary, Coppola "achieved the combination of groundbreaking expression and public acceptance that is a popular artist's holy grail." But the grail, he reminded us, was a relic that, for all its glory, exacts misery from those who seek it. And even those who find it.

How do you come to terms with being the man who directed *The Godfather*? On one simple level it is a spellbinding film, the great opera around which Coppola's career revolves, proof of his copious talents. But in agreeing to *The Godfather*, this middle-order studio gangster movie, he swayed from his chosen path, away from the small, original films that were to be the signature of Zoetrope. Like the tidy career of Woody Allen, say, delivering fresh romantic entanglements with each calendar year. Or, maybe, that of his daughter, Sofia, who has never compromised.

So he can only consider *The Godfather* with sadness. Not only did it rob him of his art and purity, on a day-to-day level, making the film was to be in a state of constant, exhausting conflict. He loved the cast, and he can see the film was something, but all that returns to him is the emotional toil. "I had two little kids and a third on the way, I was living in this borrowed apartment, and at one point my editor told me that nothing was any good. It was a total collapse of self-confidence on my part; it was just an awful experience. I'm nauseated to think about it."

Necessity might well be the mother of invention, but chaos and pressure are the mother and father of greatness.

Coppola was thirty-one years old, and owed $300,000 to Warner Bros.

Let us retrace our steps. By 1969, the countercultural dream is in a tailspin. Blows are raining down. The Manson Family had ritualistically slaughtered a pregnant Sharon Tate in her own home. The Rolling Stones had seen murder with their own eyes in the crowd at Altamont. The Civil Rights movement buckled against the establishment. Martin

Luther King took a bullet on a motel balcony, then Robert Kennedy in a hotel kitchen. A stench of corruption emanated from the White House. Vietnam loomed over everything, the psychedelic war.

What did movies even mean anymore? Hollywood was in an existential crisis. With television now a national obsession, the studios had experienced their lowest movie attendance figures ever. Corporate giants were feeding on the studios like vultures: the Kinney National Corporation had consumed Warner Bros.; MCA had feasted on Universal; Transamerica had swallowed United Artists.

Another immigrant who had toiled to success, Bluhdorn's billions had been made merging metal stamping with agricultural products to create Gulf & Western. He had bought Paramount as a plaything for $600,000. That was how low the industry had fallen.

On a whim, or an instinct he would often regret, Bluhdorn appointed the dashing Robert Evans as head of production in 1966, nominally based out of the Melrose Avenue lot. The newspapers had guffawed at the appointment of this bottom-rung producer to the upper echelons. "Bluhdorn's Folly" ran one headline. Evans was more likely to be found running operations from his Edenic, sixteen-room Beverly Hills cocoon, Woodland, with its lush veil of eucalyptus trees, rose bushes, and gardenias, and state-of-the-art screening room in the pool house: part of the deal he struck with Charlie in order the save the company. Find a house, his new employer had told him. Somewhere for business and pleasure. Beefy, balding Bluhdorn, with his big teeth and Groucho glasses, had coveted him like a sweetheart.

Born in 1930, Evans had the glow of a matinee idol. Leaving New York and a sullen dentist father – a frustrated pianist – he headed to the West Coast in search of fame and life. Even with Robert Wagner cheekbones and a tan like lacquered teak, he had proven an unremarkable actor. His gifts lay in persuasion. So numerous were the starlets led to his silk sheets, his housekeeper would place the name of the latest sleeping beauty beside his morning coffee and cheesecake.

Is there a pinch of the playboy peacock of Paramount in *The Godfather*'s Jack Woltz, the Hollywood man with his precious racehorse and extravagant Italianate estate? According to Coppola's notes, a man who lived like a king. For those sunburned exteriors he used the Beverly

Hills mansion of William Randolph Hearst – once food for Orson Welles' defiant art. The interiors were shot in the Guggenheim Estate on Long Island. These were the palaces of magnates, or was it mobsters?

Evans had begun his reign with the swooning, smash hit *Love Story*; married the star, Ali MacGraw; lost her to Steve McQueen; and schemed and plotted at the forefront of Hollywood's new wave. He was brilliant, arrogant and devious, a virtuoso on the phone, following his impeccable hunches. "He's the best producer I've ever seen," was Dustin Hoffman's take. "He has the best taste, the best memory, the best suggestions for cutting."

Not all would conform to that view.

Evans soon installed Peter Bart as his vice president. A razor-sharp former columnist for *The New York Times*, where the film industry had been his beat (he had interviewed Hitchcock and Selznick in his travels), he would serve as Evans' *consigliere* – his stoic right-hand man. Together, the beauty and brains of Paramount Pictures, they sensed change in the Santa Ana winds: those new voices spilling out of the film schools, steeped in history, wrapped in beards, with big plans behind their dark eyes. So they bet on directors.

"Everybody was looking for an answer," said Bart. "One answer seemed to be, if you found a brilliant young director with a vision, go with him. It was Kubrick, more than anybody, that had an impact on us."

By sticking with their auteur theory, Paramount would become the number one studio in Hollywood, with a slew of era-defining hits: *Rosemary's Baby*, *The Odd Couple*, *Chinatown*, *The Conversation*, and *The Godfather* films, of course.

This was all to come.

First we must circle back to Paramount, and Woodland, with its tropical pool and shrill phone. *Love Story* was a start, but Evans was urgently in need of more hits to fill a scheduled twenty-five films a year. And this thriller might serve as a profitable genre picture midway up the roster.

There are two sides to the Mario Puzo story. One belonged to the loquacious Evans and his colourful, well-thumbed memoir *The Kid Stays in the Picture*. How one afternoon an unknown author had strolled into his office smoking a cigar. Puzo was a man of appetites – gambling and spaghetti ai fagioli. His waistline documented his self-indulgence. There was a touch of Clemenza about him, the Don's *caporegime* with his "jolly ferocity", but for the heavy glasses and uneasy smile. He had a rumpled envelope under his arm. Inside were fifty to sixty pages of typescript, the beginnings of a novel. He offered to trade it to Paramount for cash.

"In trouble?" asked Evans.

With the quickened pulse of a movie set-up, we have the producer's account: Puzo was into the bookies for ten grand, and his legs were in grave danger of being broken.

So he had written a novel. A story, he said, that went against his principles. Puzo had begun his literary career in search of art. Two well-received heavyweights, *The Dark Arena* and *The Fortunate Pilgrim*, hadn't made him a cent. Now he was writing a popular novel, something knowingly vulgar and violent — a barefaced attempt at a bestseller to provide collateral for his art, and a healthy stake at the tables.

It was called *Mafia*.

Evans, according to Evans, cut a deal: ten Gs upfront, then $75,000 if it ever got made. "Could you make it fifteen?" pushed Puzo. No dice. Evans then promptly forgot about the whole thing.

Cut to: a few months later, and Evans's phone is rattling in its nest. Puzo has a change of title: "I want to call it *The Godfather.*"

Evans starts to get a hunch.

Puzo tells a different story. There was never any Hollywood meeting. True, he was in debt. True, he was an inveterate gambler. True, his book began with as blunt a title as *Mafia*. Like Coppola, he was first-generation Italian-American, born in New York's Hell's Kitchen, one of seven. Like Coppola's maternal line, Puzo's parents were from Campania, close to Naples. His father, who worked the railroads, had unsteady moods and was eventually institutionalised. The upbringing was left to his mother and an older sister. Don Vito, Puzo claimed, was based on his mother. She knew the neighbourhood, how to provide for her family, and was given to pithy remarks.

Make him an offer he can't refuse.

"My mother was a wonderful, handsome woman," he claimed, "but a truly ruthless person."

Puzo received his first communion, but gambling was his religion. Las Vegas his Holy See. And he was now seriously in debt. Aspirations to art weren't going to keep his head above water. "I wrote below my gifts," he admitted in his 1972 memoir, *The Godfather Collection*. Like Coppola, Puzo created *The Godfather* to pay his debts.

It took three years to complete the novel. While he knew the rumours, Puzo had "never met a real honest-to-god gangster." It was pure research – between bets on the roulette wheel, he would grill the pit bosses at the Sands Hotel in Vegas. And it was pure invention. He coined so many terms that were later adopted by a besotted Mafia. The concept of a "Godfather" was a Puzo affectation. Thanks to the films, the exaggerations within the book's pages would be accepted as the cultural idiom of organised crime.

Spanning fifty years from the turn of the century, Puzo delivered a crime saga. The story of two kinds of family: the bloodline of the Corleones, and the powerful New York crime syndicate that enclosed them, built from the ground up by Don Vito Corleone through a combination of old-world, Machiavellian instincts and shrewd, new-world values. In the sprawling, operatic tapestry, reaching from coast to coast, with a huge dramatis personae, the story homes in on the dramatic destiny that awaits a middle-aged Vito and his three sons: Sonny, Fredo, and Michael. Bawdy and thrilling, it was a story of America.

George Wieser was one of Evans's hive of spies, a studio tipster, locating choice material before the competition. His beat was the Manhattan literary scene. Puzo had only written a hundred pages or so when Wieser called Evans about the potential of this New York crime dynasty. It is unclear whether he had read any of it yet.

It didn't matter. Evans's telephone also delivered rumours that Universal were keen to buy it for Burt Lancaster to play the Don. He and Bart got their hands on sixty pages – which may be where Evans' recollections begin – and knew it had something. "It wasn't great writing," said Bart, but here were the stallion's head in Woltz's bed, and the garrotting of Brasi, his hand pinned to the bar with a switchblade.

The final deal with Puzo was a paltry $12,000 for an option on *The Godfather*, rising to $85,000 if they exercised that option. He would later get $100,000 upfront to write the script, two-and-a-half percent of the grosses, and $500 a week expenses.

Expectations within the studio were limited. Gangsters were old hat. *The Brotherhood*, an expensive 1968 dud about an ageing Mafioso starring Kirk Douglas, had left a sour taste.

The Godfather was pulp fiction – the chance for a quick buck. Find a competent director, a decent enough cast, and make it contemporary, shooting in Kansas City or St. Louis to keep costs down. The budget was locked at $2.5 million. Puzo's first task as screenwriter was to shed the book's evocative historical milieu and bring it up to date – 1970s America. As Coppola lamented of the first draft, "it had hippies."

Finding a director proved a struggle. A suite of credible choices had turned their noses up at this trashy airport thriller. The rumour mill lists elder statesman like Richard Brooks, Costa-Gavras, and Otto Preminger. Arthur Penn was too busy. Fred Zinnemann, Peter Yates, and *Patton's* Franklin Schaffner fretted that it romanticised the Mafia. We root for these killers? There were others. Elia Kazan even. Though Sam Peckinpah's petitions fell on deaf ears. The body count was unthinkable.

A question hangs over the choice of Coppola. Were Evans and Bart genuinely in tune with what he would offer the film? That he was the vanguard of a new vitality. Or was it simply that they were seeking an Italian–American green enough to be pushed around?

One of the chief problems with the genre, reasoned Evans, was that the films were always made by Hollywood Italians. In other words, Jewish directors with Jewish stars like Douglas. There was no intimacy, no ear for the argot of Italian-American life. Evans wanted authenticity, or as he crudely put it, to "smell the spaghetti." And Coppola might deflect the potential heat of always depicting Italian-Americans as gangsters.

"I was a writer," laughed Coppola, which meant they got a rewrite for free from the guy who had won an Oscar for *Patton*, "and I was Italian, so I seemed like an intelligent shot."

He also reasoned that *The Rain People* had played its part, for it showed he could direct acting, and serious scenes. "It was a dramatic movie; it looked good, and it was made inexpensively."

Having written about Coppola in the mid-'60s, Bart had seen the potential in his early films. He might have been Italian-American, he insisted, but he was also "the brightest young director I knew." He could bring out what Bart believed to be an underlying integrity in Puzo's writing. Bart was the first to foresee *The Godfather*.

Fifty pages in, Coppola knew he hated the novel. This was everything he was running away from: the lurid syntax of Hollywood sensationalism. All that hot air about the singer, Johnny Fontane, supposedly modelled on Frank Sinatra; Lucy Mancini, the girl Sonny was sweet on, with her gynaecological issues. The writing had an Irwin Shaw-Harold Robbins zip to it. Cheap thrills.

"Forget it," he told Paramount.

He was into Fellini and the French New Wave.

Months later, he couldn't afford to be so high-minded. Zoetrope was on its knees. They were days away from sheriffs chaining the doors of Folsom Street. Warner was demanding repayment of the development money on scripts they were never likely to make.

Any hopes of establishing their fiefdom within the Hollywood system had been dashed with *THX-1138*. An appalled Warner saw Lucas's dystopian escape movie as artsy and cold-blooded. Did they sense it was a satire of corporate menace? They jettisoned Zoetrope, suffocated the film at the box office (history and *Star Wars* would grant it the oxygen of cult appreciation), and sent Coppola a bill for the divorce.

He never forgot their short-sightedness. "They turned down what became the whole '70s cinema movement."

Bart was well aware Coppola was in a tight spot when he tracked him down to Lucas's kitchen in Mill Valley and put it to him straight. Directing *The Godfather* would provide salvation from his fiscal troubles. In the parlance of an unborn cliché, this was an offer he really couldn't refuse.

So much better attuned to the stark economics of the film business, Lucas concurred. This was a lifeboat.

"Survival is the key thing here," he insisted.

If there was to be a future, Coppola must return to the past. Yet his wasn't an overnight change of heart. He was in agony that he might be truly selling out this time.

Weeks later, he picked his father up from Burbank Airport, grumbling about having spent the previous day at Paramount, who wanted him to direct this hunk of trash.

"I don't want to do it," he remonstrated. "I want to do art films."

Well versed in compromise, Carmine spoke wisely, like a father should. Take the money, use it for the kinds of films he wanted to make so badly. Feed your children.

Coppola called Bart. He had one condition. This wasn't going to be a film about organised crime.

"Is he nuts?" said Evans.

Like a San Francisco fog giving way to sunshine, Coppola had begun to see something in the novel. "Much of the book fell away in my mind," he explained. Out of Puzo's hot and lavish detail, Mafia truths entwined with fantasy, he perceived a family saga – the theme closest to his heart. This was a tale of succession with a dying king and three sons. It could be Greek or Shakespearean in scope. Something classical, where each son possessed an aspect of the Don. "The question was which of them would prove to be the true heir?" Coppola saw beyond the Mafia, into *King Lear*, or the tragic sons of that American titan Joseph Kennedy.

"It is a film about power," he said.

We can also discern a tincture of Coppola in each brother: hot-headed Santino – known as "Sonny" – thinking with his heart and his fists; weak, wounded, sweet Frederico – "Fredo" – laid low by pneumonia as a child; and quiet, capable, cunning Michael, the good son drawn to the dark centre.

Coppola also descried a metaphor. In Puzo's world, organised crime stood for capitalism. Killing was simply a way of dealing with the competition. Market forces are laid bare. This was American morality.

Brando let that idea percolate through his performance. "Don Corleone is just an ordinary American business magnate who is trying to do the best he can for the group he represents, and his family."

There's another aspect to consider. The fact that the book was deemed no better than a commercial potboiler may well have loosened up Coppola. He had reverence for the material but wasn't cramped by it. He could play the cinematic alchemist turning trash into art.

Coppola never hid the fact he was using a studio job to fund his true calling – his new Hollywood, where he could foster personal filmmaking. But it was this quick-hit gangster picture, as heady as cigar smoke, which proved the true catalyst for change. *The Godfather* was his art film.

Of course, Hollywood existed on the other side of the looking glass. And having been courted by Paramount to direct *The Godfather*, he would now have to prove to Paramount he was worthy of the task. In short, he would have to run the gauntlet of Evans and Paramount President Stanley Jaffe, and then the bluster of Bluhdorn.

Coppola's "spiel", as Bart called it, was spellbinding.

Central to his modus operandi were Coppola's powers of persuasion. He was delightful company, able to charm a room with his self-deprecating humour, fund of stories, and startling insight. In the executive offices in Los Angeles, he held forth not only on the film, but studio policy, the world at large, all his pent-up feelings about how films should be made.

Was it now the penny dropped that they were not dealing with a pushover? This young man, without a hit to his name, was lording it like he was Mike Nichols or Kubrick.

Coppola and Bluhdorn talked through the night. When morning came round a deal had been reached, and temporary salvation for Zoetrope. Coppola would receive an upfront salary of $150,000 for directing and co-writing, and six percent of the net profits. As it would turn out, the best deal he has ever made.

As quickly became apparent, he was incapable of simply doing the studio's bidding. The film had to come from within him as much as it spilled out of the Puzo's decadent novel. Straightaway, he insisted they return to the same starting point as the novel: the last Saturday in 1945. "New York was a real character in the story," he pressed upon his new bosses, "and it had to be period, the 1940s."

He knew this world, not the immediacy of organised crime perhaps, but the texture of Italian-American life. Wasn't that why they had employed him? The palate for the film was his memories: the bright cars, market stalls, backstreets, and fire escapes; the trips to the fairyland of Manhattan; the airing of grievances at dinner tables; and the grand theatre of wedding days.

That took Evans aback. Returning the book to its original post-war setting more than doubled the budget in an instant. His modest $2.5 million thriller was now costing him upwards of $6 million. His hunch was becoming more of an uncertain itch.

"The trouble was," laughed Bart, "it became this huge international bestseller."

With the deal signed, Coppola took his family and what little money he had and set sail for Italy, with an invitation to attend the Sorrento Film Festival. It was there he met a fellow New Yorker, who could talk and talk on the subject of film. He seemed to know all there was to know on the subject. Martin Scorsese had thick black hair and a beard – they could have been brothers.

Coppola's financial woes were far from over, but he had a new purpose. Work always deferred the fear. Despite the misgivings of the captain, while on-board ship he commandeered a bar and began pulling the book apart – quite literally tearing it free from its bindings, cutting out each page, and sticking them down on a blank sheet leaving a wide margin for notes.

He had visited the local Mill Valley Public Library for anything he could find on the American Mafia, immersing himself in the struggles between these powerful families. One book was on the rat Joseph Valachi; another covered the life of Vito Genovese, one more Neapolitan immigrant, who stepped into Lucky Luciano's shoes and attempted to consolidate power in the 1950s.

We begin to glean Coppola's intense approach to material – trying to anticipate his film, to get ahead of it, to know each scene intimately before the camera turned. Back in his Hofstra days, he had learned how to make a prompt book, the loose-leafed collection of notes that became any stage manager's bible: alongside the text would be lighting and music cues, the timing of actor's entrances, etc. He was now doing the same for *The Godfather*, creating a repository of every idea he had about the project.

He marked each page of the novel with his first impressions, underlining portions he felt important. He used different coloured pens, accentuated things, Puzo's way with a glancing detail, like those "mists of blood" in the air after Sollozzo is shot.

Coppola then broke the story down into prospective scenes, jettisoning the sweatier elements, and what was untenable within his budget. Out went the lengthy sojourn in Hollywood, and the coveted flashback to Vito's youth, arriving in New York from Sicily. That would have to wait. Each scene was then deconstructed into five criteria.

First, The Synopsis: what actually happens. This established an "embryo" of the subsequent script.

Second, The Times: the immediate historical context for the scene in question. He noted that, "America in the 1940s had a certain style." Detail mattered.

Third, Imagery and Tone: images that stood out from the book, and the visual tone. "What did I see on the page of the novel that I could latch onto?" He would supplant Puzo's textures with nuance. There were pages of specifics for Connie's wedding.

The film's celebrated Long Island opening has the abundance of Pieter Bruegel, Jean Renoir, or Charles Dickens. But nothing looks planted. Here is an emerging style: theatrical yet lived in. An entire world conceived in swift, open glances.

The location was, in fact, Staten Island, and the wedding scene began shooting on April 30, 1971, the twenty-sixth day of production. Studio press releases claim upwards of 750 extras were at the Corleone compound (the "Mall") as Coppola mounted an Italian family celebration by heart: yard-wide trays of lasagne, gallons of beer and wine, a wedding cake six-feet high. The live band beating out the *tarantella*. Dean Martin-slick crooner Johnny Fontane (Al Martino) serenading the bride. The young men tossing sandwiches back and forth, the gifts of cash (it had to be cash) handed to the bride in white envelopes, the small girl dancing on a gangster's shoes.

Within this bustling, alfresco sequence we get to observe (near enough) the entire principal cast in the same space and time, and in relation to one another. The emotional lines are drawn. Fredo (John Cazale) already drunk, already weak. Sonny (James Caan) like a puffer fish, confronting the cops at the gates. Connie (Talia Shire) showing off her handsome, feckless husband Carlo (Gianni Russo). Prim Michael (Al Pacino) in his starched uniform, sitting at a side table with his starched girlfriend Kay (Diane Keaton), who couldn't look any less Italian.

"It's my family, Kay," he insists. "It's not me."

Who's he fooling?

Fourth, was The Core: this he drew from the writings of Kazan, who believed that every scene in a play comes down to a core idea, which could be summed up in a word or two. Coppola always needed at least a sentence. What validated the scene's presence in the story? The Core could be thematic or expositional, but always tuned into the audience's response. What do we learn? Catching up with Sonny after the Don's shooting, was about "taking stock before a storm..."

Fifth, were The Pitfalls: the traps he could so easily slip into. How could he screw things up? Clichés or pacing were cited, or too many scenes of guys sitting around talking. There were written warnings to his future self – be prepared Francis!

The "prompt book" was, in its bruised, battered, and glued-together glory, a first step toward a new way of making films – an entirely analogue attempt to pre-visualise what was to come. He brought a big, brown satchel to transport his filmmaking concordance, which would be with him throughout the screenwriting, and then on into the shoot, a constant companion. In fact, he consulted the notebook more often than the script.

"In truth, I think I made the notebook out of profound fear," said Coppola. "I was terrified." If the script was wrong then the foundations of the movie would be unstable. If he could create a set of blueprints – a plan – then he could sleep at night.

Tossing out the clumsy attempts to modernise the book, Coppola fell into collaboration with Puzo, quickly establishing the mechanics of their screenwriting partnership: he would do the first draft then send it to Puzo at his house on Long Island, or in his new office at Paramount, to make corrections, rewrite, change what he wanted to change, and then send it back. Back and forth the pages went, draft after draft, the film coming into focus. He enjoyed Puzo's company. Having quarrelled with their wives, they both liked to play baccarat, or poker, or shoot dice. But they worked very differently. Puzo took forever to get started, Coppola barely stopped.

He would sit at a corner table at the Caffe Trieste in North Beach with his Olivetti Lettera 32 typewriter and blank paper. Every day for weeks there he was, after the lunchtime rush, in the back by the phone booth.

"I would just sit there, looking at the people coming and going, and go through these pages. I loved it; I was living a dream. I was in a café where there was lots of noise and Italian being spoken, and cute girls walking through, and that was my dream; it was *La bohème* for me."

That was the happiest he would ever be on the film.

Casting was like a turf war. Coppola had fixed ideas about who he wanted; Paramount had their own. An irresistible force reported to an immovable object. The budget kept rising. As well as having it be a period film, Coppola was fixed on filming the passage of Michael hiding out in a sun-scorched Sicily, where he falls for the heavenly Apollonia (Simonetta Stefanelli, a vision who was only sixteen years old). The director wanted to establish the links to the old world, all the medieval towns standing vigil on stony hilltops, where the Mafia took form. The sudden contrast with New York is like passing from night into day. Evans didn't see the need. Couldn't they film in the Adirondacks?

All the while, the book kept selling (it would end up with 650,000 sales in hardback and over 10 million in paperback, liberating Puzo for evermore), and the media's beady eye became more intense. "It was getting bigger than I was," recalled Coppola. "And they were starting to wonder if they hadn't made a mistake in choosing me as the director."

At every meeting, they were aligned against him: Evans, Bart, and Jaffe. There were always assorted lawyers in the room. And somewhere in the background was Bluhdorn chaffing at this upstart. Remember Brando was a non-starter. Jaffe didn't want to hear about it.

They must have tested every Italian going for the Don. Evans was sold on Carlo Ponti, the great Italian producer of Fellini's *La Strada*, who had never acted. Coppola was interested in that. Someone already important in life. They stretched the net wider: Anthony Quinn, George C. Scott, John Huston, Ernest Borgnine. There were always so many lists. Coppola had suggested Laurence Olivier, and then Brando. Evans yelled at him for being a fool.

So Brando, swiftly: born in 1924, in Omaha, Nebraska, to a tough, unloving father and an unreliable, alcoholic mother. Did it correspond that his father made chemical feed and his mother ran a theatre? Brando's 1994 biography, *Songs My Mother Taught Me*, makes no bones about his lopsided parenthood. "Most of my childhood memories of my father are of being ignored," he recalled. "I was his namesake, but nothing I did ever pleased or even interested him." Brando frayed against authority his entire career.

Expelled from Military Academy, he followed his sisters to New York, took classes with Stanislavski advocate Stella Adler (draw from experience), disavowed Lee Strasberg (draw from psychology), and found his feet with Kazan. He had the looks of Adonis and the scuttling, ingenious mind of an inventor.

Stardom, bright as a sunburst, followed, and the status of the greatest of his generation: *The Wild One, Julius Caesar*, those Kazan collaborations, the charm of *Guys and Dolls*. By the 1960s, the light had dimmed. He became apathetic about the material and audiences felt his disdain. In pursuit of connection, he became maddeningly difficult. *Mutiny on the Bounty*, with Trevor Howard, became a self-fulfilling prophecy – infuriated at the script's shortcomings, the star would stand in front of the camera and refuse to act.

Brando's legacy as an artist is irrevocably entwined with that of Coppola. There is the wool gathering of *Apocalypse Now* to come, but for now the young director fought for an American icon.

By 1970, Brando's stock was in free fall. His last film, *Burn!* (an Italian historical drama with Gillo Pontecorvo) had been a disaster. But Coppola wouldn't let it lie. He could feel the promise. He tried again with his Brando pitch.

Jaffe exploded: "As president of Paramount Pictures, I assure you that Marlon Brando will never appear in this motion picture. And, furthermore, as president of the company, I will no longer allow you to discuss it."

That is burned onto Coppola's memory word for word.

Evans interceded. "Give the kid five minutes. Hear him out."

Coppola applied all of his persuasive powers. He was like a lawyer pleading for someone's life. He gave all his reasons why it could only be Brando. "[He] came on like stereo, singing, dancing, reciting lines, jumping around the room," recalled producer Al Ruddy. "We were all speechless."

Upon reaching his impassioned conclusion, Coppola fainted to the floor. Genuinely collapsed and began writhing around as if he was having a fit. Or a heart attack. It was a gag – a trick he used to get his way at UCLA. Jaffe just about got that, and relented. He could have Brando, but under the strictest conditions, surely designed to make him baulk: any delays would be reimbursed to the studio; and he would get a per diem, expenses, and a percentage, but no fee; and he had to take a screen test. And so Coppola headed to the hills.

Star and director found a rapport. Seeing his director's nerves, the actor, well versed in Hollywood's nettlesome games, spoke words of encouragement: "Don't get so upset, it will all work out. It's just a movie." They became allies. Coppola knew that Brando had his back. If they fired him, Brando would walk.

With his specially designed mouthpiece, padded stomach, ten-pound weights in each shoe, and that pugnacious thrust of his jaw, Brando's great talent was revived. But he resisted learning his lines, often improvising like he did with Kazan. So Coppola put cue cards beside the camera. Don't try and master Brando, he understood. Listen to him.

"His performance sets the pitch for the entire production," commended Vincent Canby in *The New York Times*, "which is true and flamboyant and, at unexpected moments, immensely moving."

Then there was Pacino. Everyone had their idea for the Leaguer, the American in the family, Michael Corleone. Ruddy wanted Robert Redford, Hollywood's golden boy. Evans wanted Ryan O'Neal, who had led *Love Story* to the top of the box office and had something of the producer about his handsome conformity. Warren Beatty claimed he turned it down. James Caan originally auditioned for Michael. And Martin Sheen.

History has Coppola first encountering Pacino on Broadway. When he read the book, his was the face he saw. But at thirty-one, the New York born, Actors-Studio trained actor had only made a single movie, the addiction drama *The Panic in Needle Park*. And he certainly didn't look the part, despite being Italian-American: only five-foot seven, favouring hippy ensembles, and hair dangling over his shoulders.

Evans hated the idea. "That midget Pacino," he kept fuming. The actor's first audition with Keaton had been a disaster. Nerves killed him.

"The self-destructive bastard," rued Coppola, "he didn't even know his lines." But the director stuck to the idea, remembering that tragic grandeur he had seen on stage. And hadn't Hoffman blown his screen test for *The Graduate*? Mike Nichols had stuck by what he saw through the lens – the twitching, anguished face of Benjamin Braddock.

Marcia Lucas, wife of George, who edited many of the screen tests, could see exactly what Coppola saw. "Cast Pacino," she told the director, having studied him closer than anyone, "because he addresses you with his eyes."

Pacino had Michael's eyes. That's all there was to it.

One by one, as with Brando, the dominoes began to fall: Ruddy, then Bart, then Bluhdorn, and, always last, Evans. Coppola wore them all down. There was one condition – he must cast James Caan as Sonny.

Pacino was stricken with anxiety. There had been so many tests and auditions his confidence was shot. "I never felt wanted," he said. Coppola empathised – he knew about self-doubt, and it was the film's most demanding role. To travel the psychological arc from Yale student to heir apparent of a New York crime family. Shedding his goodness like a skin. As an actor, he wasn't yet used to shooting out of sequence. Figuring out where he was at any time in terms of Michael's transformation. As Coppola knew, Michael's isolation was the story. We find the film in his eyes.

"Al Pacino's is the guiding performance, that whispers to all the others," wrote film historian David Thomson.

"You don't catch him acting," cooed Kael in her extended rave, "yet he manages to change…"

All the actors are now indelible from their parts – the film fixed in history, cast in bronze. Caan's trigger-happy bravado as Sonny; Robert Duvall's cold efficiency as lonely, adopted son and *consigliere* Tom Hagen; and the remarkable Cazale, discovered by casting director Fred Roos, as Fredo, itching beneath his weakness. Establishing himself as a lifelong Coppola ally, Roos had such a knack for an authentic face, all those background actors who look fully born to this world. Only Richard Castellano, as Clemenza, had the air of Edward G. Robinson or Al Capone.

How do we disentangle Talia Shire from Connie Corleone? She is Coppola's sister as Connie is Michael's feisty sibling. The slight frame and blazing eyes of a spirited young woman in thrall to the whims and casual misogyny of older brothers applies to both life and art.

Like her brothers, Talia was drawn to the arts beneath the disapproving gaze of her father. She wanted to act. For her, it was an even steeper hill to climb. "Growing up the way I did, I was prepared for marriage and to live anonymously," she said. Roman Catholic schools, cheap shoes, washing the dishes.

She had a strangeness. Where her brothers hungered for experience, she took a perverse pleasure in denying herself. She recalled going alone to Radio City Music Hall, not to go backstage and revel in the secret kingdom but to join the line on a chilly New York street. "And then when I finally got to the ticket booth, I'd turn around and go to the end of the line again. There's a real thrill in denial. My whole life has been that way."

How the Coppolas treat interviews as confessionals.

There is a wounded, resentful side to Talia – as there is to Connie. Growing up, she was classically pretty – jet-black hair, large sloe-eyes, a ballerina's waif-like frame – but painfully shy. Instinct told her to keep her ambitions hidden, especially from her brother Francis. She didn't want anything from him. Their relationship, she said, was tender and complex.

Eventually, Talia convinced her parents that Yale School of Drama would bring her out of herself. Graduating, she got serious, joining Stella Adler's class, who had stirred the demons in Brando. She followed her brothers West, and served her time with Roger Corman, acting in shoestring pictures like *The Dunwich Horror* and *Gas-S-S*. After which, she played the wife to Nick Nolte in the adaptation of another post-war family saga: ABC television's soapy rendition of Irwin Shaw's *Rich Man, Poor Man*.

The Godfather was different. She needed to play Connie. So Talia found the courage to ask her brother for an audition. No special favours; just an audition like everyone else. He turned her down. He was already under pressure, growing insecure beneath the glare of the studio. "And I think maybe he was scared of me," she said. "What if I was no good?"

It was more than that. Coppola didn't want to be bartering with the studio – asking for favours that would one day have to be returned. Never be indebted to these people. He also considered his sister wrong for Connie. "Tally's too pretty for the part," he shouted at his mother, the matter reaching a head at the family table. His dramatic point was that a pretty boy marrying into the Mafia would have "a fat little dumpy Italian girl." He saw Connie as a kind of maid.

Are the women of *The Godfather* complicit? Even as they are shuffled into the kitchen or bedroom there is a striking ambiguity in proud, isolated Connie, clinging to a terrible marriage; doomed Apollonia; the near-silent presence of Mama Corleone (Morgana King), and even Kay, the outsider, who sees the family for what it is, yet is drawn back to Michael.

History serves us well. Coppola departed briefly for England to visit Brando, who was shooting *The Nightcomers* in Cambridgeshire. While he was gone, through the guile of Roos, who had been Talia's manager (she had introduced him to Coppola), and a well-disposed Puzo, Talia landed an audition. Having married David Shire in 1970, a composer like her father, who scored significant films like *All the President's Men* and *The Conversation*, she went under her married name for fear that the Coppola tag might count for or against her.

The venue was a draughty rehearsal space in New York. Coppola refused to audition in offices where the phone might ring. He respected actors. Waiting their turn were Pacino and Sheen. "Evans chose me," said Talia with pride. Which led to a "long talk" with her brother.

Talia's intensity cuts through like broken glass. Connie comes alive for us, bruised by the men in her life. There's a great photo of her pinned to the bed during the shooting of the fight scene with Russo's combustible, no-good husband Carlo. Such were the visceral furies between the two actors, and the flying crockery, she had feared cinematographer Gordon Willis would get caught in the crossfire. But in this picture it is Coppola standing over his prone sister, conducting the moment. This is the family business.

Talia's career would flourish across the three *Godfather* films, in which time Connie grows in corruption: dead husbands and dead brothers left in her wake. A sweeter, more vulnerable side was revealed in that other iconic Italian-American role, Adrian, wife and rock to Sylvester Stallone's boxing hero Rocky Balboa, across five of the many *Rocky* films. "I'm very much like Adrian," she said.

From her second marriage to attorney turned producer Jack Schwartzman, Talia was mother to actor Jason Schwartzman and actor-filmmaker Robert Schwartzman.

"People ask about that," she said, "and I've always said we are in the tradition of a circus family. And what I mean is that we kill ourselves for our work."

On the eve of production, Coppola hosted a dinner. An icebreaker for the principal cast held in the backroom of Patsy's restaurant in New York. "Like playing at family," said Coppola. He placed Brando at the head of the table, then Pacino on one side and Caan on the other, then Duvall and Cazale: this male preserve. Cracking open the wine, Brando never broke character. "When that meal was finished," said Coppola, "that family existed for the first time..." Talia served the pasta.

"There was not one single happy day on that film," recalled Bart.

They began on March 18, 1971, with the New York streets overcast. Michael and Kay coming out of Radio City Music Hall (an auteur's touch). The mood deteriorated fast.

A plot gathered to have Coppola fired. Doubts already seeded before production began to grow among the Paramount heads on the West Coast. But betrayal came from discomfortingly close quarters. Coppola's editor Aram Avakian, who had cut *You're a Big Boy Now* and hired for his experience, was feeding back to the studio that the footage was a mess. You couldn't see a thing it was so dark. And none of it cut together. It was mutiny, a putsch. Avakian and Jack Ballard, sent by Evans to sniff out trouble, were contriving to have Coppola fired. With one directorial credit (*End of the Road*), Avakian planned to replace his boss, with first AD Steve Kesten as producer.

It was the Sollozzo footage that saved Coppola. They had shot it on the Wednesday and Thursday of the first week. Michael putting a bullet through The Turk's forehead in the quiet Brooklyn restaurant, scarlet mist blooming in the air behind him, with the director's parents among the terrified extras.

Technically tricky, the blanks and squibs would need resetting with every take, while Coppola nudged and noodled with the performances, nuances the crew couldn't detect.

It is the scene around which the entire film pivots, the moment Michael's trajectory is set – where he sells his soul to save the family. Here is the full flavour of Coppola's epic intimacy. Here is the monumentality of the film's violence. First the overreaching Sollozzo (Al Lettieri) and then, after a heartbeat in which the camera peers at the perplexed policeman, his thuggish bodyguard McCluskey (Sterling Hayden) through the throat, then the head. The crack of the shots, and then only background noise. The gun had been concealed behind a cistern in the lavatory.

A work of alchemy was going on beneath the noses of Evans and Bart and Bluhdorn – Coppola was transforming pulp fiction into a new idiom not only for genre pictures but the medium as a whole.

Let us pause to recall how the detail feels. Louis's restaurant in The Bronx, another venue sliced out of history as finely as a garlic shaving: the tiled floor, the white tablecloths, the veal and pasta, and the steady hum of quieted voices. How the director refuses to use subtitles when the talk shifts into Italian. We lean in to grasp how the words are spoken.

The orchestration of the music is inspired. How sparsely it is used. Tension rises to the insistent rhythm of the subway train – absurdly loud, a metaphorical ambience. "In the hands of another filmmaker, there would be tension music percolating under the surface," explained Murch. The notes of Nino Rota's great theme are withheld; then with the clatter of the gun hitting the ground at last the release of music. Channelling emotion, not creating it.

Even in its rough form, screened in the pool house at Woodland, Evans could see this footage was "not just good, but brilliant." Pacino's black eyes stare out from the screen, the shutters already drawn.

So it was Coppola who had Avakian and Kesten fired (Ballard was ordered home), but the director was always watching his back. That fear, heavy and dull, was a constant companion. At night, he kept dreaming that Kazan had arrived on set, there to take over. Not without cause – there were discussions at Paramount. Kazan, they thought, knew how to handle Brando. Coppola persuaded them Kazan was nearly senile. Not true at all, but he had got into Evans's head. He was learning to be devious.

Every day battle would recommence with his cinematographer. Willis had lent a dreamy, monochrome elegance to the cityscapes of Woody

Allen's *Manhattan*, and was fresh from shooting *Klute* with Alan J. Pakula in a spectrum of pewters and browns so grim it barely registered as colour. The urbane, meticulous Willis was able to foster mood and myth in the canyons of New York, but he had the disposition of a porcupine. Each shot was a matter of discipline, blocked out and made to work. He was clinical, while Coppola wanted to explore and improvise, to find the spark in the moment. Blocking was a bore – it tied the actors down. Willis thought his director was deliberately tempting chaos. Coppola's attitude, he said, was "I'll set my clothes on fire – if I can make it to the other side of the room it'll be spectacular." That went down in the history books.

Did they not realise they were working miracles? They had agreed upon a radically subdued look. A classical style to fit a classical story was how Coppola saw it. He wanted Willis's famous underexposed interiors, because that was how he remembered Italian homes, thick with shadowy intimacy. Production designer Dean Tavoularis – another commencing a lifelong collaboration with the storm-laden director – recalled the planning of sensual tableaux: men crowded into dark rooms, straight-on shots with minimal camera movement. It must seem organic. Sepia, like old photos.

As Kael grasped, "You're a few minutes into the movie before you're conscious it's set in the past."

It began with Brando emerging from the dark like the prow of a ship. It was a darkness, intuited Thomson, "not too far from wickedness, maybe, yet as close to comfort, security, and home." The diabolical gloom of the office would stand in stark contrast to the bright Kodachromey footage of the wedding outside. Two rhythms: exterior and interior. Good and evil, and the twilight that lies between. The studio was bewildered. This was an era in which Hollywood came candied in the dayglo of Doris Day or Julie Andrews movies. Even their bloated epics looked as if they had been shot under floodlights.

Despite diametrically opposed temperaments, intellectual chalk and emotional cheese, Willis and Coppola were the perfect foils for one another. Not that either saw it that way.

Disputes reached operatic heights. Shooting at Filmways Studios in East Harlem, which housed the two-storey interior of the Don's home,

Pacino stumbled down an unlit corridor. Coppola demanded to know why they hadn't prepared for that eventuality. Willis, who felt he was the only one of the set displaying any professionalism, let loose at his director.

"You don't know how to do anything right!"

The set froze.

Coppola exploded. "Fuck this picture! I've directed five fucking pictures without anyone telling me how to do it…"

He threatened to fire the cinematographer.

That resulted in Willis storming off set, and Coppola demanding that camera operator Michael Chapman step in to shoot the scene.

Caught between two masters, Chapman fled to the studio's insalubrious bathroom, lowering his trousers to stave off orders to return. Not to be outshone, Coppola stormed off to his office, half-demolishing the door. The noise was so loud the crew feared he had shot himself.

There were 120 locations across Manhattan and into the boroughs. Hereby lies another legend: that the mob, the *real* mob, took against Puzo's book and its adaptation. The "Italian-American Civil Rights League", represented by one Anthony Colombo, claimed the story unfairly stigmatised all Italian-Americans as criminals and began to orchestrate obstructions. It began as small, niggling things. Local homeowners would suddenly refuse permission for shooting. Then it got more serious: abusive phone calls, bomb threats called into Paramount's New York offices, and producers being trailed home. Coppola was left unmolested – it was the head of the snake they were aiming for. Eventually, it was Ruddy who took matters head on, meeting with Colombo at the Gulf & Western building, letting him read the script, and hitting upon an agreement. Not once in the whole film would the word "Mafia" be spoken. Three months later, Anthony Colombo's father, Joseph Colombo, narrowly survived being gunned down at a rally on Columbus Circle, a few blocks from where *The Godfather* was filming.

Still Coppola dallied and pondered, kneading his scenes like dough, refusing to be rushed. So good with the actors: allowing room for improvisations, God-given miracles plucked out of the air. Castellano, for instance, his fleshy, redoubtable Clemenza, had a way with polishing lines. After the clinical killing of Paulie, parked amid the long grass, the script simply read, "Leave the gun." It was Castellano who added, "Take the cannoli."

Is it a stretch to say that the entire ethos of *The Sopranos* sprang from the offhand idiom of that remark?

That was the day Jack Ballard had taken Coppola aside and said, "If you don't finish on time today, you're not gonna come to work tomorrow."

The music that filled his childhood homes informed his direction. There were cadences only he could hear. He was composing a symphony, where even stage fright could be transformed into realism. Montana, his burly Luca Brasi, was not a professional actor, and fell to pieces in front of Brando. "We shot the scene a dozen times, but he froze on every take and forgot his lines," recalled Coppola. "We finally gave up. Later, I wrote a new little scene where he was at the party, before his visit to the Godfather, practising his speech perfectly over and over."

Keeping one of the scenes where Montana genuinely froze, it suddenly made sense. It was Brasi fumbling his lines, not Montana.

Yet Paramount's sorties continued. Mostly led by Evans. Why was it still so dark? What was Brando saying? Will it need subtitles? Why was he taking so long? Was the violence explicit enough? Did he really need the Don's elaborate death scene among the tomato plants (so beautifully improvised by Brando)?

Coppola became increasingly depressed. "I thought my movie was a disaster," he said, after all that is what everyone was telling him. He took to wearing a badge bearing the title of the Sophia Loren film, *Mortadella*, shooting in New York at the same time. He would tell anyone who asked that he wished he was directing that film. Scorsese visited on the day they were shooting the Don's funeral, and found his friend sat on one of the gravestones crying.

There was one voice that offered hope – the screenwriter Robert Towne. He was there to help find the answer to a crucial scene.

Coppola's creative well had finally run dry. Brando was getting ready to leave, and they needed a moment between the old Don, now dying, and his son and heir apparent Michael. The master passing on wisdom to the apprentice. What they had was too explicit. He needed more emotion. Something underneath lines. Coppola knew Towne from their shared time at Roger Corman's knee. Talented and perceptive, if self-possessed,

Towne's reputation was riding high having script doctored on *Bonnie and Clyde* and Jack Nicholson's *Cisko Pike*. He had already got Evans out of a few tight spots, Hollywood's relief pitcher, and was in the early stages of his first great contribution to the New Wave: the dizzyingly complex neo-noir *Chinatown*.

Grateful for the respite, Towne flew into New York, and Coppola explained what he needed. As did Brando. "Just once, I want Vito not to be inarticulate," he impressed upon Towne. To give him a taste of what they were creating, the director showed him an hour's worth of rushes. Towne called the director straight after, raving. Coppola was too beaten up to take in the encouragement.

"I'd never seen footage with that kind of texture related to any so-called gangster movies; Francis had brought so much of himself and of life to it," remembered Towne.

Writing through the night, drunk on the rich taste of what he knew to be a masterpiece in the making, he found his scene. Inspired by the cover of the book, that image of puppet strings, he gives Vito his eloquence: "I refused to be a fool, dancing on the string held by these big shots." As with so much in *The Godfather*, it seemed to say as much about Coppola as it did the characters.

His own family was with him. This was policy: if the shoot took Coppola away for longer than two weeks, he had his kids on set. "We travel together like a circus family, with Francis on the tightrope and the rest of us holding the ropes," said Eleanor. There are photos of Gio at his father's side, with a pensive Eleanor looking on. She more than anyone could see the pressure he was under. To make matters more intense, crammed into a small, rented apartment, she was heavily pregnant with their third child. You can't help but picture young Vito's cramped tenement, and his squalling newborn in *The Godfather Part II*.

On May 13, George and Marcia Lucas stopped by on their way to go backpacking around Europe. As soon as they had left to catch a plane, Eleanor felt the contractions. Coppola was already back miserably perusing the dailies when the call came through at 11 p.m., and he rushed to the hospital. Enter Sofia, his daughter. Born into the transcendent chaos of *The Godfather*. Anointed into cinema.

Eleanor takes her to the Staten Island set where they are shooting the wedding sequence. Coppola introduces his wife and baby girl to Brando. It was "like standing in a beam of light," recalled Eleanor, imagining this was what it was to experience heroin. Brando lifts Sofia from her mother's arms, holding her with ease as he examines her fingers and toes. A few days later he sends a gold bracelet with a card.

"Welcome to the world."

Within two weeks, Sofia had a featured role as Connie's son, Michael, at the christening sequence, with Gio and Roman in attendance.

The film's finale finds Coppola expressing imperious talent. Puzo had fretted over how to contain the two threads: Michael taking the sacrament in church and the enactment of his audacious plan to assassinate the heads of the five families. Each death strikes its own unforgettable image. Moe Greene with a bullet through his glasses, Barzini tumbling down the steps of the courthouse. Edit them together like Eisenstein, decreed Coppola. Fuse baptism and slaughter for something exhilarating and terrifying. The fusion here is also between director and character – as Michael achieves full control, so finally does Coppola.

This is opera.

Back at Zoetrope's Folsom Street offices in San Francisco, examining his assembly, Coppola fell into even greater despair. "I was sure people would feel I had taken this exciting bestseller novel and transformed it into a dark, ponderous, boring movie with a lot of actors who were known to be my personal friends." William Friedkin's *The French Connection* was flying high at the box office, filled with a frantic, street-wrecking forward momentum. That is what young audiences wanted, Coppola told himself. Not this.

He was terrified the studio would take it away from him – Paramount still had final cut.

There were further clashes over the music. Coppola had hired Nino Rota, Fellini's composer, who had an Italian fatalism in his soul. The director hand delivered the cans of film to Rota's studio in Rome. He sent back a tape with the immortal waltz played on piano. Evans had gone his own way, hiring Henry Mancini (*Love Story*), who had a snazzier way with the classics.

That led to a screaming match, and Coppola carrying on regardless. For five days, he arrived at Woodland with the scored reels, sitting by the pool, awaiting Evans's response. They agreed on a preview. If the audience hated the music, Coppola would bow to fate. On the way out, people kept raving:"… that great theme!"

As it stood, the film was two hours and forty-five minutes long. Coppola loved it, but Evans had been clear – if it was over two hours and fifteen minutes (he was very exact) the edit would switch to Paramount in Los Angeles. Coppola would effectively lose control. It was a power play, a way of getting the movie back into his hands. So the editors filed down scene after scene, removing all the background texture, all the granular reality of the film. They got to a heartbreaking two hours and fifteen minutes and sent the reels to Los Angeles.

Evans's recollections are hazy, and like much in his life, spun through the prism of his ego. Reading his account of the film's final stages in *The Kid Stays in the Picture*, you will learn that he saved *The Godfather* from certain ignominy.

He had to be wheeled into his screening room on a gurney, crippled with acute sciatica (a lifelong struggle). "You've destroyed the picture," he remonstrated to Coppola on the phone. "This is a long, bad trailer for a really good film."

He demanded Coppola come down to Los Angeles. There was a conference beside Evans's pool, serenaded by fountains, and the director agreed to return all the non-narrative sequences that gave it such ambience.

"See, now it works," said Evans.

Had it been a ruse? Or blind luck?

Evans was an astute judge of an edit, maintained Bart, even from his gurney. "This guy couldn't cut his toenail," smarted Caan. Maybe Coppola had become an astute judge of Evans.

How do you get a grip on *The Godfather*? Surely now the most celebrated film ever made, or close to it. For it brings together not only the opposing poles of commercial success and critical acclaim, but encloses them in a form of cinematic nobility – the idea that Hollywood was truly capable of art. This film was the vanguard of possibility.

So it is now staggering that the reviews at the time were so inconsistent. Vincent Canby in *The New York Times* swooned in its presence: *The Godfather*, he reported, was "one of the most brutal and moving chronicles of American life ever designed within the limits of popular entertainment."

Yet there were those who found it morally deplorable. "[*The Godfather*] forces you to take sides, to form allegiances," said Robert Hatch in *The Nation*. There were those who saw it as an implicit endorsement of Mafia methods. And others still who found it pretentious, or overblown, or tedious.

Did it glamorise the Mafia? Coppola certainly maintains a moral distance from his subject. There is no judgment. As Thomson, such a cheerleader, noted, the film stands for a brief era (those consecrated 1970s) when "the details of our evil could be inspected without moral relief being insisted upon." If we come away admiring these people, longing for the family to close ranks around us, then maybe we ought to look into our own hearts. Coppola threw open the doors of moral nihilism. It was a "premonition" of the America to come.

The box office returns have an epochal ripple to them. The film opened in an unprecedented 400 theatres on March 14, 1972, and the queues began to form. After a week it had made $7.4 million. After two it was up to $17.2 million. By May 17, it was up to $53.3 million. All over the world it devoured records, and Mafia screenplays and novels piled up in Bart's office. By August 2, it had grossed $101 million. Would everyone in the country end up partaking of his lustrous saga?

The event picture was born.

Evans had his contract extended.

All the aforementioned stories have become legend. Endlessly retold, endlessly quoted. Is it even possible to see past the adoration, the anniversaries, the think pieces on its heavy legacy, and the documentaries in which A-list fans reel off the lines? "Leave the gun," instructs Tom Hanks, known to hold annual *Godfather* singalongs. "Take the Cannoli." Can we find the film that lies beneath? Coppola's great family saga.

Can he draw no satisfaction from the unquestionable triumph of *The Godfather*? That he was proven so right: the revival of Brando, the discovery of Pacino, the numinous luxury of the period setting, and the thematic reach — at once familial and national. He chipped at a cultural vein and opened up a seam of gold.

That is truly the point here. *The Godfather* is *The Godfather* despite Hollywood and because of Coppola. He is still to this day quick to acknowledge that this was Puzo's story, but it is his world. What makes the film so popular is the personal touch; we see and feel ourselves within its embrace. We know families, weddings, and dinner table squabbles. And Coppola transcended the book, finding the subtext in his own cultural identity, his sure knowledge, and his artistic ambitions.

Eleanor recalled being in New York and her husband gazing out of the open window at the lines for *The Godfather* running around the block. The excited chatter mixing with the angry traffic. Without a word he returned to his typewriter, and his struggles in adapting *The Great Gatsby* (a stopgap screenwriting assignment, and he would hate what Jack Clayton did with his script) — a tale, as it happens, of the hollowness at the heart of the American Dream.

The work made more sense.

With all their fanfare and tradition, the Oscars represented another occasion in which Hollywood was able to give with one hand and take with the other. To remind this young director, with his dark angry eyes, that he was still an upstart.

On the evening of March 26, 1973, *The Godfather's* chief rival is Bob Fosse's *Cabaret* — turning Christopher Isherwood's Weimar Berlin into a smoky blend of musical and tragedy. Another film strong on time and place, and the porous borders between genres. Each has a mixed night.

Rota's lovely score had been refused entry on a technicality, though would be repeated frequently on the night. Pacino (reduced somehow to the Supporting Actor category) loses to *Cabaret's* Joel Grey. Brando wins Best Actor only to strike that old note of defiance by sending Native American princess Sacheen Littlefeather, dignified amid the jeers, to refuse on his behalf. He was landing a blow against Hollywood's "demeaning" portrayal of natives, and redrawing old battle lines with the studios.

Coppola takes to the stage with Puzo's daughter to accept Best Adapted Screenplay. He is, of course, a natural at the podium: endearing but provocative as he slips in mention of his "wonderful, romantic financial adventure in San Francisco." He thanks Bart but makes no mention of Evans.

Wasn't this the dusty routine the Brats intended to sweep into the Pacific? It was always their great (and inevitable) paradox to hunger for recognition from the old guard.

Sweating in his bottle-green tuxedo, Coppola's jaw tightens when the Best Director category is announced. The presenting duo, Julie Andrews and a cratered George Stevens milking old Hollywood platitudes, take an eternity to tear open the envelope. It goes to Bob Fosse, and Coppola lifts his chin and valiantly applauds a travesty. Fosse slips in a joke about Coppola not having turned up yet. He knows. Backstage Coppola is heard whispering, "I was so sure…"

Another wound to add to the collection.

The Godfather wins Best Picture, no force on Earth was going to deny it that. A tetchy Clint Eastwood (what about the cowboys, he quips dully) does the honours, rasping hoary routines about picking a first among equals. "They all concern human nature and our confrontation with fate," he reads off the cue card.

Ruddy alone bounds to the stage (not Evans, not Coppola, not Puzo). "We were getting worried there," he gasps, making clear the expectation within the room. He rattles off the names of the suits, Evans, Bart, Bluhdorn, and babbles, blind to the irony, about the possibilities of the American Dream.

Not once does he mention Coppola.

"*The Godfather*," declared author and journalist Jonathan Freedland in *The Guardian*, "now functions the way fairy tales or Bible stories do. It's become a fundamental narrative deeply embedded in the collective psyche…"

Almost fifty years hence, it remains a confounding victory for Coppola. He had won like Michael. His were the spoils. He was a commercial giant with Hollywood at his feet (always a potential trip hazard). In return he had sold his soul. Who he was as an artist had been fundamentally altered. Or is that revealed?

"Coppola obviously identified with Michael," reported Peter Biskind, summing up the impact of *The Godfather*, "the prodigal son, and in Michael's pact with the devil lies the tale of Coppola's uneasy relationship with the studios, and his brave, if stumbling attempts to build his own independent power base."

Could he deny the opera in his veins?

"*The Godfathers*," concluded Biskind, "would be the most personal films Coppola would ever make."

If he didn't quite have the last laugh (Paramount made millions, Evans hailed the conquering hero), he had a decent giggle. At one of the endless, needling meetings, Coppola had put it to Evans that if the film ever reached $15 million at the box office, Paramount must buy him a Mercedes 600, the big stretch model, custom-made like a limousine. The Pope had one.

"No problem at $50 million," retorted Evans, enjoying a preposterous bet.

Two years later, with *The Godfather* past $100 million, Coppola walks into a San Francisco Mercedes dealership with Lucas. Suspicious salesmen eye the jeans and sneakers, the untucked shirts, and the Honda parked outside. They are moodily shown sedans.

"We want the one with six doors," insists Coppola. "Send the bill to Paramount."

CHAPTER 4

CONTROL FREAKS

The Conversation (1974), The Godfather Part II (1974)

Success was to his taste. *The Godfather* had made Francis Ford Coppola in the region of $7 million, and he went on a cathartic spending spree. Maybe he was trying to quieten those inner doubts. Maybe he was trying to buy off his guilt. Maybe he wanted to show off.

"The success of *The Godfather* went to my head like a rush of perfume," he said. "I thought I couldn't do anything wrong."

Imagine the montage.

The mansion is a Queen Anne-style row house in San Francisco's celebrated Pacific Heights: twenty-eight rooms, cornflower blue walls, and an unimpeded view of the Golden Gate Bridge. Orson Welles famously described (and demeaned) Hollywood as "the biggest electric train set any boy ever had," so Coppola installs a symbolic train set in his cellar. Friends nickname him, "F.A.O. Coppola". There is a Wurlitzer jukebox, a Warhol Mao print, and a ballroom transformed into a screening room with projector, Moog synthesiser, and harpsichord. The furniture is a mix of Italian modern and antiques, picked out by Eleanor.

Does Coppola dream of inviting Robert Evans up the coast to pay his respects beside the Moorish-style swimming pool shaped like a clover?

He has promises to keep. He had made *The Godfather* in order to fund American Zoetrope. And so it does. Only his ambitions have magnified. The under-the-radar collective that had run for the hills is replaced by a prestige production company, with Coppola its Korda-like mogul.

Folsom Street is abandoned (and eventually demolished), and he buys the iconic copper-green Sentinel Building on the edge of Chinatown, a survivor of the 1906 earthquake. He fills it with the latest in editing, sound, and screening rooms, with his oak-panelled, art-deco penthouse office designed by Dean Tavoularis with windows on three sides. From this lofty perch, he sees himself conducting American culture.

His mind skitters in different directions, impulses impossible to resist. He buys a radio station, a magazine (a foolhardy expedition called *City*), the 300-seat Little Fox Theatre, a helicopter, and shares in a private jet (immediately dubbed "Air Francis"). Then part ownership in the Cinema 5 chain of New York arthouse theatres (like those his grandfather Francesco ran).

He serves as producer for George Lucas, who is intent on a nostalgia-infused tale of cars and teens called *American Graffiti*, based on his memories of growing up in Modesto, with roles for Ron Howard, Richard Dreyfuss, and Harrison Ford. After the fiasco of *THX-1138*, the only studio interested is Universal. But it proves a tense relationship, with swords crossed over final cut, and Coppola left duelling on behalf of his dumbstruck friend.

Significantly warmer than Lucas's debut, it catches on at the box office, scoring $115 million worldwide on a budget of next to nothing (he had something that kid). Coppola's backend points land him $3 million. But he can only fume how those close to him (including Eleanor) had advised him not to invest his own money into Lucas's second film.

"That movie could have brought me over twenty million dollars. After that, I decided that I would try to finance all Zoetrope films myself."

Take a note of that.

Cut to Hollywood, where Paramount is in the ascendancy. On the phone, in the restaurants, Evans takes to referring to his place of work as "the mountain" after its rugged logo. The money and hubris are flowing. Chairman Charlie Bluhdorn is all for the Hollywood renaissance if it carries on delivering Coppolas and their *Godfathers*. These auteurs are their own worst enemies. "They work like slaves for themselves," he says, shaking his blunt head.

He has an idea: a company within the company, headed up by the three biggest directors of the moment. This is Coppola (of course), plus fellow first-wavers Peter Bogdanovich (prized for the small-town wonder *The Last Picture Show*), and William Friedkin (coveted after *The French Connection*). It was the usual situation – friends and rivals. Friedkin had known Coppola as far back as Seven Arts. He would come over for dinner, while Coppola tried to set him up with Talia.

They seal the deal at the Essex House Hotel in New York, with Central Park across the street. Bluhdorn tells them he was once a doorman here; he now owns the joint. He's like the Don parcelling out favours. They could make any film of their choosing for under $3 million, with an initial capital injection of $31 million. Complete autonomy. Profit sharing. And non-exclusivity. "They should have given an Oscar to the deal," quips Billy Wilder. Bluhdorn has his eye on Mike Nichols and Stanley Kubrick. Incorporating auteurs like chicken feed suppliers.

It is August 1972.

Coppola claimed he only ever signed up to the Directors Company for "vindictive, Mafia-like reasons." He wanted to get back at Warner Bros. for discarding Zoetrope. It was a chance to jam another toe into the studio door. He had one stipulation. Keep Evans away. Among the Paramount hierarchy, served a Coppola-flavoured *fait accompli*, a suspicion arose that the *Godfather*-maestro was pulling the strings. "Playing Charlie like a Stradivarius," recalled production chief Frank Yablans, certain the result would be nothing but indulgent garbage.

Maybe all of this deal making and nest feathering was a way for Coppola to avoid confronting his central quandary. In the wake of *The Godfather*, who exactly was he? There were already whispers of a sequel. It was that age-old dilemma – art or commerce? With the slush fund presented by the Director's Company he could hold back the tide.

So he made *The Conversation* his priority, exactly the kind of project that Yablans feared: a clever-clever dissertation on technology and paranoia destined never to rattle box office tills. Coppola would resume where he had left off.

No one could ever accuse Bluhdorn of not having an agenda. He wanted a favour in return. They met for lunch at the Palm in Manhattan, Bluhdorn's treat: Gulf & Western's short-tempered powerbroker, Coppola, and his father Carmine. The Austrian bullied his way through the usual pleasantries and small-talk then got down to business.

"Listen, you've gotta licence to make Coca-Cola, make Coca-Cola!"

American capitalism 101: the trouble with making so much money is making even more of it. Paramount was desperate for a sequel to *The Godfather*, and as quickly as possible: more gangsters, more family, more period, more Pacino, more of all those things they had resisted every inch of the way. QED: more Coppola.

Things were already moving. Evans hadn't hung around waiting on the whims of artists; he was on the phone, plotting, manoeuvring, and laying down a trail of golden breadcrumbs. Mario Puzo had already delivered a prospective script – a plodding rehash called *The Death of Michael Corleone.*

Returning to the bosom of the Corleones had always sounded tacky to Coppola. He let it be known that he was done with gangsters for good. "I used to joke that the only way I'd do it was if they'd let me film *Abbott and Costello Meet the Godfather.*"

Yes, he wanted to define himself as an artist. Stay out of the reach of Hollywood. But his reluctance was also born of fear. How do you top a film in the realm of the immortals? If anything went wrong, he knew, "that people would put the first one down to Brando or something." You should lay off sequels. They can ruin your past as well as your future.

But Bluhdorn was in full spate. Hadn't he been the one who had Coppola's back during the first film? Back when he was just a punk director who'd done some lousy Fred Astaire movie. Even when Evans and the others had wanted him out. And things would be different this time. Coppola would call the shots. He was untouchable. Could he imagine a *Godfather* film being made without him?

That struck an icy chord – to lose control of his world. Like a drowning man accepting the water's embrace, his ego took over. "In short," he said, "it seemed like such a terrible idea that I began to be intrigued by the thought of pulling it off." Having turned trash into art with the first film, he had a recurring daydream that he could work such miracles with anything. Turning a soap opera into the most wonderful soap ever done. Directing the plays of a cub-scout troop and having it become the most exciting theatre company in the country.

Directing a sequel to *The Godfather* was so outrageous a proposition only he could attempt it. And there was unfinished business. That Best Director Oscar had eluded him.

But he offered Bluhdorn only half of what he wanted. He would produce and supervise the sequel, lend it his precious perspective, and help choose a worthy director.

Three months later, he did. "Martin Scorsese."

"Over my dead body!" screeched Evans.

Another impasse.

Paramount vice president Peter Bart met Coppola for breakfast and laid it on thick. It had to be him. "Look, who was the star of *The Godfather*? Brando, Pacino… No, it was you."

Coppola winced. It'll be two years of misery, he protested: this big, expensive film with all the pressure, and all those people telling him what to do.

Bart improvised. "If I can get you a million dollars to write and direct, will you do it?"

On June 22, 1972, Coppola broke the world record. He signed a deal to direct *The Godfather* sequel for $1 million upfront. Front offices all over Hollywood heard the crack as the glass ceiling shattered. Within hours, Warner was on the phone asking for the $300,000 he still owed them.

According to biographer Michael Schumacher, the $1 million fee was a publicity front. There was still room for negotiation: what Coppola eventually got was $250,000 to direct, $200,000 to co-write the script (with Puzo), $50,000 to produce, and thirteen percent of the gross. And there were his demands: Evans was not to set foot on set. He wasn't even to read the script. And the film would be called *The Godfather Part II*. That got backs up. The marketing department thought audiences would be confused. Was this just the second half of the same movie? Well, yes.

Remember sequels were still relatively unknown at this time. Characters returned, there were further adventures of *The Lone Ranger* or *Abbott and Costello*, but that whole number game started with Coppola.

One more stipulation, he got to keep his sanity by making *The Conversation* first. Bluhdorn agreed to it all. He just wanted more Coca-Cola.

With his requirements met, *The Godfather Part II* started to resemble a $12 million personal project.

Coppola wanted it to be known as *Part II* for good reason. He could never bring himself to be conventional. Conformity made his bones itch. To simply tell the story of Michael Corleone consolidating his power by moving – counter to his father's legacy – into drugs and gambling, reigning supreme at the head of the family before the mandated downfall. He wanted something more operatic and structurally elaborate – a saga that would cross years.

He would tell two stories, a sequel and a prequel, intertwining Vito's origins from the book with Michael's moral decay. Or as Coppola explained it: "Two parallel stories, two generations, two men at the same point in their life – they both have young children, and they are learning to deal with power." It was about a father and a son measured against one another.

We can infer a third story, a third man at the same point in his life, dealing with power and family – Coppola.

"The daring of *Part II* is that it enlarges the scope and deepens the meaning of the first film," extolled *The New Yorker's* Pauline Kael, back before the altar.

Now he could do all those things he hadn't been able to do on *The Godfather*. Vito coming to America, his young family, and his rise to power against the backdrop of a chaotic New York. In Michael's story – expanding into Cuba, outwitting the Senate commission, rooting out betrayal – there was the chance to extend his metaphor that organised crime, the unnamed Mafia, stood for big business. And America.

"Though the Mafia was a Sicilian phenomenon," he said, "there was no way it could really have flowered except in the soil of America."

He let his imagination wander, dashing down potential scenes and ideas. Michael's ties with his Italian background have strained; Fredo has married a movie star *à la* Raquel Welch; Connie remarries; Michael is diabetic. He deviated further and further from the novel, drawing the new film closer still to the post-war America he had breathed in his own life. Puzo collaborated, but these were Coppola's memories.

He listed all the characters from *The Godfather* still alive, mapped out a family tree. How old were the children by 1958? As well as Al Pacino as Michael, he foresaw Diane Keaton (Kay) and John Cazale (doomed Fredo) taking more prominent roles. With Robert Duvall (Tom Hagen), Talia Shire (Connie), and Richard Bright (assassin Al Neri) returning to the fold.

This presented hurdles, what you might call the *Godfather* syndrome. No one had signed up for a sequel, and there was a nagging resentment among the cast that they hadn't reaped their just rewards on *The Godfather*. Insulted by the initial offer of $100,000, Pacino flatly refused to return.

It took Coppola to win him over. He sat him down, told him what he had in mind, gave it the big sell, the full-bore passion, and Pacino was compelled – for $600,000, and ten percent of the gross. And only days into shooting, he demanded a complete rewrite of his part. Coppola complied in three days flat. It was like being back on *Dementia 13*.

Any plans to use Marlon Brando minus wrinkles and hair dye as the young Vito were shattered by the actor's refusal to countenance returning. Negotiations with Paramount failed to make any progress, and there was an air of bitterness from Brando on his treatment (translation: earnings) on the original.

A blessing in disguise, Coppola turned to Robert De Niro. He had originally auditioned for Sonny, and Coppola had liked him then. But he was still a relative unknown, who had played edgy goofballs, nothing as contained as Vito. To convince his friend, Martin Scorsese flew up to San Francisco with a print of *Mean Streets*. Coppola was mesmerised. This could work: he didn't have to resemble a young Brando; he needed to resemble a young Vito. And they could play him younger.

It was an eye-opening visit for Scorsese. He stayed in the attic of the Queen Anne, clocking the growing number of hangers-on and acolytes that surrounded his old friend. Every morning he would literally be awoken by the sound of Coppola blowing his own trumpet, dressed in nothing but an open robe.

De Niro would use implants to stretch his jaw, but this was about performance – the romantic and brutal spirit of Vito Corleone.

There was no Clemenza either, which was a blow. Richard Castellano demanded both a substantial increase on his salary, and that his wife be hired to rewrite his dialogue. Coppola implored him to see sense, figuring he would crack as the start date approached. To no avail, and we learn of Clemenza's death in the opening scenes.

Casting Lee Strasberg as Hyman Roth was an act of pure cheek. Roth is a spin on Meyer Lansky, the notorious Jewish kingpin who fixed his sights on Cuba. The idea being to encode the history of organised crime into the fiction. The Cuban scenes would, as biographer Peter Cowie said, "resonate as profoundly as the Sicilian scenes had in *The Godfather*."

Strasberg was the revered head of the Actors Studio in New York, the man who taught both Brando and Pacino. But the tetchy, sparrow-like icon was rarely seen on screen. Could he walk the walk? The role called for a duplicitous ease – a kind of tensile evil compared to the still waters of Michael. Asking him to audition was an affront. Instead, Roos and Coppola got actress-friend Sally Kirkland to throw a party and invite him. As Coppola circled, asking questions, putting ideas to him, Strasberg had no idea he was being tested to play a villain.

Finally, Coppola calls Gordon Willis, his old foe, asking the cinematographer to return. Assuring him that things would be different. Words to that effect. There were whispers that he had asked Vittorio Storaro to step in, and Storaro telling him he needed Willis.

Only Willis refuses. Or tries to.

"Francis, I really don't feel like doing it this time."

"It won't look the same if someone else does it."

"This is true."

So he agreed to it, or he couldn't refuse. There was a dumpster of money from Paramount to help soothe his troubled brow, but *The Godfather* had a grip on its creators as deeply as the audience. The team was back: Willis, production designer Dean Tavoularis, costumes by Theodora Van

Runkle, Dick Smith doing the make-up effects, with producers Fred Roos and Gray Frederickson as Coppola's devoted marshals.

As he shot *The Conversation* by day, he was writing and researching *The Godfather Part II* by night. Teams amassed material. A library of faded clippings, dusty manila envelopes, newsreels, and photographs filled up the research rooms in Napa. There were histories of subway construction, tenements, and Ellis Island. And a full immersion into America's underbelly across the twentieth century: tapes of the Joseph Valachi hearings, details of heroin smuggling, gambling, and Cuba. Coppola wanted to know it all.

His voice was never clearer than in this astonishing mix of vérité and opera. His art was never finer than in the creation of mythic tapestries from the threads of life. But still he doubted that these epics were his true calling, and that doubt was crucial.

Accumulating detail upon detail, this was now solely his domain. The battle to enforce his will on a studio film was in the past. He was like Michael presiding over *The Godfather* universe unopposed.

If he saw himself in Michael Corleone, Coppola wrote himself as Harry Caul. *The Conversation* began life with an image, and the staccato crackle of broken dialogue, and then a character. Back in 1966, Coppola had got into an in-depth discussion with director Irvin Kershner about the advances in bugging technology. He still lived for the geeky particulars of gadgetry and science. Kershner reasoned that the best place to prevent being overheard was outside in a crowd. But he cautioned that there was now a scanning microphone able to eavesdrop on a conversation from the distance of a sniper rifle. They even had crosshairs to aim at mouths. As long as no one blocked the line of "sight" you could get a decent recording.

The opening of a film came to Coppola. Two people walking through a city square to the hum of telltale static on the soundtrack, their conversation interrupted as bystanders step across the remote microphone's sightline. The listener, whoever that was, wouldn't be able to make out everything being said. From that restricted knowledge a mystery would arise.

What was it the writer Eve Babitz said? "Coppola finds stories where everyone else is blind."

We can peel the onion back further, back to when he was a teenager, recently restored from polio and addicted to technology. He would plant homemade microphones in the radiators, mimicking the espionage he saw on television shows. It was innocent enough (and fairly unreliable) – he only wanted to find out what he was getting for Christmas. Yet he remembered a "tremendous sense of power" in being able to listen unseen. He had the habits of a bug-man.

Started in 1966, the script passed through the usual evolution of drafts, being abandoned several times, revived, only to fail to find funding. In which time, he had paid keen interest to the advances in microphones, even attending "bugging conventions". Kershner introduced him to Bernard Spindel, the genuine article, who once worked for Jimmy Hoffa.

Rather than a thriller per se, Coppola thought of his story as a psychological horror. He became more and more interested in who was listening. Who was the bug-man? What was it like to be a peripheral character?

"As in *The Godfather*, I want to get inside a very specialised individual, discover what motivated him."

As he assembled notes and potential scenes, he had been reading Hermann Hesse's *Steppenwolf* about a misanthrope named Harry Haller, alienated from society. "Hence, my guy's named Harry."

"Caul" was a mistake. His original name, Harry Call, was mistyped as "Caul" by a secretary, and Coppola immediately liked the insinuation of a psychological cloak or shroud.

"It gave Francis a visual metaphor for the film," said Walter Murch, editor and all-important sound engineer on the film, "of a man who wears a semi-translucent raincoat, which is a caul-like membrane, and whenever he's threatened or something bad is going to happen, he retreats behind pieces of plastic or rippled glass."

That serendipitous mistake led first to a name, then a costume, and then a way of acting. Harry has a membrane between him and reality. "The film is about the shedding of that membrane," explained Murch, "and how painful it is for the character."

This was a precise study in the loss of control.

Harry is the best wiretapper on the West Coast, but he's tuned to an odd frequency. He's "kind of a repressed being," said Coppola. Harry bugs people literally and figuratively. His only solace is playing the saxophone along to jazz records. But only we see the human side. And now, on his latest assignment, recording the secret assignation of a couple (Frederic Forrest and Cindy Williams) in Union Square, something is chipping away at his professional froideur. A barely made out comment: "He'd kill us if he got the chance." Do they really think they might be murdered? Does he know too much?

Paranoia festers like a fever. Is *he* being bugged? His mistress (Teri Garr) is asking too many questions. His landlord has dropped in a bottle of wine for his birthday — but how does he know his age? And how did he disable his alarm? Where is the Director (Robert Duvall), the man who hired him? Who stole the tapes? Past sins begin to bubble back to the surface. Guilt is a big theme.

Coppola's new partners weren't impressed. Friedkin thought it sounded like a rip-off of Michelangelo Antonioni's *Blow-Up*. Which was partially true. Coppola was using the moody, modish, 1960s thriller about a photographer who glimpses murder as a style guide. "The scenes of revelation through technology are very similar," he accepted. Beyond that, he was his own man. As far as Bogdanovich was concerned, it didn't sound much like the Hitchcock movie he'd promised. Was there resentment that Coppola was using the Directors Company to pursue his old, rusting Zoetrope projects?

Coppola had never liked the acting in Hitchcock movies — "I'm much more interested in *performances*" — but he recognised that anyone making a thriller was a student of the master. In the lead-up to shooting, he screened the classics, such as *Rear Window* (for its voyeurism), *Vertigo* (with its warped psychology and surreal San Francisco), and *Strangers on a Train* (for its devious plotting).

He had longed to cast Marlon Brando, imagining the great Method actor embracing Harry's disintegration. But when Brando passed, as he so often did (that was before *The Godfather*), Coppola's thoughts turned to Gene Hackman, who had won an Oscar for Friedkin's *The French Connection*. Hackman spoke of his admiration for *The Rain People,* which may have swayed the director. Worrying he might come across macho – Hackman was fresh off *The Poseidon Adventure* – Coppola made Harry balding, adding a few pounds, an unflattering moustache, nerdy glasses, out-of-fashion clothes and crepe-soled shoes. Hackman felt pressured by the director's high-wire act. By nature, he was an exuberant personality, and the character was so low key, so depressed, there was no space for humour, or much action.

"I tried to obtain emotions that would be passed over if the picture had been done in the usual manner of thrillers," said Coppola. Introspection was becoming a speciality. It began with *The Rain People*, and then *The Godfather*, and on into *The Godfather Part II, Apocalypse Now* (a navel-gazing war epic), and *Rumble Fish*. He preferred his films to flow inwards.

The sly delight of the story is that we remain perpetually unbalanced by Harry. Is this all in his head? In ours? Coppola was reversing the poles on Hitchcock. Could these be ordinary circumstances distorted by an extraordinarily troubled mind? Not quite, there is skulduggery, and murder, but it is secondary to a study in psychic compression. The terrain occupied by Scorsese and Brian De Palma.

No sooner had they begun shooting in San Francisco on November 26, 1972, than Coppola was firing cinematographer Haskell Wexler (*American Graffiti*), who fumed that he couldn't light such featureless, modernist settings. Coppola's hometown was chosen for convenience. But it must remain anonymous, decreed the director, no landmarks or tourist traps (another reversal on Hitchcock's grandstanding). Everything was shot on location: real offices, real hotel rooms, real bathrooms. Harry scampers into the faceless corporate monolith of the Embarcadero Center where his employers whisper and wheedle. The design is as sheerly ascetic as Lucas's *THX-1138*, but edges into delusion. Only Harry's workshop, with its clutter of splicers and recorders locked behind wire mesh, was constructed in a Zoetrope warehouse. For the record, replacement shooter Bill Butler (*The Rain People*) found the look – make the camera a peeping Tom.

The justly celebrated opening shot in Union Square features an overhead zoom from the top of a skyscraper down onto the back of Harry's head like an amplified version on the creeping zoom that begins *The Godfather*. The entire sequence required days to complete, art and life in close proximity. Harry, his dubious assistant Stan (John Cazale), and a squad of freelance techs stationed on rooftops and hidden in bushes, apply the tools of their trade to listen in to the couple swapping small-talk in the sunshine. Coppola, with crew and extras mingling among the bystanders, was using the tools of his trade, long lenses and microphones, to replicate Harry's game. The police even arrested a sound tech armed with a suspiciously weapon-like microphone. They feared an assassination was being planned.

Coppola might be the expansive, voluble family man who loves to cook and entertain, but he and oddball Harry had an awful lot in common. *The Conversation* was autobiography by stealth. "There's another side to Francis that's very much like Harry Caul," said Murch.

Like Coppola, Harry was undone by a childhood illness, and nearly drowned in a hot bath. Like Coppola, Harry is Catholic, though more devout (Coppola had wanted a scene of Harry confessing his sins to an unseen listener). Faith and technology make for uneasy companions. Guilt infects all of Coppola's characters like a sickness.

This is a film about a man whose job it is to spy on others, obsessing over line readings and endlessly, hypnotically editing (Coppola wanted to fetishise repetition). Harry feels tarnished by his work, but it is his true calling. Like Coppola, he is a director.

He left behind contemporary, sun-scorched San Francisco and caught a plane for Reno in the 1950s, his mind shifting gear, changing films, eras, scale, and budget (but not style, or effort, or moral perplexity). Coppola turned his thoughts back toward Michael Corleone, keeping the exhaustion out of reach.

With autumn closing in, Lake Tahoe gets chilly. At sunset the water turns pinkish and still, black pines reflecting on the surface. By nightfall, it is freezing. Dusted in fake snow, the Corleones' new home is a graveyard compared to the fiesta of that Long Island wedding. In ways literal and spiritual, the temperature has dropped. The heavily guarded compound is cloaked in a sorrow that permeates the entire film.

The crew carry makeshift hand warmers – small boxes containing a burning coal. A trick Roos brought back from the Korean War. Thermal underwear is a necessity.

Eleanor and the kids are staying in one of the houses on the compound, literally living on set. Cables run through the kitchen, and Sofia, only a toddler, scampers among the crew in search of candy. Gio does the child's drawing on Michael's wall.

It is here in Tahoe, on the blustering lake – in a magnificent wide shot of steel clouds fringed in holy light – the film's defining tragedy is shot. This is the fratricidal slaying of Fredo, having taken sides against the family. In the lead-up, Cazale gives the jealous, weak, lovelorn character a howl of primal displeasure – the anguish of the overlooked son.

Puzo had never wanted Fredo killed, but Coppola was adamant. This was the true moment we see the depths to which Michael has fallen.

On set, Coppola is back to his old tricks, refusing to be hurried, finding the mood and rhythm of scenes in the moment. They spend weeks at ice-cold Tahoe, this Spartan world, already behind schedule.

He is still only thirty-six.

The shoot had kicked off its nine-month slog on October 23, 1973. Unable to be in two places at once, Coppola had left postproduction on *The Conversation* – the edit and vitally the sound mix – in Murch's capable hands.

"I won't be around the way a normal director is around," he warned him. "You take the mix, do what you think is right, and then show it to me when you think it's ready to be shown."

He fled from a film still shapeless and strange, and that familiar nausea upon assembling a patchwork of scenes. Murch mentioned that time pressures had resulted in fifteen pages of the script being discarded. Crucial plot points were never filmed. He had to devise ways around the narrative, using Harry's increasingly unreliable viewpoint to his advantage.

There were many trials, confrontations with chaos, but Coppola will always think of *The Godfather Part II* as a good experience. Things have changed. Older, wiser men are at play – and the studio keeps its distance.

"We didn't have Paramount up our ass," said Willis.

"I had made my peace with most of those people and much more of the energy went into the film than into all of the ambient politics and sociology," admitted Coppola.

He and Willis were getting along.

"We had the same concept," said Coppola. "But socially, he's such a cranky, grumpy guy and I always took it as criticism. Then I would get defensive. When we did the second film, I realised that he's just a cranky, grumpy guy and it had nothing to do with me. He can also be really a sweet guy. As a result, the relationship we had on *Godfather II* is the most pleasant I've ever had. He's a guy who really sees things not only in the same way that I do but very often better."

"I can't call him a friend," reflected Willis.

In Las Vegas, where they plant dead hookers and blackmail senators, Pacino admitted he had got mad. He was a star now, a big deal, and Coppola's extravagances had broken through his patience. "How the hell does it take so long to shoot a scene?" he fumed. "Lumet shot *Serpico* in *eighteen* days! And I go up to Francis, I've got a problem I want to talk to him about... So what does *he* do? He tells me *his* problems. What do I want to hear *his* problems for? He's the *director!*"

It was a tough journey for Pacino. Michael is now Mephistophelian, an enigma being gradually eaten alive. He's been lying so long there is no truth. "He's the same man from beginning to end," acknowledged Coppola. The unwavering nature of the part is one of those incremental elements that make the sequel ultimately a lesser film. We forget that he was anyone else.

The pressures mounted on a director working every God-given hour. As he shot *The Godfather Part II* on weekdays, at the weekend he would be back supervising the edit of *The Conversation*. But in the chaos, Coppola finds his art. There is only so much control a director can have, even at the height of his power (as Michael was discovering too).

They would travel from Tahoe to Vegas to New York to Santo Domingo in the Dominican Republic, which stood in for Miami and Havana. This is where Michael is buying into the casinos with the slippery Roth, treachery warming in the tropical air. Before the Caribbean, they came to Los Angeles to shoot interiors on the Paramount lot. Did Evans gaze across the rows of soundstages and wonder? It was here they filmed the Senate Investigating Committee (including Roger Corman and Bill Feldman, Coppola's first agent, among their number), with the pensive Frankie "Five Angels" Pentangeli (boisterous New York playwright-actor

Michael Gazzo), an old mobster turning state's evidence. That was the arc set aside for Clemenza – to rat on Michael.

With his bulldog face and accusing eyes, Gazzo was a complicated actor capable of fire, and East Coast indulgences. For a dinner party scene, requiring six different angles, so six different set-ups, he drank wine throughout. With each take his chin inched toward the table. In the rushes, Diane Keaton turns to the camera and grins, "Is everyone having a good time? I know I certainly am."

The committee scene is another marvel. Pentangeli's brother from Sicily is shuffled into his eyeline like a walking wound. Salvatore Po doesn't need a line to evoke the sin against the blood and the witness clams up. Even Washington can't touch Michael.

To the side of the set, De Niro could be seen, out of costume, out of era, observing his friend Pacino at work.

In Santo Domingo in March 1974, everyone got sick, but no one got sick like Pacino. The doctor diagnosed pneumonia and ordered a month's bed rest. But Michael may finally have poisoned his system.

With Pacino felled, Coppola departed for New York and Vito's story. The footage is imperious. In the mid-1970s, there is no more assured director alive. Who can forget De Niro's Vito, limber between the chimney pots, as he tracks Don Fanucci (Gastone Moschin from *The Conformist*) in his white suit, the vain racketeer who runs the neighbourhood, wending his way through the crowd, an orange (death!) clutched in his palm.

Peer again at the sequence: the accumulated detail, the sensuous pacing, nothing hurried, gathering suspense like the intake of a breath. A 200-foot tracking shot follows Fanucci amid the street Festa, cut with the parallel motion of Vito watching from above. Between them, the vibrant press of immigrant bodies.

That street took six months to dress. Tavoularis eventually finding what they needed in the Ukrainian district of lower Manhattan on East Sixth Street. They went door-to-door, winning the approval of three hundred people: grocers, butchers, morticians. They measured it all, photographed it, then set about sending it back in time to 1918 when the roads were gravel. They built the grocery store, added the lights that crossed over the street like enchantment for the celebrations. There were over 700 extras. Coppola would walk among them eating chocolate-covered almonds.

You need to set a killing apart, explained Coppola. Movie violence is old hat. You need to finesse it with those unforgettable touches: the loosened light bulb throwing the hall into gloom; Fanucci ripping the buttons from his jacket as the bullet pierces his heart; a second bullet puckering his cheek; the towel, wrapped around Vito's gun to muffle the shots, igniting into flame to reveal De Niro's frozen features. It is the same look Pacino has after shooting Sollozzo.

With death still on his fingers, Vito walks home, takes the baby on his lap, and whispers: "Michael, your father loves you very much." The seal is set. De Niro's performance is like a work of science – not imitating Brando, but deciphering a younger, hungrier version of that performance. "Audiences already know Vito Corleone," he explained. "I watch him and I say, 'That's an interesting gesture. When could he have started to do that?'" He is spellbinding.

The shoot goes on to Sicily, the old country, to follow the path of Vito's revenge. De Niro spent three weeks acclimatising to the island, learning the local dialect. But the weather went against them, causing expensive delays.

Finally to Trieste for a month, where the fish market offered a surprising match for turn-of-the-century Ellis Island, and the extras, to Coppola's eye, bore the faces of authentic immigrants. This is where the boy Vito (Oreste Baldini) arrives in America only to be quarantined with smallpox (that echo of polio). Sitting in his tiny cell, he gazes out at the Statue of Liberty. It is one of countless moments of epiphany.

Respite and reassurance came with *The Conversation*'s debut at the Cannes Film Festival in May 1974, when the critics swooned en masse. *The Conversation* gives full voices to Coppola's gifts. He is moving beyond the traditional landscape of film, inverting old formulas: listening into a murder scene rather than showing it, the blood welling up into the toilet bowl. How can we tell if Harry is hallucinating or not? The director adds dream sequences, fumbling doubts, as Harry comes closer to a confrontation with the cruel twist of fate awaiting him – he never did listen correctly.

This is the story of spiritual impotence – a man failing to do the right thing. Through Hackman's "clammy, subtle performance," said Michael Sragow in *The New Yorker*, "the movie captures a more elusive and universal fear – that of losing the power to respond, emotionally and morally, to the evidence of one's own senses."

It is telling that all of Coppola's so-called original films are such vortices of anxiety and pressure. The ending throws people, which he liked.

Murch proved a fine lieutenant (and is arguably the film's co-creator), finding the balance between character study and murder mystery. Metals, he said, that "don't easily go together." He also sculpted an unprecedented soundscape with which the story is infected. The stabbing jazz-piano motifs from composer David Shire (then Talia's husband) are interlaced with Murch's elemental sound effects: the background throb of crowds, the metronomic clicking of tape recorder switches, the flapping of Harry's transparent raincoat... Such density of character, sensory overload, and crestfallen examination of America set a precedent for *Apocalypse Now*.

Yet Coppola is not a political filmmaker. He sidesteps enquiries about his own political stance – he's an artist! – framing the world in thematic close-up, not with wide shots of the geopolitical landscape. Even his Vietnam epic skews toward a deeply personal perspective – an entire war viewed from the boat. The backdrop of *The Conversation* is corporate insecurity, not shifty governments. It is the least overtly political of that great run of 1970s paranoid thrillers that took the temperature of the ill-favoured American times. *Three Days of the Condor*, *The Parallax View*, *All the President's Men*. Only in hindsight would Coppola's contribution be reframed in terms of the Nixon administration and their covert plumbing.

Setting out to make the film, Coppola had no idea how deep the Nixonian stink truly went. He'd never meant to be relevant. Shooting was already underway when Watergate went down. "The actual break-in, as you remember, was not considered a big deal at the time," he noted. Unknowingly, he was tuning into the world's corrupt pulse. Kershner had sent him a *Life* magazine article about a San Francisco sound expert,

Hal Lipset, who would later be summoned to analyse the notorious eighteen-minute blank section of Nixon's White House tapes.

The satellites and cyber-bugging of the surveillance state were decades away, but Coppola had heard the distant thunder of an incoming storm. Indeed, Tony Scott would pay tribute to Coppola's tight little nightmare by casting Hackman as an old hacking operative, Edward "Brill" Lyle, in the high-end 1998 thriller *Enemy of the State*. The photo seen in Brill's file is Hackman as Harry Caul in *The Conversation*. He even wears a transparent raincoat. Are we watching a covert sequel?

With its anti-American timbre, its timeliness, and versatility, European critics hailed *The Conversation* an instant classic. For Coppola it was a defining moment. He had staked out his personal turf. He would never just be "*The Godfather* guy".

There is a picture from Cannes: Coppola dressed in a corduroy suit, beside him are Eleanor and a young Roman carrying the Palme d'Or his father had just won. The director has never looked as happy.

Released on his birthday, April 7, 1974, American critics played harder to get. "Profoundly irritating," grouched *Esquire*. "A disappointment," shrugged *The Washington Post*. Whereas *The New York Times* saw a "stunning piece of American fiction."

Predictably, the Directors Company collapsed in a crossfire of blame and recrimination. It rankled that Coppola played the leader elect, holding court in his San Francisco Xanadu. Caught up with making *The Exorcist* at Warner, Friedkin's enthusiasm waned, but not his willingness to take a $300,000 slice of Bogdanovich's period caper *Paper Moon* – the company's only true hit. Resentment kicked in. *The Conversation* was lauded but made a scant $4.4 million at the box office (a notable comedown after the highs of *The Godfather*). When Bogdanovich's wretched Henry James's adaptation *Daisy Miller* sank, they called it quits. Another uneasy alliance of artists was over.

Nino Rota's laconic waltz plays like a dream, and Coppola almost bounds to the stage to accept the Oscar from goofy Goldie Hawn and Robert Wise, director of *The Sound of Music*, Hollywood gentry, old as the hills. What is running through Coppola's mind? Maybe that he has beaten Roman Polanski (for *Chinatown*), Francois Truffaut (for *Day for Night*),

John Cassavetes (for A *Woman Under the Influence*) and indeed Bob Fosse (for *Lenny*).

He has won Best Director.

"I almost won this a couple of years ago," he starts, "for the first half of the same picture."

If it is a gag, he lands the laugh.

It is April 8, 1975, and despite the torrential rain, Coppola was having quite a night at the Dorothy Chandler Pavilion. *The Conversation* had been nominated alongside *The Godfather Part II* for Best Picture. Naturally, he had worried that he would split the vote. But the *Godfather* sequel will end up with Best Supporting Actor (De Niro beating, among others, Strasberg and Gazzo), Best Adapted Screenplay, Best Production Design, Best Score (Carmine Coppola holds his Oscar aloft), and Best Picture.

What a night for Paramount, too, with three Best Picture nominees — the third is *Chinatown*, Evans's baby.

They managed a gracious exchange backstage beforehand.

"It's your night," said Coppola.

"No, Francis, it's yours," replied Evans. He had a hunch. It was a bittersweet occasion for the studio man. Robert Towne would deservingly pick up Best Original Screenplay for *Chinatown*, but Evans was out at Paramount. There were many reasons why – being exiled from *The Godfather Part II* among them.

Postproduction had brought its woes. Five hours of story had to be whittled down to three-and-a-half, with the movement between past and present a critical challenge. The symmetry Coppola had sought, matching the rise of Vito to the fall of Michael, wasn't there. The divergent plot was hard to follow, the pace too slow, the last hour irredeemably cold. Test screenings were met with embarrassed silences.

By now, Coppola had a term for what was required in the darkest hours: "perseverance of vision". But the film fought him every inch of the way. He and his editors would time those transitions to delicate emotional triggers – fading beautifully between faces across decades. By the end, they were on a twenty-four cycle.

At first, critics were not in the mood for Coppola showing off. Immediate reactions to the premiere were shockingly negative. "It's a

Frankenstein's monster stitched together from leftover parts," snarled *The New York Times*. "Essentially superfluous," said *The Washington Post*.

By now, Coppola knew this to be the way. It was as if they needed to clear his presence out of their heads before they could see the film for what it was. There were those who felt its votive power and narrative ambition. "In New York, people used to say, 'I wonder who's going to write the Great American novel?'" said Babitz, assigned to cover the film in *City* magazine. "When I came out of the screening of the final, three-and-a-half-hour *Godfather Part II*, I knew that Francis had finished off the idea."

The two films together created a greater whole – a vast American saga spiralling into despair. "The complete work, both films in unison, is an epic about the seeds of destruction that the immigrants brought to the new land," wrote Kael.

Coppola was closing in on his protagonist as he had with Harry Caul. The second film shows the "consequences" of the family business. Coppola had hung onto the criticism that *The Godfather* had romanticised the Mafia. Well, now we see the rot. From the opening shot, Michael appears jowlier somehow, his eyes bruised, his mouth twisted. If we're not mistaken, he's more like his father.

There is a symbolism in how De Niro and Pacino were both striving to resemble Brando.

The ending is a masterstroke of Coppola improvisation, fading from the young, untainted Michael alone at the family table to the older Michael, damned and forever alone. Pacino could be twenty years older. Perseverance of vision.

The Oscars renewed Coppola's lustre, after the box office returns on *The Godfather II* turned out to be merely decent. Following a flying start, the more complex film ended up at $48 million. The media were wondering if Coppola was more art than commerce.

At home, Eleanor was fraying against the role of wife and mother. She had ambitions of her own. She'd met fellow artist Lynn Hershman on the school run, and together they mounted a show at the Coppolas' San Francisco home, with over fifty members of the art elite as guests. Coppola happened to be out of town.

Hiding from view, the artists spoke to their visitors via a large monitor, inviting them to take a self-guided tour of the house, a circuit of home furnishings and conceptual exhibits. Roman and Sofia were paid to stay in Sofia's bedroom watching a video of her birth (shot by her father). In the kitchen, there was an invitation to peel a potato and then drop it into either the pot marked "Art" or the pot marked "Not Art".

Suspecting her guests were more interested in viewing her husband's five Oscars, Eleanor removed the full-sized trophies from their glass case and replaced them with the miniature Oscars given to her as the wife of a winner to wear as a necklace. His triumph shrunk to the size of a thimble.

Of course, crime pays. Whatever Coppola's feelings for *The Godfather* films, they bought him his sanctuary and second calling. Established in 1879 and founded by a former Finnish sea captain and furrier, the Gustave Niebaum estate lay in the heart of the tranquil Napa Valley countryside north of San Francisco, a 1700-acre quilt of gardens, olive groves, and vineyards. At the centre of which stood a majestic Victorian mansion, the Inglenook, with gabled porches, outhouses, and a grizzled old oak that stood guard at the top of the drive.

The story goes that Coppola and Eleanor were looking for a summerhouse with two or three acres of grapes, no more than that. "Let's take a look at the Niebaum estate, just for fun," said the real estate broker, no fool when he has an award-winning director on his books. Did he happen to mention that it was only on the market once in a lifetime?

"It looked like a movie set," said Eleanor.

Treat this as a montage: they put in an offer but lose out to a consortium of land developers. Years go by, and nothing else they look at comes close. Then the estate is zoned as an Agricultural Preserve and the consortium wants to sell. So it comes on the market twice in a lifetime. Coppola's is the offer they can't refuse. A filmmaker becomes a winemaker. He sees the similarity. You aim for a perfect balance.

He was such a good interview, so unguarded, so eloquent, projecting into the future and seeing the past for what it was. All the big magazines queued up for the *enfant terrible*'s latest pronouncements: *Playboy*, *Vogue*, *The New York Times*, *Time*. All ended up asking the same dull question. What on earth would he be doing next?

In late 1975, Coppola replied that with his next film he was venturing into an area laden with so many implications he ran the risk of irresponsibility. He was going to have to tread very carefully with this one.

"It's going to be a film about Vietnam," he said, "although it won't necessarily be political – it will be about war and the human soul."

CHAPTER 5

NEVER GET OFF THE BOAT

Apocalypse Now (1979)

Something happens at night. In the humid air, the light gains the clarity of a hallucination. The set resembles a circus: strings of lights on cables that draw coloured reflections on the black water; GI extras are thrown into relief by bonfires that the special effects boys light in the trenches. They wrap their heads in T-shirts to keep out the frenzy of insects drawn by the glare.

Orientating by the script, the Do Long Bridge is halfway upriver and serves as the last official outpost of American forces, entrenched across the water from the enemy. Every day the bridge is rebuilt, only to be blow apart again at night. The absurdity of Vietnam reduced to this slender crossing.

Captain Willard (who has the square-jawed mien of Martin Sheen) goes ashore to find someone in charge. He stops a GI, who has the sullen stare of the anaesthetised.

"Hey soldier, do you know who's in command here?"

"Ain't you?" the GI sneers.

Francis Ford Coppola wants spectacle. And futility. On the first night at the small, lagoon-side town of Pagsanjan – which will also host the temple compound of the hotly debated ending – tropical lightning strobes the sky. The air tastes of metal. There is an unusual sense of anticipation. In reality, there was only ever half a bridge here. It was blown up by the Japanese in World War II and never rebuilt. The production of *Apocalypse Now* will rebuild it and blow it up again every night for over two weeks.

Gio Coppola is an extra. He is twelve but dressed up as a GI with his own M-16 rifle.

Action is finally called at 11 p.m. – flares, rockets, and what Eleanor Coppola described as "big flame balls" soar into the sky, irradiating the omnipresent smoke. In the wide shot, the chaos becomes beautiful. The date is August 11, 1976, five months into production. There is laughter among the watching crew.

By the sixth consecutive night on the Do Long Bridge, the good spirits have evaporated. Rain is falling steadily, and they have to pack the floor of the trench with sand to make it stable. During camera rehearsal a section of the trench wall collapses, and they have to begin again.

A delay of even a day costs up to $50,000, and this set alone has fallen two days behind. Coppola adds dialogue, dwells on rehearsal, fixing unseen things. His anger is never far away. That slows things down too. Sometimes it just rains, and the mud gets deep. A grey mist is laid down by canister. Everyone is coughing and rubbing their eyes.

Thirty-six months later, on May 17, 1979, Coppola strode into the Palais, the modernist hub of the Cannes Film Festival, like a man possessed. Before him are assembled 1,100 members of the world's press. He paused at the podium to observe the throng of notepads and cameras. As far as he was concerned, the massed ranks of the enemy. They stared back at the world's most famous director who currently resembled a biblical prophet in a panama hat. He glowered through his thick glasses. He licked his lips. He rubbed his bushy beard. Then he began to speak.

Much against the better judgment of the hierarchy at United Artists, Coppola had entered his new film into the festival's competition. They were still unable to decipher whether this was a final, hell-bent act of self-destruction. What UA executive and author Steven Bach summed up as, "the most public sneak preview in the history of motion pictures." Or was it a gesture of outrageous confidence, if not hubris, to match the titanic struggle to get his film made. UA had no say in the matter – their investment was limited to domestic (US) rights, and they hadn't even been offered a look at whatever constituted the current cut.

The film was in no way finished.

Billed as *Apocalypse Now (A Work in Progress)*, for the festival and its self-regarding artistic director Gilles Jacob, who had spent months winding in Coppola like a wriggling fish, this was a major coup. There wasn't a film in the world more debated than Coppola's Vietnam folly.

So the UA executives could only look on as Coppola stood in his pulpit, doing what he did best – speaking from the heart.

"My film is not about Vietnam," he declared, his voice soaring like a Do Long rocket. "It *is* Vietnam."

Where does it begin – the great journey into the jungle, into the mire of Vietnam, and on into the annals of cinema as the ultimate symbol of the neurotic mania of moviemaking (and the first death knell for the euphoria of 1970s auteurism) and an emblem of all it can achieve? The other story that everyone tells about Coppola, when the chaos threatened to consume him. Unexpectedly, the answer doesn't lie with the man who would dare madness to get *Apocalypse Now* made.

First we must turn to screenwriter, director, gun freak, rightward-leaning philosopher, and Movie Brat John Milius, who once revelled in the mentorship of Coppola, and being his most obtuse student. His lungs and imagination loosened by the mists of marijuana that hung over late-night student gatherings at USC, Milius conjured up a new kind of war movie for their times. He called it *The Psychedelic Soldier*, and it would be a radical, contemporary reworking of Joseph Conrad's *Heart of Darkness*.

Cut to the filmmaking delirium at American Zoetrope's conception, where the future was being forged with Coppola as blacksmith. He remembered both Milius and George Lucas talking about the guys returning from Vietnam, "bringing word of the craziness of it, the drugs, the hallucination, the surfing..." And how Milius was "cooking up a script" for Lucas to direct.

Wait, though. Carroll Ballard, another lively planet circling Coppola's sun, also made a claim to being the source of *Apocalypse Now*. He had been actively planning an adaptation of *Heart of Darkness* as far back as 1967. He simply hadn't been able to pin down the rights. Something, he insisted, he had discussed with Coppola. "At one time, I was very bitter about it," he admitted. More than anything, for being left out.

Quite apart from how readily the colonial fevers of Conrad could be applied to the psychedelic battleground of Vietnam (each with their primordial jungles), the book held a grip on the imaginations of adventurous filmmakers. When Orson Welles arrived in Hollywood in 1939, his first instinct was to sculpt a film from *Heart of Darkness* (as he had done on radio with his Mercury Theatre Company). "You aren't going to see this picture," he announced. "This picture is going to *happen* to you." Welles got as far as scouting locations before the project crumbled beneath a ballooning budget. There exists a single day of test footage with Gus Schilling as the protagonist Marlow, due to pilot his barge upriver through the Congolese jungle toward Kurtz, the company man gone insane among the natives.

Lucas was driven solely by the urge to make a Vietnam movie, with no idea, as of yet, what it would be. "He didn't know *Heart of Darkness* from *Mary Poppins*," sniped Milius. The Zoetrope discussions, it should be noted, were taking place with the war still underway. Milius recalled the badges worn by hippies calling for "Nirvana Now" and with a hint of satire what was *The Psychedelic Soldier* became *Apocalypse Now*. His inclination was toward black comedy.

Coppola was keen enough to back the project, allowing Milius time and space to write his script while he pitched it as part of his deal at Warner. Milius refused to re-read the novel, saying he "wanted to remember it like a dream." Whereas Lucas had now decided he wanted to shoot it with the immediacy of a documentary, moving swiftly and cheaply with 16mm cameras, but on home turf. There were rice fields between Stockton and Sacramento. His focus would be the Vietnamese villagers resisting the brute force of America. Editor Walter Murch recognised how he would take that story of minnows against might and remove it to a galaxy far, far away from Vietnam.

Milius was on his way to becoming one of the hottest, gun-slinging screenwriters in town. *Dirty Harry*, *Magnum Force*, *Dillinger*, and *Jeremiah Johnson* were all fired by his fascination with man wrestling his animal nature – a theme central to his Vietnam epic. But he had no stomach for directing the picture.

This is when Zoetrope's deal with Warner dissolved in a mix of rancour, debt, and stagnant box office results (see: *THX-1138*).

So *Apocalypse Now* would have to wait. And wait for years. Beyond the brittle finances of Zoetrope and the shifting sands of the studio scene, there was a bigger wall of resistance – American society. No studio would be likely to provide millions of dollars for a revisionist take on Vietnam while the war was still going on. Audiences wouldn't stand for it, with body bags on the evening news.

Nevertheless, Coppola began pushing the idea of a "Vietnam picture" with the studios again. While filming *The Godfather Part II* in 1973, he had approached Paramount, for whom he was making so much money with his morally ambiguous mob classics. They were cautious. It's still too early, the subject still taboo. The response was similar across town. It's too early. Or it was too late – this from Warner, playing contrarians, still needled by Coppola.

Hostilities officially ceased on April 30, 1975, with America pulling out of Vietnam, and the striking footage of Marines being airlifted from the US embassy as Saigon fell. Frankly, it looked like a movie. But there was little doubt, however it was phrased by the government, that this was a crushing defeat, which only increased the ironic possibilities of their film.

There followed a brief period when Lucas tried to set it up at Columbia. He even had producer Gary Kurtz out in the Philippines scouting locations. Don't shoot in typhoon season he was warned. But Lucas became sidetracked by the concept of combining the nostalgia of *American Graffiti* with the futurescaping of *THX-1138* to create something he was calling *Star Wars*. He asked Coppola to wait for him. But having finally paid back Warner, and owning the rights to *Apocalypse Now*, Coppola loved the provocation of getting their Vietnam film out for America's Bicentennial in 1976. Unable to resist Coppola's tractor beam, Lucas surrendered.

"If you want to make it," he said, "go make it."

There were other forces at play in Coppola's mind. Maybe this would be the film to finally establish his new cinematic world order. "My thought was to do some virtuoso directing," he said nonchalantly, "and get on with what I'd always thought I wanted to do – which is to have my own film company, and my own studio, and really get to work."

An exalted film career is what happens while you're busy making other plans.

As it was, he would display his virtuosity – there are few war movies, indeed few films period, that come close to the visual and aural power of *Apocalypse Now* – but he nearly lost everything in order to do so.

Eleanor saw his initial motivation in simpler terms. He needed to get out into the light. After the trials of *The Godfather Part II*, he couldn't face making another intense film in dark rooms. "He just wanted to get out into the sunlight and make a cowboy movie, an action-adventure movie," she said. "Francis saw *Apocalypse Now* as a big outdoor opera."

Murch remembered Coppola's enthusiasm, and that gung-ho naiveté that allowed him to step so boldly into the unknown. "I'll have no trouble financing it," Coppola told his friend, "everyone will want to see it. It'll run like clockwork."

He genuinely thought he would be making a normal film.

Beyond any political or artistic or bravura statements he wanted to make by going upriver to meet his destiny, Coppola wanted to simply own a movie. Whatever else happened, the copyright would be his. He was still smarting over missing out on *American Graffiti*. With *Apocalypse Now*, he would at last thwart the studio paradigm.

He swiftly (and somewhat elusively) announced that his next film would concern Vietnam, was loosely based on *Heart of Darkness*, and would be totally self-financed.

Key to this was convincing foreign distributors to pay for local rights upfront, providing him with the exorbitant (but as it turned out conservative) budget of $14 million. For American distribution, he turned to the forward-thinking United Artists, who, enthralled by the idea and having the next film from Coppola, agreed to pay for marketing and completion if the budget fell short.

Milius delivered his revised screenplay in early 1975. Marlow was transformed into Willard, the special ops veteran sent, covertly, to assassinate Kurtz, the decorated Green Beret turned renegade, holed up over the border in Cambodia with an army of Montagnard tribesmen. This mad king at the "uttermost end" of the river was conducting his own insurgent campaign without permission and without moral qualm. He was the deranged endgame of American imperialism, the embodiment of war.

Coppola knew he needed to rein in the philosophical gulf that lay between him and Milius. "Basically, he wanted to ruin it, liberalise it, and turn it into *Hair*," complained the writer. Milius felt war was intrinsic to man, unavoidable. For him, the term "anti-war" was meaningless. You might as well be "anti-rain". Whereas Coppola thought war utterly abhorrent. His Kurtz recognises he is insane. The rational part of his being knows that death is the only answer to the horror of his instincts. All the great set pieces belong to Milius, Coppola readily admitted, but he orientated the drama back toward the book.

"I wanted to push for something mythic."

All he needed was a cast and crew willing to join his un-pampered foray into the equivalent tropical jungles of the Philippines – Vietnam hadn't yet cooled.

Casting was the first storm. Even if he was calling the shots (there was no Robert Evans leaning over his shoulder), he struggled to find his leading men. Or convince those he found.

He had promised his foreign partners big names. Why not? He was Francis Ford Coppola. Clint Eastwood said no, Jack Nicholson said no, Robert Redford said no, James Caan said no. They were reluctant to be away so long, reluctant maybe to follow Coppola into the jungle. His favourite, Steve McQueen, was opposed to the lengthy requirements of Willard, but agreed to the brief window of Kurtz, but for the same $3 million. Marlon Brando refused to discuss any role in the film.

The director became enraged at the demands, the cowardice, and the lack of belief. Al Pacino liked the idea of Willard but feared for his health with four months in the tropics (he'd been so ill in the Dominican Republic shooting *The Godfather Part II*). Kurtz, he felt, needed rewriting.

Coppola cracked sometime in late fall, 1975. He was at home in Pacific Heights, mulling over his troubles. How is it the leading filmmaker of his generation can't cast his next film? How many Oscars does it take to be taken seriously? With a rush of blood and that natural inclination for the symbolic gesture, he opened the window, gathered up his five Oscars, and threw them into the air. They were smashed to bits in the courtyard below. The past meant nothing if he didn't have a future.

A few days later, his phone rang. It was Brando's people. There had been a change of heart.

Eleanor's diaries bring us closer to the making of *Apocalypse Now* than perhaps any film ever made. Reading Eleanor's taut, lucid, intensely personal account, we understand that the term film production falls woefully short of what this mad, brilliant, gruelling enterprise became. What a nightmare it evolved into. Steadily, she peers into the film's moral smoke. Roman Coppola, her younger son, only eleven years old, hanging out in the make-up tent and boasting that he had learned to do a perfect bullet hit. Watching every day as her husband tied himself to the rocks as the eagle that was *Apocalypse Now* came and plucked out his liver.

On arriving in the Philippines, she was handed a camera and given a small crew and asked to document the shoot (as Lucas had done with *The Rain People*) – a chance to mythologise the very making of *Apocalypse Now*. She fretted that she would either be in the way or was being kept out of the way.

The great undertaking began on March 20, 1976, and there were times when it felt as if it would never end, as Coppola searched for the ultimate expression of the Vietnam War, and perhaps of filmmaking itself, whatever the cost (literally). Can we argue that he didn't attain his goals? Made in a fever of artistic turmoil and self-doubt, and perhaps flawed (but somehow more valuable for those flaws), *Apocalypse Now* is like no other film.

In a rare moment of lucidity while being interviewed by Eleanor on set, Dennis Hopper proclaimed that filmmaking was in "the same phase of development that art was during the cathedral-building period." In his eyeline was the great decayed temple of Kurtz's compound.

Between school-terms, Gio and Roman made their way to the shoot. Only five-year-old Sofia was with them all year round, enrolled into a local kindergarten, picking up the language. "It looks like the Disneyland *Jungle Cruise*," she told her mother when they first entered the foliage. One night, amid mounting stress, Eleanor watched as her husband sat calmly picking tiny lice eggs from his daughter's hair with a flashlight.

Coppola was master of his own destiny, and slave to a furtive vision. He would strain to find it, as he had before, in the heat of filmmaking, waiting for his subconscious to stir. He would live his film. And it would nearly destroy him. This is the legend and torment of *Apocalypse Now* – Coppola in extremis. Stories that have been recounted and distorted over the years until a mythology prevailed as strung out and vivid as that of Vietnam itself.

The problems had become evident as soon as they touched down in Manila. Transport alone was a miasma of constant negotiation. The irony was plain – they need to run production as a military operation.

With the American military disgusted by the concept of soldiers being sent to assassinate renegade officers (and leery of the film's home truths) official assistance was refused. "If [he] wants to make a bundle with this type of garbage, so be it," announced the U.S. Army's Chief of Information. "But he will do so without the slightest assistance from the Army." Coppola called it censorship. *The Green Berets*, a slab of propagandist Vietnam baloney with John Wayne strutting like a cockerel, had their pick of the U.S. war machine.

Coppola turned to the Philippine government, with the lavish, corrupt President Marcos only too pleased to lend these American filmmakers Huey and Hughes 500 helicopters from his air force. That was until an uprising of Muslim rebels in the southern islands took precedence over the requirements of irritable directors. In the middle of a camera rehearsal, the helicopters literally fled the scene to engage the rebels 150 miles further south. This also resulted in Coppola being supplied with a government bodyguard at all times. Marcos feared the famous director would be marked for kidnap and couldn't face the international embarrassment.

In the early weeks of production, Coppola conducted the great battle scene at the mouth of the river, with Robert Duvall's stiff-necked Kilgore sniffing napalm on the morning breeze, and those choppers descending like hornets onto the bamboo huts. This was Baler, a tiny village on the eastern coast of Luzon, with no electricity, no telephone lines, and no Coca-Cola.

The sequence is a bombardment of interconnected moments, a blitzkrieg of narrative: Kilgore demanding that Lance surf the local break;

the Vietnamese girl tossing a grenade into a medevac; the terrified grunt refusing to leave his chopper; Coppola's cameo as part of a television crew, screaming at the soldiers not to look in the camera; napalm (actually, 1,200 gallons of gasoline) blooming in the treeline like demonic marigolds. On set, the beach would shake like an earthquake.

Coppola accumulated swathes of footage, an editing Everest, but he knew he had a "high point". With the addition of Wagner's *Ride of the Valkyries* (Milius's imperialistic joke doubled in irony when audiences thrilled to the operatic accompaniment), it remains one of the most visceral and ideologically fractured battle scenes ever put on film.

The director's anger rose like the tide. There was a string of firings. His frustrations grew with the script. He knew the supporting characters were good: Duvall's peacock Colonel in his cavalry hat, halfway to Kurtz already, or Patton; Albert Hall as Chief Phillips, captain of the patrol boat and the film's moral fury; Frederic Forrest's manic Chef, giggling and death bound; Sam Bottoms as the golden Malibu surfer Lance, drifting into the middle distance; and the childlike Clean, skinny as a bird, and played by Laurence Fishburne, only fifteen years old.

Life on the boat, the sparring among crew too long in close quarters, has that hum familiar to all of Coppola's films. He's so good on natural interaction – simple scenes of guys bugging one another. But Willard and Kurtz were shadows. Brando was still to come, his three-week stint blocked out for the end of summer. The immediate problem was Harvey Keitel in the lead role. Viewing his first week's footage, it was now Coppola expressing doubts over what he had.

There have been many rumours (contract disputes, personal animus), but the simple truth is that Keitel didn't fit Willard. He wasn't passive enough. "Harvey is an extremely active actor," said Coppola, "and you want to look at him all the time." Willard needed to be the audience's eyes in Vietnam.

So it was never Keitel's talent, but his style. He had been cast in desperation – Coppola had loved him in Martin Scorsese's *Mean Streets* but hadn't thought things through. Producer Fred Roos, usually so unerring, had backed the idea. Keitel was clearly uncomfortable: in the role, in the uniform, in the jungle. "He was a city boy," said Roos. While the trades squawked about a troubled picture, the actor was relieved. He was paid in full for his time, and spent his last night watching a bar singer croon "My Way".

Coppola's insecurities, those doubts that closed in on him every time he stepped onto a set, swelled in the heat and humidity. Was he making a pompous film? Was he making a coherent film? A visiting television crew asked him what challenge there could possibly be left for the most famous director in the world?

"I am just trying to get through today," he replied.

Italian cinematographer Vittorio Storaro was Bernardo Bertolucci's man – a visualist of distinction who had provided the contrasts of *The Conformist* (an influence on *The Godfather* films) and the winter light of *Last Tango in Paris* with Brando. He had theories on colour and the hauteur of a Renaissance Prince, with a hawk-like nose and long brown hair that gathered at his collar, but unlike Gordon Willis he bound himself to the will of Coppola, spinning trance-like textures from his camera like gold.

Early on, Storaro was afraid he wasn't "definitive" in the American way. "Vittorio, I have a confession to make," replied Coppola in Italian. "I am scared every day that you will think that I am an asshole, because I am not definitive enough…"

The scenes with their smears of river mist and plumes of pastel-coloured smoke – pestilences of red, orange, purple, and yellow – conjoin Hieronymus Bosch and Andy Warhol. Vietnam and the hinterlands of Cambodia (via the Philippines) meet us as an alien planet fringed in a tumult of greens, a paradox of dream and intense presence. Storaro has spoken of a conflict between natural energy and artificial energy: lights against the dark trees, helicopters like UFOs.

There was a constant background radiation of mutiny. Money was an issue – Coppola was the studio now, and began to serve as his own worst enemy, nipping and tucking at the crew's expenses. While he would be flagrant when it came to his own supply of luxuries.

There was tropical disease, gastro-enteritis, parasites, hookworm, and monkey bites, while crew dabbed at cuts and sores with neat vodka. The chemical toilets ran out of chemicals. Wherever they were staying, there were ants and large, brown cockroaches that didn't seem to do anything, only watch.

At times, reported script supervisor Nancy Tonery, the atmosphere was reminiscent of the fall of Saigon. Coppola was known to storm off set. Which meant catching a plane back to his house and family and swimming pool in Manila. Things kept breaking down: the boats, the cameras, the script.

Martin Sheen arrived on April 24, the new Willard. The cut you see on his cheek covered by a plaster is real – four stitches. He passed out crossing the street, not yet acclimatised to the heat. Born and raised in Dayton, Ohio, a Spanish-Irish mix, the star of *Catch-22* and *Badlands* changed the complexion of the film. Despite a resemblance to James Dean, he was a concentrated actor. Often reducing a moment to the movement of his large eyes. He had survived his staunchly Catholic father's disapproval, and a bout of childhood polio that left him bedridden for a year.

In fact, Sheen had been the original choice for Willard, but schedules clashed. With the delay, he was now free. They met at LAX, and Sheen agreed without hesitation. He knew the script. It took four days to reshoot the Keitel scenes.

The journey upriver, the bulk of the film, had never been an issue. Guided by Milius's blueprint, Coppola began to stretch out improvisational fingers toward the purple haze of the Vietnam experience. He didn't want to see the war but enter the war. The Vietcong would stay hidden in the trees, announced only by the firework displays of combat.

Like the book, the film is structured as a string of encounters as the boat – the Patrol Boat River or "PBR" – journeys inwards, against the current, toward its meeting with fate and Kurtz. Thematically, each staging post of the odyssey both explores the *Through the Looking Glass* psychosis of this absurd war and evokes a drift backwards in time from civilisation toward barbarity (bullets are exchanged for arrows and spears). With the addition of Sheen's drowsy, hypnotic voice-over, we also experience a journey inwards towards Willard's soul. Or the space where it was once located. The secret, Coppola told Sheen, "is not to play him as a nice guy."

The tiger, briefly glimpsed as Willard and Chef scout for water, serves as a portent of nature's savagery. When the handlers coaxed it onto the transport plane, the pilot leaped out of the window and fled. He had to be coaxed back into the cockpit via the wing. Forrest had to be coaxed out of a tree. "Never get off the boat!" screams Chef, and the actor really means it.

Still Coppola toiled over the script. He carried a copy of Conrad's book filled with notes and inkblots, but there was none of the detailed breakdown that had gone into *The Godfather*.

Eleanor watched on. Writing a script, she knew, was a way for Coppola to understand himself. *The Godfather Part II* was about a man dealing with money, power, and family. "Now he was struggling with the themes of Willard's journey into self and Kurtz's truths that are in a way themes that he has not resolved within himself." This was why he always struggled. He could never simply be objective, as he mainlined espressos, his skin and brain itching.

On May 19, Typhoon Olga span off the South China Sea, made landfall and sheared into two. One half made straight for their location in Iba, leaving the *M*A*S*H*-like medevac sequence a no-man's-land hip-deep in mud. They managed to shoot there briefly. After the dolly track was dug out by hand. The scenes of the stranded Playboy Bunnies eventually surfaced in the *Redux* version. The other half of Olga made for the set two hundred miles away in Baler. The entire island was engulfed by days of torrential rain. "How can you take it seriously?" laughed Coppola, but only years later.

On June 8, accepting that filming was impossible, he called a temporary halt to production and returned to Napa, six weeks behind schedule, and already $3 million over budget.

Not for the first time, he found that his phone had been cut off. He turned to UA, pressing them for a loan. They agreed, but the details were stringent. He would be personally liable if the film didn't make over $40 million: that meant his office and homes. His life was on the line for this film. While they waited, he read a biography of Genghis Khan and revised the script. Eleanor took the kids to Disneyland, where the jungles were fake.

Phase II began in July 1976. Nobody was happy to be back. Especially Sheen. "I don't know if I am going to live through this," he told friends as he departed.

There are few scenes like Willard's introduction, filmed in a hotel in Pagsanjan. What rational film would have its leading character bear his soul in the opening moments? Yet we would always know that mania lay beneath the surface. The scene had come to Coppola in a dream. Willard comes to in a Saigon hotel, having attempted to drink away his sins. Suicide hovers over his head like the blades of a fan. The only way to clear his mind is the offer of a future sin – to rid the US army of this turbulent priest, with extreme prejudice. Sheen had been drinking all day. "I had no business being on screen," he said. Coppola called out ideas, urging his actor on, pushing through the layers – Saint! Orator! Street tough! – until Willard and Sheen merged. The character becomes the actor. Coppola's theory for finding truth in performance put to the ultimate test. The atmosphere in the room was electric and dangerous. Sheen-Willard ends up punching his reflection in the mirror. That blood is real. This was *Apocalypse* Method.

Coppola stares into the night sky. He has scaled the lighting platform and just laid down. Rain is falling, a gentle but incessant drizzle. It is September 16, 1976, they are still in Pagsanjan, below him is the ruin of Kurtz's compound, slowly being consumed by the jungle. The crew sits around, waiting. Cautious glances make their way up the scaffolding to where the director is stationed. Brando is refusing to leave his houseboat because he doesn't like the scene.

Eleanor climbs up – she has never seen her husband so miserable. "Let me out of here," he cries, "let me just quit and go home. I can't do it. I can't see it." Did it feel as if polio had felled him again? He was lucid but unable to move.

The ending – it was always the ending. Intoxicated on the ritualism of Joseph Campbell and the increased surrealism as Willard nears his goal, where he must slay the god Kurtz, he knew he had, "painted himself into a corner." Convention would never serve him. Milius's script had culminated in battle with Kurtz and Willard fighting alongside one another. That was long gone. But he felt unsure, bedevilled, haunted by the spectre of Francis Ford Coppola. "He is on some brittle edge," wrote Eleanor.

He'd been concentrating so hard on the set pieces, he recalled, "he'd left a flank open." Spectacle alone was not enough. Not for the director of the *Godfathers*. What was he trying to say about man's capacity for evil?

He had theories. "Morality is an issue we have to take as it comes. One day you lie to your wife, another day you don't." He let that thought settle, then raised the stakes. "And when morality gets up to higher levels, so that it's not just a matter of a lie, it comes into the reach of madness where it's life or death."

Watching the eerie, abstruse ending, strewn with (near Corman-like) gothic horrors, we witness Brando's Kurtz contemplating his own worth – what do I amount to? He is almost babbling, Michael Corleone's twisted, primeval cousin. We also see Sheen's Willard mesmerised by the sight, incapable of action. They are both Coppola.

"This is like an opening night," he tells Eleanor, "the curtain goes up and there is no show."

Then Storaro calls to him. He has an idea. "I've made some strange light and smoke and I think you can do something."

Coppola wearily returns to the interior of the temple set, Brando is lured from his hideaway, and they begin to improvise, trying lines in the dance of shadow and copper light. Brando-Kurtz's Easter Island features peering out of the darkness as Don Vito's once had.

Brando's arrival had only added to the director's burden. The actor was 90lbs overweight, and wholly underprepared. This is despite a promise to lose weight for the role of the former Green Beret holding court with his makeshift army. Despite the many discussions with Coppola at the summit of Mulholland Drive, and all the research material sent on by the team, food for Brando's considerable thoughts.

He was getting a princely $3 million for three weeks work, and in his arguments with the director it became apparent that he had not, after all, read the book.

For his first contracted week, he sat with Coppola in his boathouse, moored on a nearby lake, deep in discursive discussions on the nature of his character. This was surely a delaying tactic. "It felt to me as if Marlon was torturing Francis," said Eleanor, but it was a process, too – Brando's inevitable struggle to climb into a role.

Someone left a copy of the book on the boat (no one has ever owned up) and Brando finally read it. By Hopper's unsteady account, Coppola had read it to him out loud. Whatever the case, by the next morning he was a changed man, dressed in black, with a completely shaved head, Conrad's "ivory ball". He was Kurtz.

Coppola recalled his stand-offs with Brando with humour. "I always felt that Marlon was a genius, not just as an actor, but as an innovative thinker. A brilliant man. But I once told him that he uses friendship like bath soap."

Storaro's genius was to hide Brando's bulk in mystery. He is not quite human, rubbing water over his bald dome, his face like a cliff side, his voice cavernous.

Hopper was all over the place, drunk and stoned, staying at the Pagsanjan Rapids Hotel, where the cast and crew had taken refuge. His role had changed. He had been sold on the part of Colby, a previous assassin turned by Kurtz (now a silent Scott Glenn). Instead, Coppola channelled those manic energies into the Photojournalist, his version of Conrad's Russian. He is the Fool to Kurtz's Lear, jabbering truths like a halfwit.

The set for Kurtz's compound was stunning. Prodigious production designer Dean Tavoularis was using Angkor Wat as inspiration: a temple time forgot with a giant carved head (based on a beautiful Filipina maid). Some of the bodies dangling from trees were real, according to producer Gray Frederickson, procured not from medical labs but graves.

Coppola found his ending in the book. Like a Russian doll, Conrad's Kurtz quotes T.S. Eliot's *The Waste Land*, a poem Coppola felt an increasing affinity for. "Not with a bang but with a whimper," he remembered. He used Elliot, he used Conrad, he used Brando, and something emerged: a penetration into the veil of madness. "One of the most haunting endings in cinema," according to the great critic Roger Ebert.

On March 1, 1977, Sheen went jogging. As he ran, it suddenly felt as if a hot poker had been thrust inside his chest and he collapsed. He was given the last rites. Days before he had been lying in a cage, covered in snakes, and dragged upside down through the mud.

Eleanor was back in Napa Valley when Coppola called. Marty has had a heart attack. He was alive but in a critical condition. She needed to call the lawyer.

Somehow shooting continued. Somehow by April 19, Sheen was back on set, looking "like he just came back from Palm Beach," reported Eleanor.

Any hope that home comforts would bring peace of mind was soon dashed. Coppola's fevers followed him across the Pacific, and as he began to sift through 240 hours of filmed footage a new anxiety consumed him. After all this time (eighteen months of shooting), all this Herculean effort, did he even have a film? These were not unfamiliar woes. The strife of watching the assembled footage in all its misshapen glory is devastating for most filmmakers. You have to begin again in the edit suite.

But Coppola was like Harry Caul, spiralling into obsession. Barely sleeping as he sat in his penthouse office, communicating by intercom, or gazed at the footage with a thousand-yard stare. Weeks would go past without a word to the editors, then he would appear like an apparition, or the looming shadow of Kurtz, to expound at length and with great eloquence on *The Golden Bough*. At other times, he railed against his fate as an artist. From now on he would make commercial films, make his wine, and be at peace.

"To those around him," wrote Peter Biskind, "it was evident that Coppola was in the grip of a full-blown, clinical case of manic depression."

Walter Murch took charge of the sound mix (a tour de force of thrumming chopper blades, birdcalls, and the intoxicating swoon of The Doors), and became the voice of reason as they made their incursion into the landscape of the movie. It was Murch who suggested that the only way to navigate the "turbulence of the storytelling" was to reinstate Milius's original narration. This led to the appointment of war correspondent Michael Herr (a huge influence on Milius who would go on to script *Full Metal Jacket*) to rewrite Willard's distinctive voice-over in his embittered sin-city argot. Conrad's Marlow became Chandler's Marlowe.

Herr arrived to find an editing team exhausted and a director, he said, "flipping in and out of nervous collapse." Still they tramped uphill, with deadlines disappearing in the mist. There was somewhere close to forty-five recording sessions with Sheen. They added some deep cuts of 'Nam legend from cracked former CIA operative Fred Rexer, who would recount his killings as a Green Beret, and once brought a loaded .45 into the studio.

The months drifted on. The press circled like buzzards. And somewhere between narration, music, and cutting into Storaro's long distance dolly shots, a film began to emerge.

Then Coppola decided the French plantation had to go. Following the death of Clean, the PBR moors up beside a crumbling boathouse wreathed in mist. Here Willard and crew take dinner with a family of plantation owners, including Aurore Clement and Christian Marquand, an outpost of the previous French occupation. A colonial family, appreciated Anthony Lane in *The New Yorker*, getting to the nub of things, "who can no more flee Vietnam than a ghost can quit its nightly stage."

This is a ghost story in miniature. Over food and drink, and Coppola insisted on Chateau Latour being served at the correct temperature, they also tuck into the historical provenance of the war. Willard ends up in bed watching Clement's opium-loosened widow encircle him like a siren behind the veil of the mosquito net. The sequence gained mythological status after the publication of *Notes* (which detailed its slavish shooting). Everybody loved it, it was so precious, so beautifully shot, but it had to go. To stand back and register the geopolitical situation stalled the apocalyptic *Now*. Or as Murch said, it was an "ultimately indigestible lump of political information at this juncture in the film."

The undead plantation was part of forty-nine minutes restored to the 2001 *Redux* version (plus more Bunnies, more boat, Brando babbling in daylight) and what was an intrusion into the current of the story in 1979 expanded the tragic waters of the film in 2001. Coppola had caught the original in a hotel room and thought how commonplace its manic visions had become. He remembered he had more madness in the deep freeze.

UA clamoured for a delivery date. Watching as first the promised Christmas release in 1977 went unheeded. Then a promised April 7, 1978 date (Coppola's birthday) came and went. *Apocalypse When?* carped the headlines. The studio was in its own fix. Out of nowhere, beloved, filmmaker-friendly chairman Arthur Krim upped sticks to form a new company – the ill-fated Orion. The Hollywood plates began to shift again. The tremors were felt all the way to San Francisco. Krim's replacement, the inexperienced Andy Albeck, was tasked with keeping the company afloat until their two heavyweights were fighting fit: *Apocalypse Now*, and the $7.5 million "poetic" Western *Heaven's Gate*, directed by Michael Cimino.

Cimino was another thorn in Coppola's side. His previous film, *The Deer Hunter*, featuring Robert De Niro and John Cazale, had beaten

Apocalypse Now as the first revisionist Vietnam epic into cinemas, even though it had begun production over a year later. *Apocalypse First!* sniggered the headlines. And the reviews were glowing. When Cimino won Best Director at the Academy Awards on April 9, 1979, it was Coppola who had to grit his teeth and beam as he handed over the trophy.

So there he was, Coppola at the Cannes podium, confrontational, emphatic, a river in full spate. Fury cracked his voice, and possibly pain. He had delayed a hernia operation (another war wound) to be there. But he was magnetic as he blandished the press for four years of gossip mongering and insolence, gloating at his struggles, while having not one clue what lay at the dark heart of filmmaking. He dismissed their ignorant views; he dismissed their very function. All that mattered was the film.

He was magnificent.

And surely he was calculating? What better performance to sell his wares – a film about madness, and misguided missions, about Vietnam, than this? This was Kurtz.

Apocalypse Now, still untamed, would win his second Palme d'Or, and can now be considered the greatest of its kind – the Vietnam picture.

After nearly three years of postproduction the film was finally released on August 15, 1979. The returns were rousing, but the budget ended up somewhere over $30 million (close scrutinisers say over $40 million), and it will take years to show a profit. Final estimates (without re-releases) come in at $92.1 million. For his agonies, Coppola will eventually make in the region of $15 million, though he would lose Best Picture to *Kramer vs. Kramer*.

Critics have waged war over the film for over forty years: masterpiece or overheated student blather or somewhere upriver between the two? "A monument to artistic self-defeat," crowed *Time*. Brando's Kurtz was like the revelation of Dorian Gray's portrait – inevitably the dampest of squibs. "Marlon Brando, as Kurtz, is bald in several ways, shorn of hair and power, posturing, and pompous," said *The New Republic*. "It seems to have been made by people who have read Conrad with their teeth," scorned *The New Yorker*, who had found the first two hours to be full of fluid horror.

And equally there were those who trumpeted the achievement. "It towers over everything that has been attempted by an American filmmaker in a very long time," enthused the *Los Angeles Times*. Which was the point. Audiences still have no idea how to react. It refuses to let your heart soar. It refuses to lend meaning to its images. It owns the torture of its making.

We spin between versions, the original theatrical cut, the novelistic *Redux* version, and the steadier *Final Cut*, but none feel definitive, only part of a fluid masterpiece that has never ended. Part of Coppola is still out there upriver.

Writing on its re-release in 2001, Ebert saw a film that shamed "modern Hollywood's timidity." He eloquently marshalled his arguments but made his case with a single sentence: "*Apocalypse Now* is one of the central events of my life as a filmgoer."

It is one of the central events in film.

After the official screening, the great and good dressed to the nines poured out of the Palais led by Coppola (his furies not yet subsided) striding down the famous steps. By his side are Eleanor, Gio and Roman, perched on his shoulders is Sofia.

There is a scene in Wes Anderson's *The Life Aquatic with Steve Zissou*, when the title character, a manic-depressive documentary filmmaker played by Bill Murray, strides out of his screening, plucks up a small boy and hoists him onto his shoulders in identical pose. Anderson had a whole Coppola thing going on. He frequently collaborated with Roman, and in *Rushmore* he had Jason Schwartzman, Coppola's nephew, mount an ingenious stage production of *Apocalypse Now*.

The next generation was rightly in awe.

CHAPTER 6

THREE FROM THE HEART

One from the Heart (1981), The Outsiders (1983),
Rumble Fish (1983)

Physically, creatively, and emotionally exhausted; his finances drastically
exposed; his marriage teetering; his ambitions thwarted; his reputation
derided by a hostile media; and his future uncertain, Francis Ford Coppola
decided that this was the perfect time to buy a studio.

Having been frustrated in his attempts to purchase the stricken United
Artists (which had spasmed into crisis with the artistic incontinence of
Apocalypse Now and *Heaven's Gate*), Coppola decided to replant Zoetrope
behind enemy lines.

Hollywood General Studios first opened its doors in 1919. History
was written into its bones. This was where Harold Lloyd had frantically
evaded the machinations of fate and gravity. And it was here the great
Michael Powell (among others) had brought such wonder to *The Thief
of Bagdad* on behalf of Alexander Korda. Which made it hallowed
ground.

Using cash and a symphony of mortgages, Coppola paid $7.2 million
for nine acres of prime studio real estate in the heart of Hollywood.
Paramount was two miles down the road. He immediately renamed it
Zoetrope Studios: nine soundstages, four bungalows, and a clutter of
auxiliary buildings and rehearsal space. He used another $3 million loan

to bring it up to date – all the mod cons, some of which were his own inventions.

This will be his temple to a new form of filmmaking, built beneath the very noses of the establishment. "There is and can be content in technology," he preached, from his new pulpit. "New tunes that we've never heard before, because they've never been possible before." The studio streets were renamed in honour of his cinematic forefathers: Federico Fellini Lane, Akira Kurosawa Avenue, and Sergei Eisenstein Park. The nostalgic revolutionary was at his old games.

Like a repertory company, or a homeless shelter, Zoetrope Studios offered sanctuary and nurture for creative talent across the generations. Coppola swore to do away with the outmoded hierarchies of agents and executives. The legendary Powell, now 75, was given an office under some vague advisory capacity. Veteran artisans mixed with next generation insurgents, wannabe directors poured out of the walls. European auteurs like Jean-Luc Godard, Wim Wenders, and Werner Herzog could be seen sizing up the possibilities through impenetrable sunglasses.

And it was still a family business. Nineteen-year-old Gio was serving as his father's assistant. Seventeen-year-old Roman haunted the sound department. Eleven-year-old Sofia sang, danced, and acted in the Coppola tradition, though not yet for money. She had founded a group, The Dingbats, with her close friends Jillian and Jenny Gersten, daughters of Bernard Gersten, Coppola's vice president. *The Dingbat News* served as the official Zoetrope newspaper.

Briefly, Coppola could stand and admire his Trojan horse.

He had reason to be positive. *Apocalypse Now* was on its way to profit, and Carroll Ballard's dreamy horse-and-his-boy adventure, *The Black Stallion*, foaled at Zoetrope, had been a rare hit for UA. Lest we forget, he was on an artistic streak that had redefined cinema.

However, it was becoming increasingly hard to pull focus on Coppola. Was he artist or mogul? Was he challenging Hollywood or buying a stake at the table? Back in San Francisco, there was an inevitable sense of betrayal. As George Lucas pointed out, weren't they supposed to be creating "a viable film alternative?" He could only watch as Coppola leapt to the front of a new parade.

The general perception in the bars, eateries, and gossip columns was that Coppola was a showman out of his depth. He had tried his merry kingdom in San Francisco and that had come to nothing. He had tried to jury-rig his Vietnam epic outside of studio channels, and that had nearly broken him. He didn't know when to stop! There was talk of megalomania.

Few missed the irony when he backed a $400,000 restoration of the 1927 silent epic *Napoléon*, directed by Abel Gance. In a special presentation at Radio City Music Hall, with a new score by Carmine Coppola, the three-and-a-half-hour masterwork, including sections showing triptychs of images, was a triumph.

Old and new, science and tradition: these were still the twin pulses of Coppola's heartbeat. He had become fixated with the idea that technology – "electronics!" – would resolve all his past problems. In particular, the interminable, maddening postproduction on *The Conversation*, *The Godfather Part II*, and *Apocalypse Now*. Technology would allow him to find his story before filming. Technology would solve the riddle of his own artistic process. Wasn't it technology that had lifted the cloak of polio?

Where once he had lugged around his giant *Godfather* notebook with its scene analysis and mood boards, he conceived of a process of "previsualisation" using computer discs and recorded rehearsals, where he would be able to edit his film before a single scene had been filmed.

In the early days of television, cantankerous New York directors like John Frankenheimer and Sidney Lumet would direct live plays, conducting an entire world from a television control booth amid plumes of acrid cigarette smoke. So he outfitted an aluminium Airstream trailer, sleek as a bullet, with the latest video technology, espresso machines, and jacuzzis. Where once he and his earnest Brats had rigged motor homes with cutting decks on *The Rain People*, he would have live feeds from set and be able to record and edit scenes by the very next morning. Catching the blinding Californian sun in the Zoetrope car park, it was named the Silverfish. Everything was being streamlined.

Eventually, he would confine the cumbrous old studio production model to the dark ages with a new breed of filmmaking that combined television, theatre, and twenty-four-track mixing desks, with distribution by satellite. The audience would watch the story as it was filmed. Hofstra and Hollywood as one! But there was work to be done. He must deliver a fully independent slate of films, produced without extravagance. He needed to make the studio a going concern. And he was leading the way with his next film. What he promised was a simple love story told in unconventional style.

And here lies the rub. Coppola the studio boss was going to have to rein in Coppola the director.

Teri Garr is talking to the ceiling. And the ceiling is replying.

"Try not to anticipate the kiss."

Everyone on set is frozen in place, listening in.

"And try to appear more happy that he's kissed you, Teri. I know you wish it was me, but *try*."

Coppola's voice cuts out, and Garr manages to smile. Shoulder-length blonde hair framing pretty features, she had honest frequencies, and was excellent as Richard Dreyfuss's frazzled wife in *Close Encounters of the Third Kind*. Coppola had previously put her to more sinister use as Harry Caul's mistress in *The Conversation*. She had just about got used to holding conversations with the disembodied director, often detailed stuff about the emotional content of a scene, with the grips tuning in.

The director is currently seated in the Silverfish, parked by the side of the soundstage, and at the bleeding edge of filmmaking. From his shiny cocoon, he watched and edited scenes, offering advice via intercom, fashioning his film as he went.

On set it was absurd. The Wizard of Oz booming his instructions. Coppola's reputation was of a director who adored actors. Wouldn't he want to look them in the eye?

There were those who worried. Was this a reaction to his breakdown in the jungle – to hide himself away with his video playback and hot tub? The danger was he was absenting himself from the film.

One from the Heart, Coppola acknowledged, was a panacea after the upheavals of *Apocalypse Now*. Maybe it was a *mea culpa* too. For it is a story of love's endurance in the face of temptation. And that hit home. Toward the end of *Notes*, Eleanor's diary describes her distraught husband's admission that even during all the turmoil of his Vietnam epic, with all her devotion, he had been unfaithful. The other woman (who goes unnamed in *Notes*) was Melissa Mathison, his assistant in the Philippines, who would marry Harrison Ford and write *E. T.: The Extra-Terrestrial*. Coppola confessed that he didn't think it was love. More like a wide-eyed crush, pupil for professor. When he was in need of a muse. "Her confidence in me, made me feel confident," he admitted.

The marriage barely survived the storm.

So the story of *One from the Heart* is striking. Frannie (Garr) and Hank (Frederic Forrest) have been living together for nearly five years on the fringes of Las Vegas. She's a travel agent, who dreams of Bora Bora. He's a mechanic, who dreams of showgirls. Their relationship has become routine. Not loveless, but dissatisfied. On July 4th (as America parties), each will have a dalliance, and embark on a journey that will restore their affection.

The script had been kicking around at MGM. Written by Armyan Bernstein, it was a romantic comedy set in Chicago when the studio offered it to Coppola to direct for a record $2 million. He demurred, but eventually struck a deal whereby Zoetrope would make and own the film, and MGM would distribute for $8 million. The amount Coppola had thought it would cost.

Working long distance with Bernstein, Coppola finished the first draft in Tokyo on his way back from *Apocalypse Now*. He had been reading Goethe, and contemplated adapting *Elective Affinities*, about a troubled married couple, which he would shoot over a decade, following the consequences across the years. *One from the Heart* offered a more tenable alternative. Walking through the Ginza section of the city – where Sofia would one day shoot *Lost in Translation* – he was struck by how all the walls of neon resembled Las Vegas, where he and Eleanor were married.

Incidentally, this was when he agreed to produce Kurosawa's ravishing (and outdoorsy) *Kagemusha*.

Coppola's plan was to transform a classic break-up story into a ritual "in the religious manner". Part musical, part drama, he would study a modern American relationship (they are noticeably unmarried) through the prism of Vegas. "I wanted the scenery, the music, and the lighting for example, to be part of the film, not just a *background* for the action."

On the eve of production, Coppola threw a huge barbecue for cast and crew at Napa. "You just begin to smell the movie around the corner," he enthused to Gersten. But that may have been the marshmallows he was roasting.

You can feel a struggle between narrative and process for supremacy in *One from the Heart*. This small, personal, jazzy, quite European film is caught on the cusp of Coppola's technical revolution, and the proud declaration that it was all "recorded on soundstages at Zoetrope Studios" might as well be a warning.

He began by putting the script onto computer discs. That way he could rearrange scenes, or rewrite them, without returning to the ache of the typewriter. He then made storyboards of each scene, which he videotaped with the actors reading lines. That gave him the rhythm of his drama. Then cast and crew headed to Las Vegas (the real one), where he videotaped them running through the whole script, so he could see how he wanted things to look. Then came the "real" rehearsals on Zoetrope's stage, which he videotaped.

Coppola effectively made the film four times before shooting a scene. There were seventy-nine rehearsal days and seventy-two shooting days.

This didn't speak of streamlining so much as neurosis. He had simply moved the trials of post into preproduction. We have Lillian Ross's exhaustive account of the film's downfall in *The New Yorker* to thank for the full ledger and the numbers are mind-boggling: he was up to 311 storyboards, over 1200 videocassettes, and 1300 photographic stills. Eight wind machines together with eight rain machines created the weather. No more slogging through jungles, he declared, tempests can be commandeered right here in the studio. But the budget was rising.

Rather than the tangible grandeur of his hits, Coppola was faking the fakest city on Earth. Behind the doors of the nine grey soundstages, production designer Dean Tavoularis created his pop masterpiece: gigantic Warholian replicas of a city that already looked like a movie set. Coppola saw Las Vegas as a metaphor for modern America, so he wanted an ersatz Vegas, a dream Vegas, a Vegas he could control.

Carpenters toiled to reach Tavoularis's perfections. He wanted to sculpt not only a facsimile of a real place but sets that answered the pre-visualised motions of Coppola's storytelling. They constructed six paved streets, seven houses, a motel, a travel agency, a department store, a nightclub and casino, an auto-repair shop and junkyard (a Fellini-note of rusted circus pieces built on the backlot), a replica of McCarran Airport and a jet (which with a whiff of portent was made from the nose cone of a crashed Boeing). And there was the Strip itself, embalmed in a migraine of neon. They used 125,000 light bulbs – that takes ego.

"The city is a metaphor for the state of love itself," added Coppola. "I'm interested in films that *are* what they are about."

Cinematographer Vittorio Storaro advanced his theories on colour, where emotions ran to shades of red and blue, which he smeared over entire scenes to stunning effect. "I went to the physiology of colour," he said: inducing feeling in the viewer with light. His high artifice would help create the disco sheen of MTV.

Here too are tributes to the succulent MGM musicals and grand, old fantasies like *The Thief of Bagdad* – the extension of reality into a movie realm. Theatrical reality. August Coppola saw an artistic progression in his brother: "He wanted to make a fantasy out of the visual imagery itself, using electronic means." After *Apocalypse Now* where else was there to go but inside?

Part of the problem is that it danced around the idea of being a musical. The barrel-bottom, bluesy croon of Tom Waits and creamy upper notes of Crystal Gayle provided twelve songs, but not to be performed within the film rather than on the soundtrack. They serve as a chorus. Mood music, you might say.

Where once Coppola had worked with Fred Astaire, now he had that other master Gene Kelly – now sixty-eight – figuring out the choreography as Zoetrope's "executive of musical production and development". But there are few true dance sequences, beyond Frannie being drawn through the syncopated crowds of the Strip in the flush of new love.

It was visionary stuff. But what was left for the actors to do? The scenery was giving the performance. Along with Garr and Forrest, we have Raul Julia as the singing waiter who tempts Frannie, and Nastassja Kinski as the angelic tightrope walker who tempts Hank. Old pros Harry

Dean Stanton and Lainie Kazan are on hand to listen to their friends complain.

It was a now familiar story. What set out to be an agile, intimate form of filmmaking grew into another quest for the ghost of perfection. Coppola was like a creative gas that fills all available space. The budget was up to $23 million.

On the other hand, who's to say that *One from the Heart* didn't shape the future? Video assist and pre-visualisation are now standard practice – and entire worlds are built with green screens and computers.

And it was not only *One from the Heart* that was draining Zoetrope of funds and stability. Impressed by his early work, Coppola had invited Wenders to direct a film noir that thrust the crime writer Dashiell Hammett (Forrest again) into one of his own stories. *Hammett* had turned into its own quagmire of reshoots and rethinking. A year after it supposedly finished shooting the film was suspended in limbo, awaiting Coppola's ruling.

With the MGM pot drained, the studio head had to find other investors, extending himself yet further. It wasn't only the film; the studio needed backing. He took out weekly bank loans of $1 million, brought in outside investors – a Canadian real estate agent named Jack Singer, an unreliable gaggle of German investors – anything to keep going.

He was moved to tears when the crew voted against a union-mandated strike with the payroll not met. They started to wear badges: "I believe in Francis C." Coppola put up the studio, his office buildings, and his homes as collateral. His life again wagered for his art. He was gambling everything on his Las Vegas romance, which came in at a staggering $27 million.

Over five thousand gather at Radio City Music Hall on January 15, 1982, including five hundred of Coppola's close personal friends. This is the final preview of his new film, a grand affair, and a chance to turn the tide. So he's putting on a show. And this venue is filled with happy memories. Sofia and her fellow Dingbats wear top hats and tails for a tap routine. While the movie plays he paces back and forth, occasionally swerving toward an aisle door to listen.

He is struggling to cement distribution. The film has confounded the studios, rumours are growing that it's unreleasable. The situation has brought out the brinkman in Coppola. If one studio expressed a doubt, he would move on to the next. First, MGM, then Paramount, and now he's wondering if he can distribute it himself.

Afterwards he confronts the press, and he can hear knives being drawn. Has he accomplished his purpose?

"When I make a film, I take a jump into something I am interested in," he responds, citing show business, gambling, love, fantasy, and music. He thinks his film is beautiful. Years from now, he knows, people will see it as an original work.

Will this film be commercially successful?

"How the hell do I know?"

Months later, the critics were perplexed. What has the mercurial giant done now? Couldn't they see that he was doing what he always did – pouring out his heart.

Lavish praise is bestowed on the iridescent visuals. There has never been a film like it, as he had promised. But where was Coppola's great facility with character? The story beneath the light bulbs is trivial. "Coppola has thrown out the baby and photographed the bath water," complained Andrew Sarris in *The Village Voice*, a line that would stick.

Eventually picked up by Columbia, it is a lost cause. *One from the Heart* leaves audiences cold. Barely scraping $2.5 million, it is the biggest flop of his career. His creditors began to prowl. All of it – Zoetrope Studios, The Sentinel Building, the Little Fox Theatre, the homes in Los Angeles, New York, San Francisco, and the estate in Napa Valley – were now at stake.

When Singer called in his loan, Coppola went bust.

It says something about the great contradictions of the director's nature that it was not the monster of *Apocalypse Now*, but this giddy tale of love lost and found – his recovery film! – that would ruin him (he declared bankruptcy on April 20, 1982). He has said many times that what people view as the derailment of a magisterial career, where he supposedly sold out to the sordid, studio dollar, was to pay his debts on *One from the Heart*.

The era of the auteur was over.

In November 1982, Coppola made it to New York for Martin Scorsese's fortieth. Both were poor company. Pacing his loft like a restless cat, Scorsese bemoaned the failure of *The King of Comedy*. He was so broke that his business manager had confiscated his credit cards. Coppola took a breath. "Marty, would you calm down? You're broke, I owe $50 million!"

The letter came from Fresno, California. Jo Ellen Misakian was a librarian's aide at the Lone Star Junior School, and she had put together a petition of over 300 signatures. The undersigned had decided that Coppola was the ideal director to adapt S.E. Hinton's *The Outsiders* – a tale of teen gangs in 1965 Tulsa, Oklahoma: the north side, working class Greasers and their rivals, the entitled, south side Socs (pronounced "*so-chez*"). This had been sent optimistically to Paramount's office in New York and forwarded to his Manhattan address. This was a fortuitous turn of events. So few letters landed on Coppola's East Coast desk, while they piled up into unanswered snowdrifts at Zoetrope Studios in Los Angeles.

So it caught his eye, that he was being pitched a movie by eleven-year-old students from an elementary school in blue collar California. They were also good enough to enclose a copy of the book.

Misakian explained that she often struggled to get her boys to read. And it was only ever this book that turned their heads. The directness of the story spoke to them. And she got thinking about how it would make a good movie. Why Coppola? Well, he had produced *The Black Stallion*, based on the children's book by Walter Farley. Misakian mentioned she had recently read a review of that film in *Newsweek*, and "the critique said that Coppola followed the story really well." Carroll Ballard's contribution notwithstanding, this was a simple entreaty from a modest source, untainted by Hollywood thinking.

Coppola handed the note and the paperback to long-time producer Fred Roos. "Check it out, if you want to."

Weeks later, on a flight back to the West Coast, Roos opened the book he'd left forgotten in his briefcase. Gliding over the American heartland, maybe even Tulsa, he knew the librarian was right. This would make a damn good movie. The students of Lone Star would eventually get a credit, a private screening, and the chance to greet some of the stars. But they never got to meet the famous director.

There have been many motives behind Coppola's artistic choices, some spontaneous, some provocative, some desperate, some maybe cynical. But what brought him to adapt *The Outsiders* was an act of purification.

In the aftermath of *One from the Heart*, Coppola needed somewhere to regroup, and take stock. That always meant another film. This $10 million show, backed by Warner Bros. (sold on the elixir of youth), was a chance to "forget my troubles and have some laughs again." He was in a vulnerable place, beaten up by the business, staring down the barrel of ruin, and this was, absurdly, a tonic. That letter contained honeyed words – simple, innocent enthusiasm for movies. That spoke to him.

"Rather than go through six months of being whipped for having committed this sin of making a film I wanted to make, I escaped with a lot of people to Tulsa and didn't have to deal with the sophisticates."

He always loved the company of kids. Drawing sustenance in the darkest hours from the presence of his three beautiful children. Way back, he had been a camp counsellor, working with teens. "And it appealed to me that kids could see *The Outsiders* as a lavish big feeling epic…" he explained. "Those kids have gargantuan romantic feelings."

Born, raised, and still firmly rooted in Tulsa whatever her success, Susan Eloise Hinton wrote her most famous novel in high school. It was her third. *The Outsiders* came out in 1967 and has since sold more than thirteen million copies. With a shelf of teen dramas, most set on the streets of Tulsa, Hinton is widely considered the progenitor of the Young Adult novel, which puts Coppola – yet again – ahead of his time. Stirred by Hinton's emotionally frictive world, the YA genre expanded exponentially, but his film was long gone.

Novel and film tell the story of Ponyboy Curtis (C. Thomas Howell), the youngest of three brothers like Michael Corleone, who runs with the Greasers. We meet other gang members, bequiffed and denim-clad, such as his best friend Johnny (Ralph Macchio), his brother Sodapop (Rob Lowe), and the volatile Dallas (Matt Dillon), fresh out of prison. We get the undulating rhythms of their lives. We ponder their empty prospects and absentee fathers. The catalyst for trouble comes with both Ponyboy's interest in Soc girl Cherry (Diane Lane) and Johnny killing a foe in self-defence. Tragedy lies on the burnished horizon, along with one last rumble.

"It was overemotional, over the top, melodramatic," accepted Hinton, looking back on the book on its 40th anniversary. "But its vices are its virtues, because kids feel that way."

Which is precisely what drew Coppola into its pages. There is a microcosm here of the mobs that pervade his more famous films – the hierarchies, power games, and possibility of redemption. The opera. And he knew precisely the approach he would take with the material.

Hinton and Coppola got on well. With a dry, disdainful wit, belied by sad eyes, Hinton was an artist uninterested in the thoroughfares of fame. "I get letters from all over the world, saying, 'It changed my life.' Who am I to change somebody's life? It's not me. It's in the book." But she remembered writing it, and the feeling of burning up that came with creation. Coppola knew those fevers well.

"I wanted a movie told in sumptuous terms," he explained, vowing faith to the source material. "Putting the emphasis more on that kind of *Gone with the Wind* lyricism, which was so important to the young girl when she wrote it."

Coppola's power base may have been ebbing, but his powers of foresight were undiminished. He peopled his bromance with what would become the next generation of superstars. We can gaze upon Dillon, Macchio, Howell, and Lowe, plus Patrick Swayze, Emilio Estevez (son of Martin Sheen, who had seen his father crack during *Apocalypse Now*), and a puppyish Tom Cruise long before they were declared heart-throbs and headline acts.

The audition process had the looseness of Coppola's old Hofstra games. All the prospective actors thrown together in one room, watching each other try out lines, aiming for certain roles, unsure whether they were rivals or co-stars. The director shimmied between them, moving parts like chess pieces, seeing how things evolved.

For those lucky enough to be cast, he moved onto character building. Handing Macchio a $5 bill and telling him to get through the day on that alone – to understand the poverty of these characters. Macchio took that to heart and spent the night in the park under newspapers as his character does. Dillon was encouraged to try his hand at shoplifting from a drugstore – on the promise that they would bail him out if anything went wrong.

Next Coppola videotaped a two-week rehearsal of the entire film, so they could study the individual scenes. He was taking what he could from the wreckage of *One from the Heart*, honing his pre-visualisation techniques to gain a look at the movie to come. Pained as they were, sitting on the floor watching their school play version, the actors started to trust the director.

He gave them emotional courage.

The cast was put up at the Excelsior Hotel, Tulsa – the Socs getting much better rooms than the Greasers to heighten the tension. There was never a question about whether they were going to shoot on Hinton's home terrain. This was the soil of her story. Straddling the Great Plains and prairie land, Tulsa is an oil town, slave to boom and bust. It's got its bumps: a fringe of rundown districts, empty buildings, and hardscrabble parks.

As promised, the film is as ripe as a peach. These are punks and tearaways who admire the sunset and quote poetry. They are young Coppolas, with their hearts on their dirty sleeves. The film has no qualms about sentiment. "It's a heartbreaking story, with nobility," announced the director, as they went into production on March 29, 1982. The mood is deluxe, Hollywood storytelling: *Rebel Without a Cause* mixed with *West Side Story*. The score, Coppola knew, would be key – something schmaltzy and classical, and offered the task to his father Carmine. The family were on the move: Gio served as his father's apprentice, Roman a production assistant, and Sofia had a cameo. The Silverfish made the long trek across the states.

The reclusive Hinton took to having the movie business in her backyard, playing den mother for the cast – who were far from home without adult supervision – and taking a cameo as a nurse. She would sit next to Coppola as he filmed, a vital voice in the writing of the script.

The atmosphere was good-natured but juvenile – actors would swindle keys out of dumbfounded maids and raid one another's rooms. Pranks included smearing Lane's toilet seat in honey, or turning Howell's entire room upside down, including his bed. Not all that funny when you've just completed a seventeen-hour shift. Coppola approved. This was about bonding, expressing something natural. He was happy in his work in a way he hadn't been since *The Conversation*. Dillon took to calling him "Father Film".

Tulsa brought relief in other ways. It may have been temporary, but his various creditors delayed their numerous foreclosures, waiting to see if he might prove able to repay his loans. His most valuable asset was still his talent, and this pearly teen drama allowed Zoetrope Studios to stay one step ahead of closure.

Things were still bleak in the outside world. There was no white knight in what was left of the Zoetrope slate – all the talk of artistic freedom was looking like too much interference from head office. Clearly patched over, Caleb Deschanel's *The Escape Artist* – about a wannabe Houdini (and written by Mathison) – found few takers. When *Hammett* finally emerged, its period soundstage aesthetic betrayed Coppola's fingerprints and the critics descended like hounds. Wenders's ersatz *Chinatown* barely gained a release. Coppola's patronage was like a cartoon piano tied to a director's ankle.

Little wonder he stayed in Tulsa to grab another movie as Roger Corman once did. *Rumble Fish* was pure impulse. Keep running, keep shooting, stay ahead of the heartache. When Warner passed on the idea – Universal stepped in six weeks into production – Coppola was not to be dissuaded from his path, writing into the night while he finished *The Outsiders*. This was who he was, the artist, shooting from the hip.

"I really started to use *Rumble Fish* as my carrot for what I promised myself when I finished *The Outsiders*."

Keeping cast and crew together, and with barely two weeks between productions, he dived into his second Hinton adaptation.

Coppola had overheard some of the kids on *The Outsiders* talking about this other book. "It just stuck in my ear, the odd words, 'rumble fish'," he recalled. He was gratified to find it was a very short novel, and written when Hinton was, in his words, "older – and drunk, I think." It is the tale of the listless Rusty James (Dillon) left behind in Tulsa and The Motorcycle Boy (Mickey Rourke), the prodigal brother who returns.

Her third published novel had a very different sensibility: it was stylised and dreamy, and harboured more complex themes, things you felt rather than understood. So Coppola was intent on what was "deliberately an American art film," said film historian David Thomson. We are reminded of the extent to which literature shapes his cinematic ideals. Everything from J.D. Salinger to Greek mythology would season the mix.

And he was back experimenting with form, shifting into an expressive European mode, heedless of commercial imperatives. The hot summer months in Tulsa provided the perfect sweltering backdrop, and he planned an incandescent black and white.

"Who but Coppola would make this film?" wondered writer Roger Ebert. "And, of course, who but Coppola would want to?"

This is his most consciously imitative work. Visually, Coppola is quoting the Orson Welles of *The Magnificent Ambersons*; the German Expressionism of *The Cabinet of Dr. Caligari;* the hallucinations of film noir; and how in French New Wave movies kids walk and talk, floating around town with the aimlessness of life, not following the paths of plot.

They ran production out of a school building, where the designers and camera crew sketched scenes on a blackboard, which they filmed as a rudimentary animatic. Coppola videotaped his rehearsals again for his "rough cut". From there, he could experiment to his heart's content.

Ideas came quickly. The Motorcycle Boy is described as being "colour blind", which he pictured as black and white, with a flash of virulent colour when we see the Siamese fighting fish in a pet store. They are the central metaphor: how we're defined by nature. This is long before Steven Spielberg soaked up the applause for his daring a red dress in *Schindler's List*. Liberating the animals (and the rumble fish into the river) linked *Rumble Fish* to *The Rain People*, where the troubled Killer frees the baby chicks.

The film aspires to music, dream, tone poem, even theatre – street fights were choreographed by Michael Smuin from the San Francisco Ballet; Stewart Copeland, the talented drummer from The Police, laid down a percussive score to which Coppola timed his drama.

"*Rumble Fish* will be to *The Outsiders* what *Apocalypse Now* was to *The Godfather*," he declared. And he had a point.

Another impulse was Rourke. He had auditioned for *The Outsiders*, and Coppola had been impressed. But there was no real role for him to play. Now that unreadable, pugilist's face was ideal for the older brother, known only as The Motorcycle Boy, who bikes back into town. Roos suggested they team him with Dillon as Rusty James, pacing the streets with his gang, yearning for his idolised sibling, shattered by the reality. Existential despair hangs in the hot air. There's a no-good pop somewhere in the picture too, an unreliable drunk conjured up in a flurry of cat-on-a-hot-plate improvisation by Dennis Hopper.

This is why Coppola related to the book — it was another story of brothers, and fathers, and America.

"It's very personal," Coppola would say, doing the full confession for interviewers. *Rumble Fish* was his film for August — the brother *he* idolised. Augie was the leader of the gang, the one with the looks, the one who wanted to take on the world. "[He] just took me everywhere," he recalled, "and taught me everything."

Growing up, trying to become a man, Coppola emulated all that Augie did. Without thinking twice, he handed in a batch of his brother's short stories to his writing class at high school. Not to cheat, rather than as an act of transference.

Augie had big dreams and read big books, filling his brother's head with Andre Gide, Jean-Paul Sartre, and James Joyce. "...The jacket that his son wears, you know Nicolas Cage, that wild goose jacket?" Coppola pointed out. "That was *his* jacket; it was a copy of his real one."

So Rourke's character, with his Albert Camus mystique and tilted cigarette, was a cypher of August, albeit with artistic licence. August was not borderline insane. He had lived up to his brother's billing: leaving UCLA to publish papers on Hemingway and teach comparative literature at Cal State. While Dean of Creative Arts at San Francisco State University, he doubled as an executive at American Zoetrope, assisting his brother on the grand revival of *Napoléon*. He married the dancer Joy Vogelsang — diagnosed as a schizophrenic — and had three sons, three brothers. The youngest one had the real name of Nicholas Coppola.

The first appearance of Cage in one of his uncle's films is as Rusty James's doe-eyed and treacherous lieutenant Smokey. This was partly a piece of thematic casting. He brought August's genes. It's something that would bug his nephew — the idea of nepotism. That his career had benefited from the family brand. That's why he changed his name, dropping the "h" and borrowing a punchy surname from comic-book hero Luke Cage. He wanted to stop walking into auditions and seeing the eyebrows go up. Those insecurities were in the genes too.

There is a family legend: Cage, still nominally a Coppola at fifteen, being driven by his uncle. "Why don't you put me in one of your movies?" he cries, his heart bursting with the need to act. His uncle, the great director, said nothing. In the silence, Cage knew he had to prove himself.

"Revenge fuelled so much of my ambition."

Born in Long Beach in 1964, schooled among the brats of Beverly Hills High, he admitted (he's got that confession thing too) to growing up resentful of his rich cousins in their San Francisco manor. He cultivated a place as the family crank – pet sharks, Elvis obsession, shrunken heads in his Bel·Air pad – but Cage was the biggest success of them all, a genuine Hollywood star. His films add up to billions, mixing blockbusters like *The Rock* and *Face/Off* with high-risk, far-out roles.

So he was very much a Coppola. He had his uncle's maverick blood. "I thought I could change acting," he once said. Everything he touched, even the epics, gained a surreal edge. His doleful eyes and long, maudlin good looks are countered by shocks of impudent energy. He admitted to being diagnosed as "superfrenetic" like Charlie Chaplin.

"You either have the proclivity to open up your imagination or you don't," he said.

The effect can be thrilling (*Raising Arizona, Wild at Heart, Moonstruck, Bringing Out the Dead* with Scorsese), or insufferable (*Vampire's Kiss, Captain Corelli's Mandolin*). He will work with Uncle Francis on two further occasions – and always be a fly in the family ointment. His choices have been questionable. As have his methods, or Method. Would Brando eat a cockroach to play a vampire? For the Vietnam vet in *Birdy*, Cage wrapped bandages around his face for five weeks.

Preparing to audition for the jailbird Dallas in *The Outsiders*, Cage locked himself in a room for two weeks watching Charles Bronson movies and guzzling beer. He didn't get the role, but Coppola asked him back for *Rumble Fish*.

Released in March 1983, as the librarian had predicted *The Outsiders* found an audience, making $25 million. The critics couldn't seem to decide what was wrong with it. But they had to try. "It may be a case of the wrong man for the job," bemoaned *The Hollywood Reporter*, wondering why it had to be both clichéd and detached. "Highly conventional," sighed *Variety*.

Did they miss that it was a film about belonging? That there is an angelic nobility to these insignificant kids.

Coppola was unapologetic. He could have made the film sixteen different ways, but this was how he saw the book.

"I liked the film on that basis. It's how I made it and why I made it. But if you think about my career, I've never made two films that were alike... maybe the two *Godfathers*. But every one of my films is very different from one another..."

Rumble Fish fared worse. Roundly booed on its debut at the New York Film Festival (leaving Coppola devastated), the studio was at a loss what to do with this oblique movie and it sunk without trace commercially. But there are those who consider it one of Coppola's most beautiful and personal films.

"*Rumble Fish* is a myth as beautiful as *Orpheé*," announced Thomson in *Film Comment*, "but is also a confession on the maker's own early life and abiding psychology."

Life moved on, and Coppola began thinking big again. To make the kind of film that would make his brother proud. If film was even the right word. He wanted to write a big novel like *Ulysses* or something by Thomas Mann, but not on the page, written in cinema. He had a name – *Megalopolis*.

"It all takes place in New York. And it's contemporary. It has many characters, and it all takes place in one day."

He will draw from Roman history, Plutarch and Cicero. Explore the idea of utopia, and the city as a living organism. Grapple with big questions: Where did we come from? Where are we going? What is the human race at this point?

CHAPTER 7

HISTORY REPEATING

The Cotton Club (1984),
Peggy Sue Got Married (1986)

If Mario Puzo had wanted to make a quick buck by writing the salacious, airport version of a Francis Ford Coppola production it would be *The Cotton Club*. Though even he may have baulked at how far-fetched things became. As many critics would eagerly point out, what occurred behind the scenes of Coppola's twelfth film would have made a more entertaining movie than the uneven cocktail of gangsters and dancers out front.

It is a making-of story that has, in a more tawdry fashion, a mythology to rival *The Godfather* and *Apocalypse Now*. In 1984, on the heels of the film's release, the high-profile *New York* magazine devoted twenty-two sensational pages to what went into the film rather than what came out of it. On the surface it is a familiar aria: an ever-changing script, reckless spending, demanding stars, and a director consumed by grandiloquence. But underneath is a Scorsesian welter of drugs, hoods, hookers, arms dealers, and murder. Fact was masquerading as cliché.

Coppola was still in the ebb and flow of his own financial disaster. The fallout from *One from the Heart*, including the prospective sale of Zoetrope Studios and the potential loss of the Sentinel Building and Napa estate, the symbolic heart and soul of Coppola's kingdom, was

147

mired in an endless succession of legal prevarications and delays. Things had stretched on so long that industry bible *Variety* had reclassified his spectacular downfall as "boring."

There were always potential projects. *Megalopolis* gathered pages, and he was keen to do the New York crime comedy, *The Pope of Greenwich Village* with Al Pacino, and had a "down-and-out" George Orwell style in mind. But that was getting delayed.

The fact was that Coppola needed work to make his interest payments. Symbolically, his American Express card had been cancelled.

When his phone rang, it was a ghost on the other end of the line. Robert Evans was in a bind. He needed someone to rewrite a script called *The Cotton Club*.

"I have a sick child," he said, his tone unctuous and wounded. "I need a doctor."

Evans had decided that *The Cotton Club* was his ticket back to the big time. His heyday at Paramount was receding into the distance. Whizz kids were running the show using predictive curves and audience data. For old times' sake, he still had a deal at the studio, but his last two films, *Black Sunday* and *Players*, were frankly embarrassments. His hunches were off. His phone quieted. The lustre was dimming.

"If he can't be Bob Evans," observed close friend and effervescent production designer Richard Sylbert, "he's dead."

So he planned something big – a showstopper. Based on James Haskins's pictorial history of a Harlem nightclub in the 1920s, Evans saw *The Cotton Club* as a mix of two genres – the gangster picture and the musical. This was the club that had launched the careers of Cab Calloway, Ella Fitzgerald, Lena Horne, and Duke Ellington. That was what gave it political spice: the hoofers, players, and comedians, plus the leggy chorus line, were all black, while the clientele was whites only, and tended toward the criminal. This was the era of Dutch Schultz and Lucky Luciano dividing up the Manhattan rackets. Evans promised the "*Godfather* with music." With unprecedented brio, he planned to make this epic of the jazz age his directorial debut.

But the studios didn't bite. There was wariness around musicals, especially with a black cast, and he had yet to produce a script. Or even describe the plot. In his frustration, Evans began a treacherous quest to find a backer through non-traditional channels.

In early 1981, he is introduced to Arab arms dealer Adnan Khashoggi (who would go on to star in the Iran-Contra scandal). Keen to try the movies business, Khashoggi offers $2 million seed money, but Evans pushes for the $20 million budget upfront. Hardballing his new partner, he splits for New York in Khashoggi's private jet. Onboard, Evans described, "an extraordinarily beautiful girl" serving him champagne, before changing into a negligee. "Let's go to bed," she purrs, but for once he thinks better of the proposition. He later learns Khashoggi has a recording of the conversation. Still, he returns for the seed money, and basks in the party thrown in his honour at the Dunes in Vegas with thirty violins playing the *Godfather* theme. Looking for some of that old magic, he approaches Mario Puzo, who charges him $1 million to turn out a script everybody hates. Including Khashoggi, who wants Evans's precious Woodland as collateral.

"It's over AK, I'm outta here," he informed his backer, leaving behind the promise of "twelve big ones." That is $12 million without the lingo.

Next Evans lines up a posse of willing Texan millionaires, only for the bottom to fall out of the oil market.

Enter Sylvester Stallone, who agrees to star for $2 million, but when *Rocky III* becomes a smash (Hollywood's rebirth as a franchise machine writ large) he doubles his asking price. Exit Stallone.

In late 1982, Evans's luck changes. He is introduced to brothers Ed and Fred Doumani, grinning sons of a Lebanese immigrant flower salesman who prospered planting hotels in the Nevada sand. His offspring had continued in casinos, partnered with a Denver insurance magnate named Victor Sayyah. They wanted to give the movie business a go.

Only they hate the Puzo script. Evans tries his own rewrite. They hate that, too, but they see the potential. *The Godfather* with songs. So he calls his old, Machiavellian nemesis, Coppola, conscious that he too is in a tight spot. According to *New York* magazine, even after *The Outsiders* and *Rumble Fish,* Coppola was still $20 million in hock.

On the phone, Evans can't help but boast.

He had Astoria Studios in Queens, near to where Coppola had grown up.

He had Gregory Hines, the fleet-footed Broadway star who began tap dancing at the age of two. Evans had been holding out for Richard Pryor, but he was asking for $4 million, and barely moved at all. Hines had leapt onto his oak desk and improvised a tap routine before his eyes.

And he had Richard Gere, nearly. The handsome, intense star of *An Officer and a Gentleman* had agreed but didn't like the script. He was trying to bolt. So Evans applied his slippery charm, swaddling him in the Woodland guesthouse, where Gere struck a hard and wacky bargain. He would get $1.5 million, ten percent of the gross, script approval, be a sympathetic character (not a hood), and play the cornet. This final condition would prove particularly irksome given that no white musicians ever played at the Cotton Club. This was kind of the point.

But with Gere he had landed a $10 million distribution deal with Orion. And $8 million in foreign distribution rights.

What he didn't have was a decent script.

Listening to Evans describe his dilemma, Coppola might have felt a spike of vindictive pleasure. But he found he empathised with the producer; charting a course outside of studios waters had nearly lost him everything. And he relished the idea of being Evans's artistic saviour.

"I offered to read the script and give him any help that I could. For about a week for free."

He reported back that the script was, indeed, dire. But fatal imaginative juices were beginning to flow, and he invited Evans, Gere, Hines, and choreographer Dyson Lovell to Napa Valley for a *Cotton Club* summit, where he instantly took charge, tap dancing with words. This should be the rise and fall of the famous club, he proposed, as seen through the perspective of two peripheral characters. "Rosencrantz and Guildenstern Harlem style," he proclaimed. Enthusiasm flowed. And Evans offered him the chance to write his version of the story.

Coppola knew gangsters, he knew New York, he knew musicals, but knew nothing about jazz. But with $250,000 being dangled by Evans, he accepted the assignment.

So where are we? March 1983, with Coppola heading off to New York to research the Harlem Renaissance, excited by the potential of a story divided along racial lines. He pictured the film swaying back and forth

Petula Clark, Tommy Steele and Francis Ford Coppola take tea on the set of *Finian's Rainbow* in 1968.

For Coppola, studio musical *Finian's Rainbow*, was a chance to finance his smaller, more personal films.

Coppola and wife Eleanor Coppola during the troubled shooting of *The Godfather* in 1971: day-to-day the director was in constant conflict with the studio.

Francis Ford Coppola examines the equine blood pooling on silk sheets for one of *The Godfather*'s multitude of signature moments.

The Corleone fraternity: Sonny (James Caan), Don Vito (Marlon Brando), Coppola, Michael (Al Pacino), and Fredo (John Cazale).

Gene Hackman and Coppola getting deep into *The Conversation* (1974).

The Godfather Part II in 1974: Coppola directs the Corleone's expansion into Cuba—filmed in the Dominican Republic.

Vindication for the family: Carmine Coppola embraces his son and daughter Talia Shire at the 1975 Academy Awards as Eleanor Coppola looks on.

The strains of *Apocalypse Now* in 1976 and 1977: Marlon Brando and Francis Ford Coppola debate the elusive ending . . .

. . . Coppola struggles to rein in the wildly improvisational flurries of Dennis Hopper . . .

. . . and heading upriver: director and star Martin Sheen find a moment of introspection.

For small, musically inclined romance *One from the Heart* (1982), Coppola built a giant replica of Las Vegas across his own soundstages.

A young at heart Coppola directs (from left) C. Thomas Howell, Ralph Macchio, and Matt Dillon on the set of *The Outsiders* (1983).

Friends reunited: director Francis Ford Coppola, producer George Lucas and the gleaming star of *Tucker: The Man and His Dream* (1988).

Sofia Coppola as the doomed Mary Corleone in *The Godfather Part III* (1990).

Nine years later, Sofia directing Kirsten Dunst in her sparkling debut *The Virgin Suicides* (1999).

The son also shines: Roman Coppola directing *CQ* in 2000.

Sofia and her droll muse Bill Murray on the promotional trail for
Lost in Translation (2003) in Rome.

Portrait of a lady:
Sofia Coppola
and Kirsten Dunst
on the set of the
controversial
Marie Antoinette
(2006).

Third generation:
granddaughter
Gia Coppola
(second from
right) directs
Palo Alto (2013).

New York story:
the irrepressible
Bill Murray and
Sofia during
the making of
On The Rocks
(2020).

between the neurotic, scheming gangsters, bragging among the tables, and the black musicians, sliding on and off the lime–lit stage. A version of what he had done with the two time periods of *The Godfather Part II*.

But the new script found old adversaries redrawing battle lines. Evans hated it – it was so immersed in historical detail it could almost be a documentary. He wanted guns and molls and jazz hands, something slick, and Gere's part had been reduced to a bystander. Where were Rosencrantz and Guildenstern?

Evans demanded a rewrite. Coppola demanded another $250,000.

There's another twist. The Doumanis were growing testy at all the wanton spending. Preproduction was already underway in New York, with Sylbert applying the same fine-boned nuance he had brought to *Rosemary's Baby* and *Chinatown* to the lavish club interiors and cluttered dressing rooms. The tall, professorial New Englander was a real intellectual, who spoke of integrating set design with costumes and cinematography. Everything should work toward a holistic realism. Which was currently costing $140,000 a week. And the Doumanis were running dry.

So Evans went fishing for more investors – enough to keep preproduction going, enough to build their fabulous club. Somewhere on the outer limits of his network, he found Elaine Jacobs, whose background among Miami coke dealers didn't bear scrutiny, unless you were a narc. She introduced him to former vaudeville producer Roy Radin. Here things get labyrinthine, with Puerto Rican holding companies, the promise of a slush fund of $35 million, and favourable cuts for Jacobs and Radin. Suffice to say, things quickly went sour, with Radin refusing to pay a percentage to Jacobs.

According to the police report, around the end of April 1983, Jacobs and Radin agree to meet to talk things through. At 9.30 p.m., Radin climbs into his limousine. As per his instructions, Radin's bodyguard tailed him, armed with a pistol. But the last he ever saw of his boss was the scarlet taillights disappearing round a bend. A month later, Radin's decomposed body was found in a canyon north of Los Angeles. He had been shot in the head like Sollozzo.

Now a suspect in a murder investigation (he would be cleared after a four-hour police interview), and terrified he might be targeted next, Evans's enthusiasm for directing *The Cotton Club* began to waver.

Gere had already been pressing for Coppola to direct, and when they reconvened in Napa to discuss the amended script (there is estimated to be in the range of thirty different drafts of *The Cotton Club*) Evans put it to his old adversary. Want to direct? Coppola decided it was an offer he could easily refuse. And keep refusing. Yet Evans wore him down, or something in the glamorous milieu woke him up.

But he had his demands: $2.5 million, twenty percent of the gross, and absolute authority.

Should Coppola have sought the root of his love affair with *The Cotton Club* (or at least its potential), he might have recalled those boyhood afternoons backstage with the Rockettes. And maybe recognise the fact that Bob Fosse beating him to Best Director with *Cabaret*, indeed a mix of drama and musical based around a nightclub, still needled. He wanted to put on a show.

In his suite at the Sherry-Netherland, drinking coffee and pacing the room, he tried to find a way into the story. He joined forces with Pulitzer Prize-winning novelist William Kennedy (*Ironweed*), who was staggered at the brevity of words required in a script. What you wrote one day, he joked, would be cut in half the next. They studied classic gangster flicks and read up on the jazz age, with Duke Ellington filling the air.

Between them, they fashioned the story of dashing, egalitarian trumpeter Dixie Dwyer (Gere) who falls for Vera (Diane Lane), who tended to be found on the arm of firebrand mobster Dutch Schultz (James Remar). Alternatively, we have Hines as tap dancing prodigy Sandman Williams, working his way up the ladder, but falling for elusive chorus girl Lila Rose Oliver (Lonette McKee). Both had brothers. Encircling the drama is Bob Hoskins's seasoned Irish gangster Owney Madden, who ran the Cotton Club, granting favours from his ritzy office.

Coppola then fired most of Evans's crew, requiring heavy payoffs, though wisely retained Sylbert. The whole thing was like history repeating. As he had on *Finian's Rainbow* aeons before, he dispensed with the choreographer, likening Lovell's routines to "an Ice Capade salute to Duke Ellington." *Rumble Fish*'s Michael Smuin was parachuted in to help devise and shoot forty-eight separate dance numbers, which had to be edited, staccato-like into the story.

He also fired a group of secretaries after they were short-tempered with Sofia and her friends, who were trying to help around the place. "I simply can't abide that nine-to-five attitude," he smarted. Don't cross the family.

Having rolled on to August 28, 1983, things got off to a bad start when Gere didn't show for the entire week. They were shooting at Prospect Hall in Brooklyn, with over 700 cast, extras, and crew waiting for the leading man. It turned out Gere was still smarting over the still evolving script and was perturbed by Coppola's willingness to improvise lines. He wanted everything on paper. There were whispers of replacing him with Matt Dillon, but Gere and the director would learn to tolerate one another.

The shoot took on a familiar cadence, with Coppola driving for perfection, accumulating footage, and ever more complex set-ups. With no one sure of what was going on his head.

Sylbert remembered Coppola's mood swings. One day he would be in despair over money or art, the next he talked about buying the old movie theatre he frequented as a child or having an office at the top of the Chrysler Building. He was torn in two. Every cell of his being wanted artistic integrity, to reclaim the period vitality of *The Godfather*, but he knew he had to deliver a commercial hit.

"I don't want to make a gangster picture and I don't want to make a musical," he lamented. "I want to make something nobody's ever seen before."

"Francis just flails around, hoping he'll pull it out of the air," said Sylbert. "He desperately wants to be Kurosawa, Fellini, Bergman."

Meanwhile, he was contending with the Doumanis's economy drives. Sylbert reckoned ten of the sets he had designed ended up not being used. But the interior of the club was something to behold, with the designer's pursuit of authenticity found in every drink stirrer, menu, or ashtray.

It was all so inordinately slow. Lane would spend hours getting into vintage costumes once worn by Jean Harlow, having her licks of kohl applied and eyelashes curled, the look hovering between romantic innocent and femme fatale. Then an AD would arrive. "Miss Lane, it's okay to go. We're not going to use you today."

Sofia would press her mother to take her over to the costume department after school, so she could see the showgirl's beaded dresses and bias-cut lingerie. The brilliant costume designer, Milena Canonero, would one day design for Sofia on the final part of *The Godfather* trilogy.

On set, family ties granted no favours. Nicolas Cage, cast as Dixie's trigger-happy younger brother Vincent "Mad Dog" Dwyer (whose rash ambition marks him for a flamboyant death), smashed up his trailer in frustration. He had been slated for three weeks and was there for sixth months.

Evans would occasionally put up a fight. Try to horse trade like the old days. Why, for instance, did Coppola want to cast Fred Gwynne as Madden's major domo Frenchy Demange? The towering, long-jawed Gwynne boasted an illustrious career, but was known to most as television's jovial Frankensteinalike Herman Munster. Which appalled Evans. But when Coppola stood firm, there was nothing he could do.

Coppola knew better. He had seen the subtle giant in a stage production of *Cat on a Hot Tin Roof*, and the wry Gwynne and Hoskins share the best scene in the film. Away from all the razzamatazz and rat-a-tat-tat, the two old friends reunite after Frenchy's brief kidnapping. In a beautifully improvised moment, guided by Gwynne, an irate Frenchy petulantly smashes his boss's pocket watch on the table, only to retrieve a brand new platinum model to replace it. Hoskins's goofy, emotional openness at being fooled offers a tender study in enduring friendship. Coppola knew how to portray gangsters as human beings.

Behind the scenes, we can count Joey Cusumano as the most absurd development yet. He was billed as a "friend" of Anthony Spilotro, according to FBI reports the head of the mob in Las Vegas (you picture the suspenders and silk underwear sported by Robert De Niro's Ace Rothstein in Martin Scorsese's *Casino*). Cusumano had one conviction for labour racketeering, and the diligent FBI were determined to unearth more through a decade of wiretapping, bugging, and trailing him.

Remember, this has nothing to do with the plot of the film. Cusumano was the latest heavy hired by the Doumanis to try and intimidate Coppola into finishing as frugally as possible on the scheduled date of December 23, 1983. He would stand quietly observing filming, maybe pose the odd question to crew (you picture the amiably hulking presence of Lenny Montana's Luca Brasi from *The Godfather*). Slowly but surely, he became enthralled, especially with Coppola. They were like brothers: Cusumano would offer his opinion, watch rushes in the Silverfish, dine on the director's spaghetti, while sending back missives to Vegas assuring his bosses great things were being accomplished. One morning the putative hood arrived on set to find a seat labelled "Joey" pulled up next to Coppola.

With the spending unabated, Cusumano was summoned back to Vegas and reminded of his duties. Though it must have pained him (this was business not personal), he reverted to character with Coppola.

"You see this Silverfish? If we go past the twenty-third, this is going to be in the ocean with the rest of the fish."

After all his yearning, his effort, his fraying nerves, and dreams of a prodigal's return, it was Evans who became the (figurative) fall guy. Unable to tame the director, with the Doumani well dry, he would have to relinquish any say in order for Orion to provide $15 million to complete the film. As if delivering the final insult, with Corman-like haste Coppola then scrambled to finish. No more script revisions, no more improv, no more ostentation. There was a three-day stretch where he got through over forty set-ups. Principal photography was finally completed at 6 a.m. on Christmas Eve.

The Cotton Club was not yet simply a film. For now the lawsuits began. Evans sued the Doumanis. Among his volley of grievances, he listed the sullying of his professional reputation. Sayah sued Evans, the Doumanis, Orion, and *The Cotton Club* production company, claiming the budget overruns were a breach of contract. Restaurateur John Rockwell sued for a finder's fee having introduced Evans to the Doumanis. Actress Susan Mechsner claimed damages for mental distress upon discovering she had been cut out of all but one scene. Evans had, allegedly, promised her a starring role. Sylvio Tabet, a B-movie producer hired and fired as the Doumanis' first ineffectual watchdog, sued for being slighted. He wanted $6 million and a co-producer credit.

Striking an amusing tone of cinematic facetiousness, U.S. district court judge Irving Hill, the man juggling these cases, likened the conflicting statements to Akira Kurosawa's *Rashomon*. Surely, Coppola smiled at that.

He may also have stifled a smug laugh at the knowledge that he – merely a director for hire – was not in the line of fire. Though he would have to appear as a witness.

The star turn was reserved for Evans, who broke down sobbing in the witness box. The producer would win a reprieve, and kissed and made up with the Doumanis, but only got a say on marketing and distribution. The final cut was out of his reach. Not that this stopped him from paying to attend a San Diego preview, which garnered a positive response. Not so from Evans. In his opinion, here was the same calamity that had befallen the initial version of *The Godfather* – the best stuff was on the cutting room floor. The razzle-dazzle numbers were herky-jerky, and so much of the period texture, racial commentary, and unpredictable relationships had disappeared.

The subtext being to remind everyone that he was the man who had saved *The Godfather* from extinction. A thirty-one-page letter filled with detailed suggestions and words of reconciliation was delivered to Coppola who set about ignoring everyone.

Evans may have had a point.

There is a decent movie in *The Cotton Club*, somewhere.

Through a warm partnership with British cinematographer Stephen Goldblatt (*The Hunger*), Coppola offers a dazzling recreation of the era. In the longer Director's Cut, which took a bow at the New York Film Festival in 2019, the musical numbers stretch into a jazzy panache to which even Fosse would have doffed his hat. Hines and his brother Maurice (a fictional spin on the legendary Nicholas Brothers) work miracles of simpatico movement.

The secondary characters are terrific, not only the phlegmatic Abbott and Costello routines of Gwynne and Hoskins, Lane's edgy portrayal of a girl looking to survive, Maurice Hines as the neglected Williams brother, even Cage's cartoonish hoodlum is a welcome reminder of genre traditions. There is a hint of spoof to the gangsters. Drawn from his extensive research, this was an era of organised crime where the German, Irish, and Jewish hoodlums held sway, small-time guys who would cede power to the Mafiosi – somewhere in the background you like to think a young Vito Corleone is quietly gaining influence.

However, with all those script revisions and star demands, *The Cotton Club* struggles to find a use for an inert leading man. Gere may have played all his trumpet solos, but he gives Dixie so little passion the film almost tries to avoid him. At one point, he is packed off to Hollywood to become a movie star.

The New Yorker's Pauline Kael, who had lavished such praise on *The Godfather* films, scorned the director for empty stylistics. "[Coppola] seems to have skimmed the top off every twenties-thirties picture he has seen, added seltzer, stirred it up with a swizzle-stick, and called it a movie." Yet *The Washington Post* saw "theme, mood, symmetries of structure, and jazzy style."

At an estimated final budget of $47 million, it was destined never to recoup its costs. For Evans it was a personal fiasco. Murder trials and turkeys left him untouchable, and even Paramount cut their ties.

It was a bittersweet time for Coppola. How had his latest film become another exhausting exercise in hubris and hope? Should he have known better than to get back into bed with Evans? Moreover, Zoetrope Studios was finally bought by the creditor Jack Singer for a low-end bid of $12.3 million, who rechristened the lot Singer Studios and auctioned off Zoetrope's trove of props, costumes, and high-end technical equipment.

If that was wounding, Coppola could find some relief in a final agreement that saved his homes, his office, his Silverfish, and the right to the name Zoetrope. Somehow the dream lived on.

Coppola ended up directing *Peggy Sue Got Married* through a fit of pique. But it was not the volatile director having the tantrum. The fury belonged to actress Debra Winger – her fuse ran notoriously short – around whose rising stardom the romantic comedy was being packaged. So this was another troubled production. Or at least, jinxed. Jonathan Demme was all set to direct. But Winger, wielding the clout afforded by the success of *An Officer and a Gentleman* (with Richard Gere), demanded Penny Marshall instead. So Demme was out (creative differences!), and Marshall was in. Except that Marshall tangled with screenwriters Jerry Leichtling and Arlene Sarner and was swiftly shown the door. This stirred Winger's outburst, and she made it abundantly clear she would walk unless an appropriate director was found.

Asked who she meant by appropriate, Winger replied, "Francis Ford Coppola."

It so happened that Winger's ire was being directed toward Rastar, the production company backing *Peggy Sue Got Married*, and owned by Ray Stark. The same Ray Stark that gave Coppola his first screenwriting contract at Seven Arts twenty years earlier. Aware of Coppola's financial tribulations (who wasn't?), Stark took Winger at her word. Thus the unlikely assignment of a time-travelling romance fell to the director of *Apocalypse Now*.

Coppola had hardly been idle. With *The Cotton Club* not yet dry, he completed a television adaptation of Washington Irving's *Rip Van Winkle* for HBO's *Faerie Tale Theatre* series, with Harry Dean Stanton and sister Talia Shire. Shot in five days, it was a goofy experiment in artifice, mixing contemporary video opticals and traditional theatrical illusion. For the mountain over the Hudson River Valley he had a group of actors huddle under a blanket shivering to evoke the cold.

With George Lucas, he produced Paul Schrader's *Mishima: A Life in Four Chapters*, a brilliantly controlled and commercially out-there biopic of the Japanese writer Yukio Mishima. And he was presently endeavouring to adapt *Cotton Club* co-writer William Kennedy's novel *Legs*, the life story of bootlegger Jack "Legs" Diamond, who was remarkably resilient to assassination.

Pure pragmatism drew him to *Peggy Sue Got Married*. With interest payments due on his properties, the $18-million project was both ready to go and openly desirous of his services. He had no idea his old friend Steven Spielberg was planning a rival time travel comedy called *Back to the Future*. Or how that might help or hinder his film. These were uncharted waters for Coppola – the headlong rush of studio populism in the 1980s. He simply took a breath and jumped in.

But not before an ironic (though hardly *Cotton Club* fiendish) twist. Winger, the catalyst for so much disruption in the film's genesis, was also forced to drop out, having been hospitalised with a back injury from a bike accident.

Despite the Hollywood packaging, Coppola's most successful film since *The Godfather Part II* – with $41 million, it was a hit, a bona fide hit! – achieved more than advertised. If nothing else, here was a simple demonstration that Coppola was as fine a Hollywood craftsman as anyone. But once he got his hands on the superficial script – "like a routine television show" – he began to ponder themes of nostalgia and agency, the ties that bind us to marriage and family, and the yearning for paths not taken. He thought of the meta-dynamics of Thornton Wilder's stage play *Our Town*: "… that kind of small-town charm and emotion."

Breezy and light-hearted, and occasionally light-headed, this is still a Coppola film.

Take his knack for casting. Kathleen Turner was an inspired replacement for Winger as Peggy, the depressed housewife who passes out at her high school reunion only to awaken back in high school in 1960 (it's an inverted *Rip Van Winkle*). With all of her adult memories still intact, she is remembering events as they happen. The sublime idea is to have the adult Turner play her seventeen-year-old self. According to Coppola's poetic licence, it is only the audience who notice the difference. Will Peggy make the same mistakes again? Including falling for Charlie Bodell (Nicolas Cage), who she knows will prove to be an unfaithful husband and poor appliance salesman.

Born in Springfield, Missouri – of "missionary stock"– and brought up in London, where she was saved by theatre, Turner was blessed with comic timing, terrific legs, and a voice like oozing honey. Such a combination allowed her to range from the sexually charged (she made for a fabulous femme fatale in Lawrence Kasdan's *Body Heat*) to the adorably klutzy (throwing herself with gusto down jungle-strewn hillsides in spirited action-adventure *Romancing the Stone*). A string of recent hits had made her, in current Hollywood parlance, "box office". Winger's bike accident was looking like a blessing. Coppola clinched the deal by taking Turner for a drive along the boulevards of Los Angeles while serenading her with Buddy Holly songs. "Francis is a damn good singer," she was happy to report.

Every dilemma had an upside. When Turner was rushed into making *The Jewel of the Nile*, a flabby sequel to *Romancing the Stone*, Coppola used the year-long delay to begin again on his cherished biopic of automobile pioneer Preston Tucker, and expand his range of vintage wines, including the Niebaum-Coppola Rubicon, a plummy red that became his bestseller. He even dabbled in science fiction, reuniting with Lucas to direct *Captain EO*.

Far removed from those youthful Zoetrope ideals, Lucas had been asked by Disney to apply his wizardry to a theme park attraction. His answer was the fifteen-minute space epic *Captain EO*, in which (then superstar) Michael Jackson and his crew of aliens and robots defeat the She-Devil Supreme (Anjelica Huston) using the power of song and laser beams. The Supreme's lightly Giger-esque planet is transformed into a candy-coloured Eden. This is no more than a narrative coat hanger for a giant-screen presentation, "3-U" effects (basically, 3D), and quintaphonic sound. With memories of New York toy stores, the science geek in Coppola was back among the gadgets and gizmos of screen technology, even convincing Vittorio Storaro to shoot such trippy marvels as Fuzzball, a flying monkey with butterfly wings and fur the colour of Kool-Aid. The Italian maestro may have wondered how far upriver they had got.

With this bright bagatelle, Coppola briefly joined the blockbusting ranks of Lucas and Spielberg. And gained the ironic satisfaction that at a cost of $20 million per minute, *Captain EO* was the most expensive film ever made. *Time* magazine declared it a "triumph of the artificial."

So he was in fine mood when he began *Peggy Sue Got Married* on August 19, 1985. It was shot on the unblemished streets of Santa Rosa and Petaluma in Northern California, where Hitchcock had hidden murders in *Shadow of a Doubt*, and close enough to drive home to Napa Valley each night. Did the comforts of home add to the air of contentment? Was this meta-comedy the elusive panacea to the bite of *Apocalypse Now*?

So there was a skein of cynicism to Coppola's motives. He asked for the film not to be credited as a "Francis Coppola film." In interview, he vaguely disowned it. "It's not a brilliant Francis Coppola film," he told reporters. This wasn't one from the heart. He was having an out-of-body experience. But critics greeted this sweet, disengaged vintage of Coppola with a round of applause. Yes, it was all vaguely familiar to that other time-travelling nostalgia trip, and sentimental too, but you can detect the pull of the artist.

We see it in the veil of satire as Reaganite-era Peggy ponders a more diverse 1950s spectrum, including her pipe-chomping Eisenhower pop (Don Murray), and quietly liberal mother (Barbara Harris, who went all the way back to *You're a Big Boy Now*). "I forgot you were ever this young," says Peggy poignantly upon greeting her pretty mother.

This is 1960, John F. Kennedy's New Frontier rhetoric rings out, and Coppola is waking up to his own potential. We catch his scent of nonconformism in Kevin J. O'Connor's would-be beatnik writer, the romantic alternative to that dumb lug Charlie. But even Charlie reveals forgotten depths, explaining the magic of (Coppola favourite) Shostakovich to a record store customer.

With softer notes, *Peggy Sue Got Married* plays a similar tune to *American Graffiti*. Music is vital to its sensibility. Doomed Buddy Holly is a spirit guide. There are no shadows of Vietnam quite yet, but there are edges to the shoo-bop mood. Peggy must learn her life anew.

Turner would deservingly be Oscar nominated for Best Actress for her performance. She walks an ingenious line: Peggy has to have the sweater sets of a teenager, but the shape and spirit of a disillusioned adult. Half the time her classmates (with Joan Allen, Catherine Hicks, Jim Carrey, and Barry Miller's science geek doing a fine job of re-tuning themselves to a juvenile station) think she's lost her mind. This was the rarest of things in a Coppola film – his first true female lead since Shirley Knight in *The Rain People*. Turner got along far better with the director. "He's an intensely caring man," she said, touched by the attention he lavished on her performance.

Turner was no pushover. When Coppola asked if she would be bothered if he directed from his Silverfish, she replied pointedly, "No, I'll go act in mine." He agreed to stay on set.

The recreation of the past – that Coppola speciality – has the hazy quality of a dream (then Peggy could be dreaming). If more white-picket and sun-dappled, Coppola was pursuing the heightened reality of *One from the Heart* – his romantic register. He's hinting at *The Wizard of Oz*, where Dorothy crashes into a land of conformity. Nostalgia can be a trap. Peggy's past has the patina of a movie set.

Coppola got on well with cinematographer Jordan Cronenweth (who had lit the antiquated future of *Blade Runner*). Saturate the colours, keep it light, were his only instructions. Cronenweth was surprised to find he was a "hands-off director".

The truth was that cinematographers generally enjoyed his company, with the notable exception of Gordon Willis.

We see Sofia again, reprising her template role as the chatterbox younger sister from *Rumble Fish*, and re-establishing a bond that Peggy has let slide. It's a small, sweet performance – possibly Sofia's best work as an actress (depending on where you stand on *The Godfather Part III*).

The only truly odd note the film strikes is in his nephew's performance. Cage took winning over. The idea of casting Charlie with a twenty-two-year-old Cage worked in the opposite direction to Peggy. He would give off immature vibrations as the no-good adult version and have exactly the right frequency of youthful impetuosity in the past. Still wary of accusations of nepotism, and concerned about repeating the interminable grind of *The Cotton Club*, Cage opted for the absurd.

"Look," he told his uncle, "I'll do it if you let me go really far out with the character."

In his head adding to the dreamlike texture, he affected a nasally, cartoon voice, and had make-up fashion him an overbite. Coppola left him to it, and he appears to be in a film all his own.

"Jerry Lewis on acid," Cage laughed.

The studio tried to fire him, but Coppola stood firm. "Young Nicky's doing this," he insisted. Critics were aghast. "What is it with his malted-milk falsetto?" asked *The Washington Post*. Time has rendered his antics more charming: this tiny portion of Coppola-style provocation amid the polished furniture.

After eight weeks, Coppola was done. And in what was perhaps an unintended irony, having brought the film in on time and on budget, the studio took out an ad to congratulate him.

When Robert Zemeckis's more mind-boggling, action-orientated *Back to the Future* became 1985's must-see summer movie, a shiver passed through Rastar and distributor Tri-Star. Would they come off second best? Old-hat? Coppola remembered how *Apocalypse Now* managed to be beaten to the screen by *The Deer Hunter* when no one made Vietnam films. He avoided seeing *Back to the Future*, unwilling to be dragged into orbiting dramas. He made a simple suggestion – hit the pause button. Let's delay by six months. This would allow him to reshoot a colourless ending that had fallen victim to a tired production.

When comparisons were inevitably made, it turned out that Coppola was far less interested in the mechanics of time travel, or ructions in the space-time continuum. He almost sends up his own premise with the kooky rituals that finally send Peggy back to the future (the weakest strand). In the revised ending, there comes a more personal note – husband and wife are reunited. For all their faults, the family unit prevails.

CHAPTER 8

FATHERS AND SONS

*Gardens of Stone (1987), Tucker: The Man and His Dream (1988),
New York Stories (1989)*

Of course, he has made two Vietnam films. One was a masterpiece soaked in the gasoline of its own incendiary making. The other was a softly spoken, elegiac ode to the dead soaked in the tears of real-life tragedy. Did it always have to be this way for Francis Ford Coppola? Film and life knotted together. That question would never be more savagely asked than during the making of *Gardens of Stone*.

Victor Kaufman, the head of Tri-Star, had offered him the script over lunch. The studio man was impressed with how things were coming along on *Peggy Sue Got Married*, and thought Coppola might be interested in an adaptation of former *Newsweek* reporter Nicholas Proffitt's novel about the Old Guard. This was the division of the U.S. Army responsible for burying the dead in Arlington National Cemetery in Washington D.C.

Proffitt had written a sympathetic but simmering account of the officers and soldiers who counted the cost of Vietnam in the late 1960s. They called them "drops" – all the body bags and burials. The title referred to the headstones. Ron Bass had delivered a decent if methodical script.

Framed by the ornate formality of a military funeral – shot with fetishistic precision – it is a countervailing story to not only *Apocalypse Now*, but the flash flood of Vietnam exposés that followed. *Coming Home*,

164

Platoon, Hamburger Hill, Full Metal Jacket. There is a pristine simplicity, as the story loops back to throw light on the surrogate father-son relationship between veteran Sergeant Clell Hazard (James Caan) and recruit – another "toy soldier" – Jackie Willow (D.B. Sweeney), frustrated at his detail. Willow wants to be in Vietnam fighting for his country. The weary Clell, who served in Korea and two terms in South Asia, sees only senseless waste in the American excursion.

The focus is personal not political. Moral debate remains on the periphery with Anjelica Huston's anti-war *Washington Post* reporter and love interest for Caan.

Coppola was intrigued for a number of reasons.

The setting recalled his time at military school: all the rituals and marching. He remembered a "certain appeal".

He was drawn to the idea of showing the army as a specialised family. To depict soldiers, he said, in "emotional" terms. Not as gung-ho clichés but as "complex individuals". These were men capable of love.

There was a quiet satisfaction in the fact the production had the U.S. Army's full approval. He had permission to shoot in Fort Myer, Arlington Cemetery, and Fort Belvoir. They were even assigned technical advisors. In return the army got script approval – unthinkable for the firebrand sinking in the Philippines. But this was a film about honour codes, ceremony, and a very particular facet of army life. The camera dwells on the insignia, caps, medals, boots, starched shirts and folded flags: the emblems of rank and order. So he wanted their eye. Above all they wanted to tone down the foul language.

It was a small film, but the numbers were impressive: 450 soldiers for a precision march, 600 further soldiers as extras. "Enough men and material to invade a small country," he joked.

Coppola danced around associations between his 'Nam stories, but *Gardens of Stone* is almost an inversion of *Apocalypse Now*. They become a commentary on one another. This was the view from the graveside: a tale of disciplined, honourable men dealing with the war from within the system. Yet similar doubts emerge. "No one hates this war more than those who have to fight it," says Willow.

Given this was a story of family ties, ritual, honour, tradition, and loyalty it was as much a companion to *The Godfather*.

And there was the simplest reason of all. He was taking the check. This was his fifth film in five years. "I've just decided to pay everything off," he said. No more high-stakes gambling, stability was what counted.

Was he a hired gun?

"Very definitely," he said, without hesitation.

This entire book maps out the synchronicity between Coppola and his subjects. How the making of *Apocalypse Now* was a refraction of the war itself; and *The Conversation* pierced the veil of his creative manias.

Give enough of yourself to it, said Coppola, and "a film can *create* your future."

With *Gardens of Stone* that connection became bleakly absurd. A tragedy made in the midst of tragedy. Even years later, Coppola's words were slow and unsteady, as if he can't quite bring himself to say them. "I was going to a funeral on the set every day. Then I had to go to a funeral *off* the set — and in my life."

It was her husband on the other end of the line, but she had never heard his voice like this: strangulated, as if he wasn't breathing. Eleanor Coppola gripped the extension as Coppola spoke the words.

"Ellie, we've lost our beloved son. Gio is dead."

Twenty-two-year-old Gian-Carlo Coppola — always "Gio" — had been in a speedboat on the South River, near Annapolis, with his friend Griffin O'Neal, son of Ryan O'Neal, who had a small role in the film. Gio was supervising all of the electronic elements. His father was up to his usual tricks, videotaping rehearsals for what he called his "Off Broadway" version. The Silverfish was parked at the side of the set like Harry Caul's surveillance van.

It was May 26, 1986, and Gio's girlfriend Jacqui de la Fontaine watched from the shore. At around 5.15 p.m., they were picking up speed when O'Neal steered between two vessels, without seeing the towline between them. O'Neal managed to duck, but the rope struck Gio, knocking him off his feet, and he crashed onto the deck. He was pronounced dead on arrival at Anne Arundel County Hospital due to massive head injuries.

O'Neal would eventually plead guilty to "negligent operation of a boat". Despite rumours of firings and recrimination, it was the actor who asked to be released from the film. Coppola wasn't about to apportion blame. This was a terrible accident – why ruin another life? Revenge is for the movies.

The inconsolable Jacqui revealed she was two-months pregnant. "He left us a gift," said Eleanor.

When he was sixteen, Gio wrote his father a letter. In his scattershot handwriting, he implored Coppola to take him out of high school – he found it hard to concentrate and was struggling (he was later diagnosed as dyslexic). He wanted to work at his father's side, to learn everything he could about filmmaking, and one day follow in his footsteps. He would become apprentice to the family trade.

Eleanor recalled how as teenagers Gio and his brother, Roman, used the old housekeeper's apartment next to the laundry in Napa as the headquarters of their new film company. They hung a sign on the door, "Wild Deuce Productions", and busied themselves with writing a script. There were beer cans and coke bottles everywhere.

"I took him out of school," said Coppola, "and from that point on he was my constant companion."

Films became Gio's education, and his life. He was associate producer on *The Outsiders* and *Rumble Fish*, he directed montage footage for *The Cotton Club*, and second unit on *Captain EO*. Following *Gardens of Stone*, he planned to intern on Steven Spielberg's anthology of adventures *Amazing Stories*, and then film second unit on the Penny Marshall comedy *Jumpin' Jack Flash*. The path was set. He was a gentleman, a sweet kid – casts and crews liked him, and liked seeing the bond with his father.

"I think there is something unique about the relationship of a father and his first child," said Eleanor. Even as a boy, on set, where his younger brother and sister would wriggle impatiently, Gio exuded a strange calm (he had his mother's temperament). They called him an "old soul", and his presence often soothed his fraught director.

Father and son were inseparable, observed the mother, "and this was the most profound blow imaginable."

"He was my best friend and collaborator," said Coppola. "He was perfect, like Pinocchio."

How did he carry on? There were those in the cast and crew that were concerned. Caan wanted Coppola to confront his grief. "Get him to a hospital," he told the studio. The director collapsed briefly on set, and they feared a heart attack. But it was nothing more than exhaustion. He took four days to find his feet again, and then returned. He knew no other way. Huston called those weeks an agony – to be making a film about grief, while grief fell across each day like ash. They would see Coppola crying, but he couldn't face home.

"I just didn't want to go somewhere where all I'd do is think of him, over and over, day and night. I dreaded the nights, and specifically the mornings most of all, because what had happened hit me anew…"

Eleanor knew that the demands of the production would be familiar for her husband, and prevent the agonising reality from invading every moment. Film was offering him relief. His grief was being channelled through a story about grief, and honouring the dead. "I wanted to use the rituals of the Old Guard to accompany their personal lives and the central theme, which seemed to be how we are entrusted to protect our children; we're sworn to protect our children; we want to protect our children, but… can't."

Eleanor and Sofia would join Roman in the Silverfish, where he had taken over from Gio.

The resulting film is like a photographic negative of Coppola's anguish: steady, subdued, and emotionally distant. Caan is good as the good man, and the salty camaraderie among career soldiers has an authentic ring, but it is going through the motions. Numbed is the word. Coppola is withholding himself. For the first time in his career, he was unwilling to pour his heart into celluloid.

"It is impossible to watch *Gardens of Stone* without remembering the tragedy that intervened in Coppola's own life," said the *Chicago Tribune*. "The film is so distant perhaps because it is so close."

Its subsequent whimper at the box office (making just over $5 million) would hardly have registered with Coppola.

Eleanor's memories of that time come to her like cuts in a montage. Staring at her face in the mirror, unrecognisable. Sinking to the sidewalk in front of the Hyatt hotel, sobbing hysterically, her husband's cousins trying to support her. The memorial service held in Arlington Chapel, where the afternoon sunlight was beautiful enough for a wedding. The bouquet of white roses sent by Bobby De Niro. Jacqui coming to live with them in Napa, and Gia Coppola, Gio's daughter, being born on New Year's Day 1987.

Following Gio's death, Roman hit the road in a VW van and drove across America on his own, without a film to make. Eleanor knew it was an "exorcism". A year later, he formed a band and played dates, out on the road again, avoiding home.

Sofia saw a therapist. She didn't want to carry it around with her. A vital link in the family chain was missing.

Coppola was a different man, a different filmmaker. Did the death of Gio take the fire from his art, as some contend? Or is that too easy? He was battle weary and chaos averse. But the debts still needed paying. And the itch remained.

There was a note he had found in the computer Gio had installed in the Silverfish when he was only sixteen – he could fix anything that boy. He pinned it to the wall.

"Art Never Sleeps".

Even as he put the final touches to *Gardens of Stone*, Coppola was shooting his next, a more personal story, one that went back to his childhood, about an inventor who dreamed too big. He was shooting closer to home than ever: Napa, Sonoma, and Petaluma.

On the horizon stood *Megalopolis*, which he promised he would make someday.

The work would sustain him.

In 1948, Coppola gazed upon the man and his dream.

Picture the scene: a father taking his eight-year-old son to an exhibition put on by ebullient, would-be motor-magnate Preston Tucker to promote his slinky new automobile. The Tucker Torpedo, boasts the publicity material, is "The Car of Tomorrow – Today!" Coppola's eyes virtually pop out on cartoon stalks. Able to cruise comfortably at 100 mph, it featured disc brakes, a central "Cyclops" headlight, seatbelts, and innumerable innovations that would reshape an industry – eventually. But it was the look that counted. The Tucker had the aerodynamic curves of a rocket ship from *Flash Gordon*, its streamlined shell tapering to a fin. Here was the suavity and style of a movie star.

Father and son share an obsession with cars. It brings them close. Carmine is so smitten with this vision in Waltz Blue, green, black, or maroon, and the fast talk of its creator, there and then he signs up to purchase one of the first off the production line, and invests $5,000 of the family's hard-won money into the new company. Carmine believed in America.

For months, Coppola pesters his father: "When's the Tucker gonna come?"

It would never come, and the money was lost. Tucker's dreams proved beyond him. But with his *Godfather*-riches, Coppola purchased two of the forty-four remaining Tuckers (only fifty-one were ever made), and the family got their car.

Born in 1903, in Capac, Michigan, Preston Thomas Tucker grew up obsessed with cars after a Buick ran over his foot when he was six. He was close enough to fall in love. Tucker was a man of gumption, selling and inventing cars of all sizes. Tall, good-looking, a real natty dresser, he exuded self-confidence. He was also a family man, with five adoring children. He described himself as an "imagineer" (a designation borrowed by theme park designers), and set about taking on the hegemony of Detroit's big three – Ford, Chrysler, and General Motors – with his swish Tucker Torpedo.

Coppola will revel in the scenes of the sedan's extravagant launch with marching band and long-legged "Tuckerettes" framing the gleaming car.

But the establishment didn't take to Tucker's fancy ways, or the threat he posed. There were charges of mail fraud and improper stock offerings (to which Carmine fell foul), along with a smear campaign in the press. He fought to clear his name, and was finally acquitted, by which time he was bankrupt, and the image of pearly Tuckers gliding the American highways was only ever a dream.

Tucker is the funhouse reflection of Coppola. The charlatan with his heart in the right place, a loveable American conman, and a shameless showboat: these are the director's descriptions. The entrepreneur certainly lived it up. Staying in the best hotel suites, riding in private planes, throwing the biggest parties, hiring the best people, and rarely counting the cost.

Upon his untimely death (at fifty-three, from cancer), *Collier's* magazine famously eulogised the inventor as "a bewildering combination of P.T.

Barnum, Henry Ford, Jimmy Walker, and Baron Munchausen, with a talent for telling stories and a genius for spending money."

Naturally, Coppola coveted the idea of telling his story.

There was a stage play written while at Hofstra. At UCLA, Coppola contemplated something almost neo-noir. Dark side of the American Dream stuff like *Citizen Kane*, with Tucker swallowed up by the corporations. Fellow student Carroll Ballard revealed that his father had sold Tuckers. Briefly. In 1976, before setting sail to *Apocalypse Now*, he bought the rights to the industrialist's life story from the family (just the one codicil: could he refrain from mentioning the affairs?). Returning from the jungle a little wired, he proposed a "Kabuki-style" musical based on Tucker's life, combined with a celebration of innovation.

"It was a dark kind of piece," he admitted, "a sort of Brechtian musical in which Tucker would be the main story, but it would also involve Edison, Ford, Firestone and Carnegie." He was thinking big: Jack Nicholson as Tucker, music by Leonard Bernstein, choreography by Gene Kelly, and lyrics by the Broadway duo Betty Comden and Adolph Green, who wrote *Singin' in the Rain*.

Invited out to Napa, Bernstein gave it to him straight: "This isn't *Apocalypse Now* where we just go improvising around."

He needed a plan.

Soon after, Coppola approached Frank Capra, Hollywood's champion of the little man, with the offer to produce. Imagine *Mr. Smith Goes to Detroit*! Only Capra didn't get it. Tucker didn't realise his dream, he pointed out. Coppola argued differently. True he was beaten by the system, but he got to show the world his car. He had seen it as a boy, gleaming like a flying saucer. That was something.

Both the Bernstein and Capra models were lost to the collapse of Zoetrope Studios in 1981. "Everything fell in a black hole," he said. Even as his career steadied, the project was still treated warily by studios, fearing another of those eccentric and expensive Coppola dreams. "They thought my pet projects were too grandiose," he sighed. He gradually let it lie.

Then Gio reignited the flame. His eldest son made for a third generation of car buffs. As a kid, he would sneak into his father's editing room and re-cut the chase sequence from Lucas's *THX-1138*. In 1985, the year before his death, he persuaded his father to enter one of the Tuckers into the Calistoga Independence Day antique car parade. With the assistance of Roman and Sofia, Gio rolled it out of the garage, washed and polished it, and then drove it down Calistoga main street to rapturous applause, with Coppola waving from the passenger seat.

In 1986, having reunited for the pinballing *Captain EO*, George Lucas suggested he was the one to help get the Tucker movie out of storage and onto the road again. He would serve as producer just as Coppola had backed *American Graffiti*, which had boasted its share of cars and Americana.

"He needs someone to hold him back," smiled Lucas. "With *The Godfather* it was Mario Puzo; with *Tucker* it was me."

In its final guise, *Tucker: The Man and His Dream* is simply a Francis Ford Coppola film – an American parable set in a lavish past. It is whimsical, upbeat, and polished like *Peggy Sue Got Married*. Lucas had leant on him "to candy-apple it up a bit," he said. Yet it yields ironies about the surrendering of the American Dream to corporate machinations: the vectors that may have given us a film noir. And contemplates the foolishness of dreamers, and the price their families pay for those dreams. This inside-out *Godfather*, where a man fails to take control, but proves his worth.

Using screenwriter Arnold Schulman had several advantages: he had written Capra's 1959 *A Hole in the Head*; he was a bona fide Coppola fanatic, who once approached the director on a plane and offered to work for free; and he would bring an outsider's eye. But Schulman had to confess that he hated cars.

Lucas set him straight.

"This is not a film about cars. It's about Francis."

So Schulman took a spell with Coppola in Napa, drinking wine, and making notes, while getting paid. He realised that while all of Coppola's films come to reflect the life of their maker, *Tucker: The Man and His Dream* was the first conscious allegory of his struggles.

Only the studios still weren't buying. At $24 million, not one of them would touch it. Lucas despaired. They wanted quick, high-concept beats like *Crocodile Dundee* or *Three Men and a Baby*, pitches the marketing department could spread like butter. So Lucas backed it himself, offsetting the risk with a distribution deal with Paramount.

The script is key: it manages to play comedic, thrilling, and tragic notes, almost at once. With the war over, Tucker (played with giddy charm by Jeff Bridges) plans to build his car of tomorrow. He enlists crook-turned-businessman Abe Karatz (a magnificent Martin Landau) to raise enough money to buy a plant and work on a prototype. They are Don Quixote and Sancho Panza. Or maybe that is Coppola and Lucas. Can we read the duplicitous boardrooms as sneering studio executives?

Joan Allen is his long suffering but devoted wife Vera, corralling their brood (Schulman would have looked to Eleanor for that portrait). There is also a resonant part for Christian Slater as Tucker's eldest, Junior, who tells his father he wants to quit school and join the enterprise.

Bridges draws us close to an edge in Tucker. The rationale slips away to reveal the obsession. The trickster emerges. Coppola finds dark currents: Dean Stockwell as Howard Hughes, a dangerously kindred spirit, or Lloyd Bridges (father to Jeff) uncredited as the bent Senator Homer Ferguson.

After the success of *Peggy Sue Got Married*, Coppola opted for the same soft glow of nostalgia. But with a more Disneyesque intensity: what you might call the colour options of the American Dream. Cinematographer Vittorio Storaro gilds the film with the silky lines and lacquered finish of a Tucker. Postproduction took place at the Skywalker Ranch, Lucas's state-of-the-art, 3,000-acre filmmaking complex built in Maris County to the north of Napa – based on an idea by Coppola. With its Victorian mansion, redwood-panelled offices, and stained-glass dome, Lucas had refurbished the Zoetrope dream as a spotless, risk-less paradise.

There were those who only saw a hood ornament. "Here, the message is the myth, clamouring like a cast-off hubcap on a lonely night," sneered *The Washington Post*. But there were those who savoured grandeur in a minor key. "The movie's costumes and décor, their color and light, lend the expansive action extraordinary visual vitality," said *The New Yorker*.

If it failed at the box office, making $23 million (art film results not mainstream success), Coppola could be satisfied that he, like Tucker, had created a thing of neglected beauty.

After the convoy of Tuckers parades around the square, and the credits roll, comes the realisation that this isn't really a film about cars, or mad inventors, or mad directors, but that common theme that ties all of Coppola's diverse work together – the binding strength of the family unit.

The film is dedicated to Gio.

Outside on a sweltering New York street, the Silverfish shines in the hard sunlight. It is June 1988, and somewhere within the grand Upper West Side apartment block where Coppola's roving nerve-centre is parked, the director glances with satisfaction into his monitor. The electronic image shows a girl, about twelve years old, fixing a pitcher of strawberry daiquiri. She pours two, passing one onto her mother, who has the fine cheekbones of Talia Shire.

Wherever Coppola could have predicted his nomadic art would take him, this is a long way from the young man who walked out of an Eisenstein screening with a fire in his belly.

To fix the cinematic co-ordinates, Coppola is shooting *Life Without Zoe*, his first short since he was a student, and it was all Woody Allen's idea. An anthology of short films connected by the theme and location of New York, each with its own distinctive (yet harmonious) director, like a collection of novellas.

Allen and producer Robert Greenhut debated where to send the invitation. Martin Scorsese made immediate sense as the city's other (contrasting) movie laureate. Ingmar Bergman? Wonderful, but would a foreign language entry fit New York? Bob Fosse and Mike Nichols were too similar in style to Allen. Steven Spielberg? Too busy. Coppola was the porridge that was just right to sit between Allen and Scorsese: a fascinating (if unpredictable) filmmaker, who hailed from New York, and showed a relish for experimentation.

Studios were sceptical. Anthologies were rarely the sum of their parts. Who was in the market for a $15 million touchy-feely version of *Twilight Zone: The Movie*? It was Touchstone (an outlet of Disney) who eventually agreed, spying an opportunity to indulge *three* major directors at once.

Coppola was certainly curious about such a compressed form of storytelling (as opposed to wrestling with five-hour rough cuts), but his motivation was Sofia. Thirty-four minutes long, *Life Without Zoe* marks a significant juncture – Sofia's first steps as a filmmaker. She had made her cameos, of course. Always been a part of things. But now the seventeen-year-old was making a credited contribution to the script – and a style is peeking through the blinds.

Coppola's New York story, loosely based on Kay Thompson's *Eloise* books, is about poor, misunderstood Zoe (Heather McComb). She may have an apartment in the Sherry-Netherland Hotel on Fifth Avenue, with her own butler on call, and can waft about Manhattan on the magic carpet of her own credit card, but Zoe is an adult before her time.

Sofia had set her father right on the inner life of a pretty little rich girl, the mixed advantages of privilege. The stab of loneliness and lick of satire are worth recording. We catch a glint of the spoiled worlds of *Marie Antoinette* and *The Bling Ring*. Sofia also designed the costumes and credit sequence.

Father and daughter had holed up in a Las Vegas suite, ordering room service, and working on the script every day. "It was his scriptwriting workshop with me," recalled Sofia. Make it personal, he told her. By night, Coppola would hit the tables.

While filming in New York, the Coppolas are staying in *their* Sherry-Netherland Hotel apartment, one of five homes, including the Victorian in Napa Valley, apartments in San Francisco and Los Angeles, and the family retreat in Belize.

In the early 1980s, Coppola had fallen for the Central American paradise, and in a rush of blood purchased the abandoned Blancaneaux Lodge. He devised plans to build a media outpost, filling the airwaves with live cinema and culture, but instead developed a select twenty-room luxury hideaway, enclosed in the rainforest like Kurtz's compound with plunge pools and Guatemalan fabrics.

The carefully cultivated 1940s chic of the Sherry feeds *Life Without Zoe* an old Hollywood classicism.

Doubling down on the biographical inferences, Shire plays Zoe's distant, socialite mother and Giancarlo Giannini her flautist father, so often absent, travelling the world to play for others. Watch closely and you will see Carmine cameo as a street musician.

Life Without Zoe has a poignant vein in the dangers of having a famous artist for a father. Coppola saw it as a father-daughter relationship story, but it was in honour of all his children, who had developed into fine people. That translates as an airy piece about fitting in, lavish birthday parties, and returning a stolen diamond earring belonging to Carole Bouquet's Arab princess. That one of Zoe's richling schoolmates is named Abu references Coppola's childhood joy *The Thief of Bagdad*. The theme of magic also connects the three stories.

Released on February 26, 1989, the collection lived down to most expectations. Critics wavered over whether the best was Allen's opener *Oedipus Wrecks*, a wry, magical-realist tale of a Jewish lawyer (Allen) who wishes for his domineering mother (Mae Questel) to vanish. Or Scorsese's sensuous concluding episode, *Life Lessons*, tackling the mysteries of the muse as ageing artist Nick Nolte falls for assistant Rosanna Arquette. They were united in opposing the self-indulgent filling. "Coppola's head doesn't seem to be in his filmmaking," rued Pauline Kael.

Back beneath the hum of Manhattan air conditioning the year before, an unsettled Coppola is almost in agreement. "Two weeks from now, I'll be done here," he relishes. "I'll be free to do what I want."

Every film becomes a prison cell. Working to another's bidding. Listening for the rapacious note from head office. Waiting for the critics to bite. He swears *Tucker* will be the last studio film he will ever make. This is no more than a distraction.

"I have to focus on what I want to say," he implores. He is becoming more philosophical in his writing – observations on life he'd like to incorporate into his work. He'd like to make a simpler kind of movie. Or maybe retire.

But just when he thought he was out... You know how it goes.

CHAPTER 9

THE DEVIL YOU KNOW

The Godfather Part III (1990), Bram Stoker's Dracula (1992),
Hearts of Darkness: A Filmmaker's Apocalypse (1991),
Jack (1996), The Rainmaker (1997)

Take a look at him – Francis Ford Coppola at fifty. With his high
forehead, piercing eyes (behind thicker lenses), thinning hair, expanding
waistline, and a beard crested with grey, he has cultivated a rabbinical
demeanour. This is a kind man, a wise man; he has plans – Coppola the
elder statesman.

Yet his debts from *One from the Heart* still hang over him like the
sword of Damocles. He is as much journeyman as auteur. He still speaks
of slipping away from the binds of Hollywood to make ones from the
heart. But fate won't let him escape. He has been shattered by tragedy,
but persisted.

"Family remains the endless riddle in his life and work," wrote film
historian David Thomson, and now the Corleones are about to come
back into his life.

Paramount had made numerous attempts to get a third *Godfather* off
the ground. It was almost an obsession at the studio. The permutations
were dizzying. CIA agents; Costa Rican dictators; Castro's Cuba; South
American drug cartels; Michael's son Anthony taking over the business,
abetted (or challenged) by his hot-headed cousin, Sonny's boy Tomasso;
Michael dies; Michael lives; Kay commits suicide. Charlie Bluhdorn even

took a turn at the typewriter, producing a sixty-page treatment with Mario Puzo. But it was all too modern, too action-packed. There was no space for character.

With Coppola still making it abundantly clear he was done with gangsters, Paramount explored the possibility of Martin Scorsese, Alan J. Pakula, Sidney Lumet, or Michael Mann as a possible replacement. Briefly, Sylvester Stallone was signed to star and direct.

By the mid-1980s, Evans was gone, Bart was gone, and Bluhdorn had died of a heart attack on his private jet. Well-groomed, one-time usher Frank Mancuso had taken charge at Paramount, and insisted that Coppola was the essential ingredient. He was able to get the current script to Talia Shire, who handed it to her brother, who after perusing the first few pages tossed it into the fire.

But with court cases pending, Coppola was unable to move forward, and the Napa Valley estate was again at risk. So he returned for the very same reason he took the first film – he needed the money. But if Paramount wanted him so badly, he wanted total artistic control in return.

The days of Evans instigating deals by his begonias were long gone. Modern Hollywood had an accelerated life cycle in which release dates were the immovable object that even irresistible forces must heed. Paramount set a non-negotiable Thanksgiving launch for the third and concluding episode in the august trilogy (the marketing department was in full swing), and Coppola found himself in a race with his own legacy. He had six weeks to complete a script with Puzo, and a year to shoot and deliver a film.

With a budget of $54 million, a third *Godfather* was an expensive business, including $4 million for Al Pacino, $1.5 million for Diane Keaton, $1 million for Robert Duvall, $500,000 for Talia Shire, and $3 million for the director.

Coppola immediately made familiar proclamations, almost as if he is trying to convince himself. He wanted it to be Shakespearean. Not a story of gangsters, but an attempt at redemption. He posited interesting ideas: Eddie Murphy as a Harlem drug dealer; Frank Sinatra; Gene Hackman; a second timeline following the young Sonny played by Eric Roberts. There were informal discussions with Robert De Niro about doubling back into the story to play Vincent (the grandson of his own Vito) with Madonna as Mary, Michael's daughter.

Holed up at the Peppermill Hotel Casino in Reno, Coppola and Puzo would work on the script by day, then hit the tables at night: roulette, craps, or Blackjack. "We're losing thousands downstairs," laughed Coppola, "but we're making millions upstairs."

Out of Reno a story emerged.

The year is 1979, and an ageing Michael Corleone is intent on making the family legitimate. He has moved their riches into banks, real estate, and as the story begins, the Catholic Church. He is intent on reconnecting with his family: ex-wife Kay (Keaton), his sensitive, opera singing son Anthony (Franc D'Ambrosio), and daughter Mary (Sofia Coppola). The sins of the past weigh upon him.

Coppola and Puzo had wanted to call it *The Death of Michael Corleone*. "The point of the movie was to illuminate our original story, rather than continue it," insisted Coppola. He wanted to explore a moral death for Michael. But *Part III* was something else that was non-negotiable.

There are certain parties who are not as keen that the family go straight. Paramount, for one, pushed back. The studio wanted Vincent (Andy Garcia, the film's shining light), Sonny's illegitimate son, to have a more prominent part. Hence the womanising hothead gets a feud with Joe Mantegna's New York hood Joey Zasa (a subplot that has the legitimate tang of *Godfather* lore), and a yen for the family business. Falling for his cousin Mary will not help his cause.

In June 1990, Coppola was dealt a devastating blow to his plans. Duvall had rejected the offer of $1 million. Director implored actor, promising him choice scenes, rewriting the script. But he was met with silence.

Once he came to terms with the fact that Tom would not return, he began to write around the problem, eliminating his name entirely. But that absence is a wound the film never recovers from. "In the early script stages, *Part III* was designed to be symmetrical with the other films," explained Walter Murch, who served as one of three editors. Each was about the death of a brother: in *The Godfather* it was Sonny, in *Part II* it was Fredo, *Part III* was due to centre on Tom's death.

Shire's Connie takes up much of the dramatic slack, effectively becoming Michael's *consigliere*. Especially in the revised cut of 2019, her character blooms like a black flower. "Like Lady Macbeth," savoured Coppola. With her hair tightly pulled back from her face, she begins to resemble Vito.

Puzo and Coppola became increasingly absorbed by the nefarious connections between the Vatican and the mob, loading the plot with a thicket of scowling Catholic businessmen and crooked priests. The idea was for more of that real world resonance, with Helmut Berger's Keinszig a direct reference to Vatican banker Roberto Calvi, who was found hanging from London's Blackfriars Bridge in 1982. Calvi was rumoured to carry a copy of *The Godfather*, "rather like a priest with his Bible."

Ever the scorpion stinging the frog, Coppola resisted what he called "the easiest route another *Godfather* could have taken." In what looked like a supreme act of subversion, he even cut Pacino's dark, Byronic locks into a greying crew cut, appalling make-up artist Dick Smith so much he quit.

Shooting in Cinecitta in Rome from November 27, 1989, was a sentimental plan — these were the footsteps of Fellini, Leone, and Bertolucci — and an excited Italian escort greeted Coppola at the airport. "Welcome to Rome. You are the director of the film *Stepfather*." Christmas was spent at Shire's rented apartment with views of the Eternal City: Pacino, Keaton, Garcia, the Coppolas, and extended families eating octopus and spaghetti.

But the grasp of America had been all-important. This was an immigrant saga. New York needed to bleed into the frame.

Things soon became fraught. Time was their enemy, and the story in a constant state of turmoil. "With Francis, the script is like a newspaper — it comes out every day," quipped Garcia. Coppola struggled to keep his doubts at bay. Not an unusual climate for the making of a *Godfather* movie, but his relationship with producers Fred Roos and Gray Fredrickson — old allies — started to fray, and he dispatched them back to America, to plan for the reduced New York section, but more because he didn't feel protected.

Gordon Willis was hardly a changed man. In fact, the cinematographer was so curt with the Italian crew, Coppola was forced to write an open letter explaining the foibles of a maestro. "Each artist has his own way of working based on his personality," said Coppola. Wasn't Toscanini the same?

On December 28, Eleanor Coppola recalled the phone ringing. The jovial assistant director sounded serious – could Sofia come to the studio immediately.

Winona Ryder had nervous exhaustion. That was the doctor's considered opinion. The eighteen-year-old actress due to play Mary had been delayed filming *Mermaids* in New England. Jumping on the first plane to Rome, she collapsed in her hotel room, unable to move. She had to quit. "They'd be working with a wet noodle," she implored. Coppola was left with two choices.

Either he suspends the shoot indefinitely while he recasts: Madonna was still keen, and Annabella Sciorra had impressed in auditions. Or go with the girl he had in mind even as he wrote. If Coppola thought of himself as Michael, then naturally they would share the same daughter. So he asked Sofia to play the pivotal role.

Studio, producers, reputedly some actors, and even the sound designer tried to get Coppola to see sense. Think how this will go down. The press will have a field day. Eleanor had worried about the pressure. But Coppola only became more entrenched. He liked the symbolism, that Mary and Sofia were both the apple of their father's eye. He fired back lengthy missives to Paramount, pointing out that Mary had to appear as if she was the offspring of Keaton and Pacino, half Wasp, half Italian. He had only cast Ryder because, "she was the most like Sofia." And Sofia had read the part during taped rehearsals. She was more prepared than anyone.

"I was game," recalled Sofia. With only twenty-four hours' notice, she dropped out of Mills College, where she was studying art history, and committed herself to Mary Corleone. "You want to prove you're good and that you're not just the director's daughter," she said. "It was very controversial to put me in it."

Little Sofia who scampered round the set was now this young woman at the centre of things. She and Pacino would play chess to the side of the shot. He quoted Brando, "Whenever you get the urge to act, wait until it passes." Keaton told her to enjoy the love scenes. You get to kiss married men.

Ryder would later call from Los Angeles to apologise, promising she would make it up to Coppola.

There were moments of levity. During the shooting of the party scene, when Michael and Mary are waltzing, Coppola's three-year-old granddaughter Gia ran into shot and grabbed hold of Sofia's skirt, unaware that this was anything more than life. The director kept the cameras rolling – this was the naturalism in which the previous films were imbedded. That made the final cut.

The climactic Sicilian sequences – bringing the saga full circle – were reworked and reworked again. Originally, Michael was destined to die in a hail of gunfire on the steps of the Teatro Massimo in Palermo, but Coppola decided that was too easy. "Just to shoot Michael doesn't make him pay," he wrote to Puzo, "he doesn't really suffer…" When the final accounting comes, it should end like *King Lear*, where his daughter dies, and he has to live with the horror.

Eleanor would never get used to the film's agonising final ten minutes. Watching her child die.

Amid the blur of postproduction, the film was delayed, if only briefly, to Christmas Day. But the final cut was another defeat. It wasn't the film that Coppola had in mind. "I'd kept pleading for another few months to do the film properly," he said. Hence the revised version in 2019, given the prolix title of *The Godfather, Coda: The Death of Michael Corleone*. It is much improved, but not transformed.

As for the original cut. Well, the prevailing air is confusion. The Vatican was a distracting choice of conspiracy when these films had from the opening line defined themselves in America. Wasn't Washington Michael's implacable foe? And the ease with which he is brought back from damnation. As *Part II* drew to a close, we looked upon a man beyond reach.

The negativity bent toward Sofia was overwhelming. It's as if she had single-handedly, and purposely, ruined the franchise. "Hopelessly amateurish," chided *The Post*. While *Time* denounced her "gosling gracelessness." In truth, the absence of Hagen is a far greater blow than any deficiencies in her performance. She is a little willowy when you want the Corleone fire, but far from a ruinous dead weight.

Nevertheless, Sofia's confidence was badly knocked. She may have already known she didn't want to act, but this was like being expelled. She would enrol in the California Institute of Arts to study painting and photography, start on a more significant path. Out of adversity comes art.

"The metaphor is now obvious to me," said Coppola in hindsight. "When the film came out and everyone attacked, the bullets that went for Sofia were really coming for me. The criticism that was launched on this eighteen-year-old girl who didn't even want to be an actress was meant to hurt me, and it did."

There were positives, of course. The excellent Garcia, Shire, and the grandeur Willis unfailingly provides. The operatic climax – at the opera! – resounds with Coppola's authority over the medium. The superbly orchestrated intercutting between riflescopes, silent stabbings, poisoned cannoli (take the gun, leave the cannoli!), and the production of *Cavalleria Rusticana* recalls the dramatic rush of the original.

At first, born aloft on its reputation, the film soared, making $14 million in three days. But it soon slowed, stalling at $67 million in the USA. The eventual worldwide total was $136 million. Hardly a disaster, but it was noticeable that Mancuso was out of his job the following spring.

Scant months before Scorsese had stripped the veneer from the myth with his hyperactive hit *Goodfellas*. The Corleones looked stuck in their ways.

Coppola is on the run. He is aiming for Belize, with a stopover in Guatemala. *Bram Stoker's Dracula* is being readied for release on November 17, 1992, and he has fled the country, determined not to get caught up in the painful autopsy of the box office results. But it is so hard to escape CNN. They go deeper. To the town of Panajachel and a cottage overlooking Lake Atitlan, where there are no phones and no televisions.

You can escape Hollywood, but you can't escape yourself. Coppola has to know. So Eleanor is dispatched to the telephone company in town, the only place to make an international call.

Having successfully completed her mission, the crackling line connecting her to the excited voice of Fred Roos, she decides to torment her husband a little, and writes down a series of numbers on scraps of paper.

"Okay, tell me," he says, girding himself for the worst.

She hands him a slip of paper with "17" written on it.

"It made $17 [million]?" he says, trying to keep the disappointment from his voice. That was an okay result, nothing more.

She hands him another slip of paper.

"$4 [million]? What does that mean?"

"Add it up."

"You mean it made $21 [million]?" He brightens up.

She hands him several more pieces of paper, until he has them all.

"It made $34 million?" He is incredulous.

"It did!"

Bram Stoker's Dracula would go on to become the ninth biggest film of the year, earning $215.8 million worldwide. With his share of the profits, Coppola could pay the last of his debts from *One from the Heart*, ironically enough another film shot entirely on soundstages.

A dissolve. Back to early 1991, when Ryder paid a visit. She felt she needed to mend bridges. And she had a script in her hands. Jim Hart's *Dracula* had been proposed as a USA Network TV movie, but it had ambition. Best known for Steven Spielberg's prettified folly *Hook*, Hart had approached the classic with two intentions: stay faithful to Bram Stoker's novel and make it a "woman's movie". He sidelined the old bluster of Victorian guys tracking down the monster. This was a story of undying love. And by a stroke of very good fortune (and agent cunning) the script had fallen into Ryder's hands, who was fixed on playing the heroine, and object of vampiric ardour, Mina Murray.

So it was Ryder who put it to Coppola. Did he want to make a *Dracula* movie?

He and August had gone to revivals of the Universal classics: *Dracula*, *Frankenstein*, and *The Wolfman*. From Max Schreck (hairless in *Nosferatu*) to Bela Lugosi to John Carradine (whose *House of Dracula* Coppola favoured) to Christopher Lee, the Count was an archetype of sexuality and terror.

Flashback to 1958, when Coppola was a camp counsellor – "teaching drama, baseball, and so on"– who enthralled his charges by reading them *Dracula* by firelight.

"The vampire myth speaks to the latent fears and desires in all of us," he relished. As he had rejuvenated the clichés of the gangster picture, he would find new life in old bones.

Songs of revolution may no longer be sung, but Zoetrope was productive. An *Outsiders* television show had been commissioned by the Fox Network (but will only last a single season). Coppola was serving as executive producer on Carroll Ballard's yacht-racing movie, *Wind*. Though far from finished, he expected *Megalopolis* to go before cameras within two years. So there was room to slot something in to film beforehand. The biopic *J. Edgar Hoover: The Man and the Secrets*, written by Curt Gentry (*Helter Skelter*), was showing promise. Or maybe his adaptation of Beat-icon Jack Kerouac's *On the Road*, which he thought might suit Ryder. Or going with a live-action musical version of *Pinocchio*.

Classic Coppola. Spinning plates. Firing out ideas, hundreds a day. Creating storms. There were those extramural distractions too: winemaking, resorts, communications, and his passion for electronics. Keep running. Keep working. Stay ahead of his frustrations.

For instance, how *The Godfather Part III* was gleefully being labelled a flop. It might have fallen short of the blockbusting figures set by the original, but so had *Part II*, and in the current era was that ever likely? "Especially for a long picture with adult subject matter," he said. And there were Oscar nominations for Best Film and Best Director.

"What is there about me that invites this controversy? Why do I have to be an oddball on the edge of extinction? Why do people enjoy that?"

A deeper, more primitive fear was also at work. Was he out of touch?

So *Dracula* was a ripe opportunity. Vampires played young, and this was the ur-text of the genre, brimming with symbolic purpose. What Coppola particularly loved was that in returning to the book, Hart had unearthed a tale of "passion and eroticism". He had framed the Victorian story with the legend of Vlad the Impaler, Dracula's living incarnation, and his great love Elisabeta, who killed herself, believing him slain in battle. Death proves a mere inconvenience to matters of the heart.

While championing the commercial prospects of parchment-pale throats, fangs, werewolves, bats, rats, and Monica Belluci writhing over Keanu Reeves, the old contrarian was going back to Stoker's awkward epistolary book.

The 1897 novel, born out of a mix of European folklore and vulgar sensationalism (also known as genres), tells of Count Dracula (Gary Oldman), the immortal vampire, and his search for his resurrected love, who has taken the form of Mina (Ryder), an English rose due for a sensible marriage. Mina's fiancé, the stoic lawyer Jonathan Harker (Reeves, stricken with a horrible case of English accent), will be waylaid in Dracula's castle, high in the postcard-bleak Carpathians. So Dracula heads for the vibrant streets of London, accompanied by crates of ancestral earth, leaving a trail of madness and bloodsucking that draws in Mina's best friend Lucy (Sadie Frost) and deranged fellow lawyer Renfield (Tom Waits). Vampire hunter Van Helsing (a zesty Anthony Hopkins) and a suite of Lucy's suitors are all that stands in his way.

Coppola's devotion to tradition was not sufficiently served by keeping faith with the plot and cluttered ambience of what he considered the author's intentions. And to provide some literary ballast he expanded the title to *Bram Stoker's Dracula*. In a frenzy of attribution, Sony's marketing department took to declaring it Francis Ford Coppola's *Bram Stoker's Dracula*.

The challenge was to find a fresh approach: to do away with the Lugosi cliché of scarlet-lined cloaks and patent leather hair, the debonair monster flitting in through the virgin's window. You picture Coppola hissing as cinematic convention is held before him like a crucifix. Where he had found a new way with gangster pictures – mixing opera and life – he envisioned a film that would embrace its own artifice.

He was back among the nodding-dog surrealism of *Rumble Fish*, the more derivative the better. To prepare for the $40 million Columbia Studios production, he watched a host of ornate classics: F.W. Murnau's expressionistic silent *Nosferatu*, Sergei Eisenstein's *Ivan the Terrible*, the Orson Welles duo of *Citizen Kane* and *Chimes of Midnight,* and Akira Kurosawa's florid *Kagemusha*. He wasn't simply filling out a gothic playbook; he was seeking a technique. "I wanted to make the picture almost in the style of the turn of the century, when motion pictures were the domain of the magician."

The late 19th century was an era of technological turmoil, and Coppola layers his imagery with blood transfusions, typewriters, phonographs, zoetropes (of course), cinematographs, and even early pornography. This was realism dancing with phantasmagoria: tangible fantasy. And a deranged love song to cinema.

Fourteen actors and crew come up to the Napa estate, where Coppola has turned the old barn into a rehearsal stage. Ryder, Hopkins, Oldman, Reeves, Waits, and Cary Elwes sit around the dinner table. Reeves's easy lope reminds Eleanor of Gio. Coppola cooks bowls of pasta, garnished with basil, and veal with sautéed zucchini. They end up on the porch as night falls sipping grappa. Hopkins and Oldman do impressions of Brando.

Familiar squalls blow through preproduction. His reputation would always go before him. Columbia became increasingly wary of his artistic approach – was he actually making a horror movie? To head off his esoteric drift they locked down the budget. Old compatriots like Vittorio Storaro and Dean Tavoularis were deemed too likely to tempt the director into expensive excesses.

Coppola countered by firing the special effects team, who were claiming the only rational way to achieve old-time "naïve" effects was by aping them with digital technology. He replaced them with his son, Roman, who simply learned antique in-camera methods. It was like time travelling to the silent days: triple exposures, variable film speeds, mirrors and silhouettes, and the use of an original, hand cranked Pathé camera for one sequence. This was standard Coppola practice, where the themes of the film extend into its making. He was almost making his version of the august *Napoléon*.

The choice of Japanese designer Eiko Ishioka (*Mishima*) was inspired. She had joined Coppola for the theatrics of *Rip Van Winkle*, which he saw now as a "crayon sketch" for *Dracula*. Ishioka would foment an Oscar-winning flux of the avant-garde and the grandly gothic in sets (with Thomas Sanders) and costumes: Gustav Klimt by way of Kabuki theatre.

"By bringing in Eiko," said Coppola, "I knew I was ensuring that at least one element – the costumes, which were so important in my scheme of the production – would be completely atypical, absolutely original and unique."

For the alluring count, he swerved into controversial territory. London-born Gary Oldman was a captivating actor who had brought fire and brimstone to Sid Vicious, Joe Orton, and Lee Harvey Oswald.

But he wasn't the matinee idol vision of Dracula most had in mind, and there was the usual kerfuffle in the press about Coppola's eccentricities.

"Gary just seemed to be the most far out," he said. Oldman was not unlike Brando, throwing out ideas, imposing his will on the performance, making unconventional choices as he ranges from the centuries-old relic licking blood from a razorblade to the Jim Morrison-esque squire who sashays to Mina's side. Though Oldman and Ryder never quite saw eye to eye as he climbed deep into the performance and away from social graces.

Shooting at Sony Studios in Culver City, Los Angeles began on October 14, 1991, and Coppola was in his element, mounting the largest pantomime in history. It was a world made entirely of sets, spilling over the soundstages, with an entire Victorian mansion, furnished in muted colours, giving way to a garden, complete with fountain and rose arbour, built on the pit where the swimming pool for Esther Williams's movies used to be. In Hollywood, films are haunted by the ghosts of other films.

Coppola elaborated on his improvisational games. Blindfolding actors, herding them to the centre of the castle set, and then unleashing Oldman in Dracula's wolf-man guise to nuzzle their faces, snarl obscenities, and make perverted threats. "So that when they *do* meet Dracula they *react*," he explained. For Renfield's scenes in the asylum, where the walls ooze slimy water, the bug wrangler provided maggots, beetles, and strange orange worms to fill his tin plate. Waits struggled to pick out the jellied insects from the writhing mass. Reviewing shots in the Silverfish, Coppola sees the actor spitting out a beetle and laughing.

Was the film too exquisite? We never want to turn away from the screen. Quite the opposite: we hunger to see what ravishment is lurking around the next corner. "How can we be in suspense when we know that our appetite for lurid visual truffles will be fed without a moment's stinting?" noted Adam Mars-Jones in *The Independent*.

That is the problem. Even the bugs are fetching. The horror has been left out. And the performances are a tonal jamboree – only Oldman holds to a gothic spirit. Among the critics, curious to see what *Dracula* drew out of Coppola, there is an even split between those who saw something exuberant and bloody: "Baroque!" squeals *Esquire*; "Luscious!" clamours

The Austin Chronicle. And those who saw a mess: "Blighted!" sneers the *AV Club*. Audiences swooned.

With the money that the vampire gave them, Coppola was able to purchase the property adjacent to his 19th-century Niebaum-Coppola home, restoring the original estate with another ninety acres of vineyards and a gothic chateau.

"*Dracula* bought the rest of it," laughed Coppola. "We paid cash."

An interlude: while Coppola was working on the *Dracula* script, *Hearts of Darkness: A Filmmaker's Apocalypse* was released. This startling, feature-length making-of had finally put to use over sixty hours of footage Eleanor had reaped in the Philippines. So frank (and frankly disturbing) was the material, that the United Artists marketing department didn't know what to make of it. So it had lain dormant.

Eleanor had joined directors Fax Bahr and George Hickenlooper in the edit suite, encouraged that they were using *Notes* as a guide. There to make sure the footage was used without distortion. Coppola still had final approval and cringed at what it revealed. "This film is a $20 million disaster! Why won't anyone believe me?" come his agonised wails from the set. But he can't bring himself to interfere. It was a wise choice.

Symbolically debuting in Cannes, the documentary was heralded as a masterpiece of the form, enriching his status as an artist and mythological figure. "There have been few sharper portraits of the filmmaker as alchemist than *Hearts of Darkness*..." extolled *The New York Times*.

So why did he make *Jack*? More than any of his films, triumphs and misadventures, no title raises the critical hackles like his tender-hearted comedy about an overgrown boy – quite literally. Jack is suffering from a rare and fictional genetic disorder that causes his cells to grow at four times the normal rate. By the time he is ten he resembles Robin Williams. What had happened to the great figurehead of the 1970s?

"I know I should be ashamed of it, but I'm not," said Coppola. He liked it, he thought it was sweet; he always had a dumb Disney movie inside of him.

There was a little more to it than that.

By 1992, Coppola estimated he had been making films continuously since UCLA. Released from his debts, he could afford to sit back and see what the present held. He took a greater interest in managing the vineyard, releasing the Pennino Zinfandel in honour of his maternal grandfather.

Under his Zoetrope banner, he produced that other gothic mainstay, *Mary Shelley's Frankenstein*. After Roman Polanski passed, the versatile British director Kenneth Branagh would direct, with Robert De Niro as a creature that, Coppola promised, would look nothing like Boris Karloff. Which might have been a mistake, for Branagh fumbles Coppola's expressionist excesses and delivers a heated nonsense.

He continued to give sagacious interviews, holding forth on his pet subjects: the future of cinema and his complicated past. He never had the "God-given" talent of peers like Steven Spielberg or Carroll Ballard, he said, but he has a theatrical prowess, and persistence. He was not what people thought he was. His heart wasn't all darkness. Years before, between movies, magazines, and launching radio stations, before the next rise and fall, Coppola had turned to the journalist compiling the latest profile, deadly serious. "I'd like to start this place up in the North Pole… A sort of toy factory where all the toys were made by little people…"

You wouldn't put it beyond him trying.

He always adored the company of children, but had he ever made a film for children? *Finian's Rainbow*, perhaps. *Rip Van Winkle* and *Captain EO* hardly counted as feature films.

Gia, now nine years old, put it to him straight. "When are you going to do a film with kids in it that I can see?" How could he refuse his granddaughter?

Coppola turned first to his remake of *Pinocchio*, which he saw as a chance to go back to Carlo Collodi's original stories, so much darker than Disney. He spent time in the Collodi archives in Florence and wrote a dozen songs. This was to be a large production, in the realm of $40 to $50 million. Pinocchio would still be a puppet, but he would utilise the computer effects Spielberg had pioneered in *Jurassic Park*. If all went well, he'd be shooting by early 1995.

But Warner Bros. – his old nemesis – baulking at his directing fee, resisted committing. Things got tense. *Pinocchio* was plunged into a legal quagmire in which Coppola claimed the studio had no intention of making the film but was preventing him from setting it up elsewhere (Sony eventually pulled the plug). The whole case hinged on the validity of a verbal agreement, which would have huge repercussions across Hollywood. It was set for a long, Dickensian trial.

That's when *Jack* came along. This straightforward Disney project: a script by James DeMonaco and Gary Nadeau, a budget of $45 million, and Williams (Coppola's friend and neighbour) already attached.

Undoubtedly, Coppola was channelling a lot of *Pinocchio* energy into *Jack*. It is the story of a boy that wants to fit in. The kinetic, often untameable Williams was a veteran at such man-child showboating. His breakthrough role was as the credulous alien in hit television comedy *Mork and Mindy*, and he had recently been locating his inner Peter Pan in Spielberg's indifferent *Hook*. The plot has Jack, a very grown up ten-year-old, starting fifth grade, and struggling to adapt his predicament to school life. There are wispy subplots involving his fraught mother (Diane Lane), his attractive teacher (Jennifer Lopez), and the awkwardly flirty mom of a fellow pupil (the peppy Fran Drescher).

He was genuinely touched by what he read. *Jack* brought back memories of being pinned beneath the sheets of his childhood polio, and the longing for friends. "There are no children in his life," he noticed.

Among his warm vineyards, he found himself thinking about lifespans, and how well we use the time allotted to us. Do mayflies know they only have a day? Inevitably, his thoughts circled back to Gio.

"My son Gio only lived twenty-two years, but it was a complete twenty-two years."

He was making it for Gia and Gio, and for himself.

They shot from September 18, 1995, around Ross to the northeast of San Francisco. It had been three years since Coppola had last directed a film. Rather than his usual rehearsals, he had instituted a kiddy boot camp, in which Williams participated in character, relearning what it was to be a ten-year-old. By the end of the week, he was one of the gang.

Jack is an extreme version of *Peggy Sue*, with an actor being required to assimilate the body language of a much younger person. The added challenge for Williams was that there was no ostensible fantasy involved. He would have to evolve an approach that was childlike but still informed by adult genes. His body would have different opinions to his head. Though the film coyly avoids the potential for any sexual tension in a grown man with a ten-year-old's lack of inhibitions.

Critics could see the catchy concept, but the schmaltz was unforgiveable. Wasn't this the very pap he had railed against? "A feelgood casserole that got left in the microwave too long," sighed Owen Gleiberman in *Entertainment Weekly*.

Sell-out.

Audiences, no doubt encouraged by the offer of Williams doing his hyper-verbal routines rather than the reputation of the director, made for a moderate success with a total of $58 million at the box office.

Coppola is holding court, raising his glass and waxing lyrical. A Venetian glass chandelier hangs over the table. Italian pottery is artfully positioned around the room. Lamb shanks and marinated fall vegetables have been served, with lemon tart to come. The great patriarch begins to list his current achievements: he has launched a magazine (*Zoetrope: All-Story*), and produced an Emmy-winning television show, *The Odyssey, Parts I and II,* with Armand Assante as the Greek Willard. "Television is like cooking," he jokes. "Cook it, serve it, eat it, and go on to the next thing."

Films have a habit of becoming odysseys.

Between mouthfuls of lamb, the assembled press are held in thrall. He has also completed another film, a courtroom thriller entitled *The Rainmaker*, screened in his converted barn.

The inevitable question comes. Why did he feel the need to make a mainstream studio thriller?

"I became a sucker for Grisham like everyone else," he laughs.

John Grisham was publishing heroin. The Arkansas-born lawyer-turned-novelist was the equivalent of Mario Puzo (swapping out the Mafia for the vicissitudes of the law). He was selling in vast quantities and making hay for Hollywood. *The Firm, The Client, The Pelican Brief, A Time to Kill.* The recipe was relatively simple: take the latest novel (and he was churning out these things faster than Stephen King), add an A-list movie star as the greenhorn lawyer out of his or her depth, serve with a garnish of character actors on the witness stand. Heavyweights from the 1970s like Sidney Pollack and Alan J. Pakula had been signing up for duty.

Coppola had simply picked up a copy of Grisham's latest novel at the airport. It went by the intriguing title of *The Rainmaker* and was already number one. He downed it in a single gulp from New York to Paris. When he landed he decided to buy the rights and cut a deal with Paramount for a budget of $40 million.

As taken as he was with the young David who takes on the medical insurance Goliath, he was still trying to learn something about the appetites of a modern audience.

The Rainmaker is the story of Rudy Baylor (Matt Damon), fresh out of Memphis law school and hard up. He's a humble kid. So he resorts to a job with "Bruiser" Stone (Mickey Rourke) and his slippery ambulance-chasing outfit (the Roger Corman of law firms). When Rudy finds new clients, he gets paid. Or, in legal parlance: when he makes it rain.

The Rainmaker, appreciated Coppola, was about a kid who didn't sell out. All the smart kids in Harvard or Stanford have all these high ideals. But when they get out into the world, he said, "they are manipulated by money."

Teamed up with wise and wisecracking Deck Shifflet (Danny DeVito), in quick succession Rudy falls for beaten wife Kelly (Claire Danes) and takes on the case of Donny Ray Black (Johnny Whitworth) being denied medical care to treat his leukaemia on wanton grounds.

Did bedbound Donny Ray stir memories of his polio? Did his heartbreaking death rouse thoughts of Gio? There was always more to Coppola's choices.

As befits the formula, Rudy will take on the insurance giant, defended by oil slick corporate lawyer Leo F. Drummond (Jon Voight), and have his day in court.

Maybe not to the transformative heights of *The Godfather*, but Coppola found his old self in this routine potboiler. You can see it in the lovely, rough-edged feel for character. You can see it in the use of hot and bothered Memphis locations, where they filmed over Christmas 1996. You can see it in the daring little choices he makes to elevate the material. Calling up Elmer Bernstein – it had been a while – to provide a 1950s-style, jazz-inflected score. You can see it in the moral uncertainty that infects the law. Justice can be a matter of the highest bidder. You can hear it in Rudy's sardonic narration, care of Michael Herr, capturing the dilemmas of his calling.

He got up his old tricks. Before a scene where Rudy gets fired, Coppola took Damon aside. Listen, he deadpanned, the studio is so unhappy with the rushes they are thinking of replacing you with Edward Norton. Before star witness Virginia Madsen was cross-examined on the stand, he got the cast to hurl insults at her. And he wasn't beyond throwing out the book. For the courtroom showdown, he realised Rudy's path to victory was too easy. So he rewrote forty pages, legalese and all, adding a series of missteps to stall the hero's progress. Unimpressed actors were required to relearn reams of dialogue.

Damon was an excellent choice. Rudy is the most straightforwardly decent character Coppola had ever put on screen, and he wanted that hint of James Stewart, or Michael Corleone before the fall. The studio was pushing for Sean Penn or Norton, provocateur types who could be hard to handle. DeVito, Voight, Danes, Rourke, Madsen, Roy Scheider, Dean Stockwell, and an uncredited Danny Glover – as the judge with a soul – provide that old ensemble charge.

Maybe it was too charming, or too off-beam, or maybe the Grisham wave had peaked. For Coppola's fine adaptation – arguably the best of the Grishams – did only a mediocre $45 million in business.

Of course, life would get in on the act. While Coppola shot a courtroom thriller about the little man against the corporate behemoth, his *Pinocchio* saga with Warner landed its designated day in court. He would win $20 million in compensatory damages, and $80 million in punitive (an entire budget, maybe two). But in another boom and bust, Warner used their deep coffers to appeal the ruling, and he ended up with nothing. Which is not so different from the outcome of *The Rainmaker*.

Late one night in Paris, while promoting *The Rainmaker*, Coppola and Eleanor strolled past a cinema. There was a midnight screening of Luc Besson's loose-limbed science-fiction blockbuster *The Fifth Element*, and a queue was already forming. On a whim, they joined, buying crepes from a nearby street vendor.

The film had panache, something appealingly European and decadent in its approach to the *Star Wars* formula, although it made little sense. Eleanor's brother Bill Neil had been Director of Photography for Visual Effects.

Outside, a group of young people approached them. Their elected leader addressed Coppola firmly, "We are film students. I want to be a director. Your films have influenced me most of any director. I see them over and over, but why did you make *Jack*?"

Crossing the street by their apartment, another young man plucked up the courage to approach Coppola.

"My favourite film of yours is *Rusty James*," he said, citing the French title for *Rumble Fish*. "...Why did you do *Jack*?"

The next morning, Coppola brooded over the encounters. Why did he give himself up to these commercial movies? He hadn't written an original script since *The Conversation*. Hollywood was now hell-bent on concept films, where all that mattered was to land the right star. The director could be anyone.

Eleanor attempted to console him, quoting one of Brando's improvisations from *Apocalypse Now*: "...to be free from the opinions of others."

He shakes his head sadly. "But it's my opinion too. I've let them down; worse, I've let myself down. I should have been writing original work all along."

PART II
SOFIA

CHAPTER 10

THE NEW BRATS

The Virgin Suicides (1999), CQ (2001)

She was always so wary of the inevitable labels. Still is – *daddy's* girl. And there was that streak of teenage rebellion. So no, she didn't want to be a director. "Everyone in my family worked in film so it made me less inclined to." Sofia Coppola was proud to be different. Doing her own thing: actress, photographer, model, fashion designer, icon – uncertain which suited her best.

But it came, that urge. That affliction. And there was no escape. She had to make *this* film.

The novel had been recommended by Thurston Moore, the lead singer of Sonic Youth, who was part of her hip Los Angeles scene. She loved how the cover was just ribbons of golden hair fringed in shadow.

Jeffrey Eugenides's *The Virgin Suicides* whispered secrets to Coppola, things she knew to be true. This was the story of the five Lisbon sisters, as blonde and ethereal as angels, who live with their strict Catholic parents in the leafy suburbs of Grosse Point, Michigan, back in the sun-bleached 1970s. And it was the story of the boys that watched them, and loved them, and despaired when one by one they committed suicide.

Straightaway, she knew how it would look. How it would feel. The film leapt into her head with a certainty that evaded her father. She began writing a script in secret. It was a private project, only for fun. In fact, she would just try the first chapter; she could see it so clearly. "I wasn't planning on showing anyone or even finishing it, but before I knew it, I'd written the whole script for something I didn't have the rights to, which is something you're never supposed to do."

Timing was key. Where her father had once been thunderstruck by Eisenstein, after years of denial and doubt, trying things that never stuck, at twenty-seven Coppola had started to realise who she was.

This was 1998, the same year she had made her first short *Lick the Star*, and realised she knew how to do this. Some kind of osmosis had occurred from all that time spent on set of her father's great productions, and having listened to George Lucas and Steven Spielberg and Werner Herzog and Akira Kurosawa or any of the celebrated directors who ate at their table. "We were always there with the adults, playing, talking, listening," she recalled. That was the Italian way.

With its high school rituals and waspish clique of mean girls, *Lick the Star* points the way toward *The Virgin Suicides*, *Marie Antoinette*, *The Bling Ring*, even elements of *The Beguiled*. It also featured her cousin Robert Schwartzman, who would appear in her feature debut.

Directing was making sense.

Then came the heartbreak. She found that the rights to *The Virgin Suicides* had been snapped up, and a script was already being written by Nick Gomez (*Laws of Gravity*). Someone else was making her film. Find something else, her father advised, that way it won't tear you apart.

But word got out that the production company, Muse, were unhappy with Gomez's script – it was too dark. She didn't wait on ceremony, pushing Muse for a meeting. Did the name help? Did it get her in the room? Whatever the case, she made her pitch. It needed a female touch, her touch. Not only should they take her script, they should let her direct. She knew how this film felt.

Written in a lush, almost musical voice, *The Virgin Suicides* chimed with Coppola's experience of being a teenager: the longing, the melancholy, and the mystery of sexuality. She connected with all the lazing around in bedrooms; the tentative first encounters with boys. Each of the Lisbon girls needed their own outward appearance. That was important, she said, for we see them through the eyes of the local boys. They are forever elusive. We will never know why they did it.

She knew her themes: the way we are shaped by time and memory, and the unfathomable. This was to be a ghost story, and an art film for teenagers.

With a budget of $6.1 million, she was given her chance.

The story is recounted by one of those bewildered, lustful boys grown into a man (he has the voice of Giovanni Ribisi). How back then they worshipped the teenage Lisbon girls: Cecilia (Hanna R. Hall), Mary (A.J. Cook), Bonnie (Chelse Swain), Therese (Leslie Hayman), and the central girl, promiscuous Lux (Kirsten Dunst).

Aside from being one of the few young stars not put off by the word suicide, there was a depth behind Dunst's eyes she liked. She was like a doomed cheerleader, beautiful but faraway. Lux was the sister Coppola could see herself in. That was true of Dunst too.

The suicides begin with Cecilia (on the second attempt). "You're too young to know how bad life gets," insists the doctor. "Obviously, doctor, you've never been a 13-year-old girl," retorts Cecilia. She will leap from a second-floor window. Lux will have a foolhardy romance with school heart-throb Trip Fontaine (Josh Hartnett), and the girls will fatefully attend prom.

Kathleen Turner and James Woods play the girls' paranoid parents, both against type. Coppola knew Turner, they had been sisters in *Peggy Sue Got Married*, and she wanted this unyielding woman to have "a certain amount of sympathy". They are victims and villains. After she got Woods, who really committed to the story, the financing fell into place.

After a curfew is broken, the Lisbon parents will take their elf-like daughters out of school and beyond reach. Confined to the house, they call the boys, sharing records over the telephone line: Carole King, Todd Rundgren, and ELO, the music charting their moods. Then they decide on a suicide pact and invite the boys to find them.

Only much later did Coppola realise that she had made a film about Gio. His death when she was only fifteen, she said, "gave me a connection to *The Virgin Suicides*." It was the story of the sister who went on ahead and called to her siblings from beyond the grave. And it was the story about those who were left behind.

Stung by the response to *The Godfather Part III*, Coppola had retreated from the limelight, returning to college, choosing the California Institute of Arts in Los Angeles where she studied art, before trying photography. She developed connections with the fashion labels, having interned with Chanel at the age of fifteen. She was not naturally glamorous, nor did she seek it out, like a runway model, or pop star, or actress. But her reserved beauty and intelligence made her hip and mysterious. "She is beautiful in an imperfect way," said Eleanor, a compliment only a mother could give. You could never quite know what she was thinking; only that she spent a lot of time behind her dark eyes.

Francis recalled going to some party during the shooting of *The Cotton Club* in 1980s New York, walking into a room and finding his eleven-year-old daughter sitting on Andy Warhol's lap, deep in conversation. Coppola has a Marc Jacobs handbag named in her honour. It all seemed preordained.

She worked for Karl Lagerfeld's studios in Paris and took pictures for *Vogue* and *Interview.* "Every girl goes through a photography phase," says Charlotte in *Lost in Translation.* "Take dumb pictures of your feet."

The limelight was done with her. In 2001, she was chosen as the face of Marc Jacobs' new fragrance. She was pictured at Paris fashion shows, magazines talked about what she was wearing, and how easily she wore it.

Still, she swore off acting after the backlash of *The Godfather Part III*, though featured as a handmaiden in George Lucas's *Star Wars: Episode I – The Phantom Menace* (a sci-fi pudding that found more profound ways to crash its legacy). She and best friend Zoe Cassavetes (who carried the burden of having John Cassavetes as her father) tried their own cable talk show called *Hi Octane*, dashing round Hollywood meeting their cool friends. It lasted four episodes.

And there were paparazzi-magnet boyfriends like Keanu Reeves and Anthony Kiedis of The Red Hot Chili Peppers. And with them came a patina of gossip and intrusion, photographers at her gate. But it never seemed her – the celebrity. As of 1998, she was dating Spike Jonze, a hip new filmmaker fresh out of the video scene being feted by the studios.

With her mother's sleek, outré poise and father's gravitational pull, Coppola became a generational icon.

Could she do it? Francis had worried for his daughter. "She's a slip of a girl," he said, but he also worried that she had a personality big enough to deal with what filmmaking would throw at her. Yet he had always shared his wisdom as if he expected her to follow in his footsteps. Passing on what he knew.

"I remember being eleven or something," said Coppola, "and [my father] talking about story structure. He made these notepads, breaking down the story, and he'd give them to us. What other guy would be talking to his eleven-year-old about screenwriting?"

As filming loomed, Eleanor recalled a conversation between father and daughter at the old Polo Lounge of the Beverly Hills Hotel, a relic swarming with Hollywood ghosts.

"I want the camera to be static, not move around," says the daughter.

"So use a forty-millimetre lens. I shot the whole *Godfather* with that," replies the father. "Beware of high angles or low angles. Say the actress stands up, do you want the camera to pan up? No, you don't want to be looking up her nose."

Coppola takes notes from her father's lectures in a red leather agenda he had given her for Christmas. Sit next to the camera so the actors can see you're in control. Remember their hands. Hands are expressive. At some point, they both knew, she was going to have to be herself. She was so very different from him: Zen, but unshakable, introverted but confident in what she wanted. Calm, she said, doesn't mean she isn't "superopinionated" about what she does and doesn't like.

They shot through July 1998 in the balmy suburbs of Toronto, and it was still a family affair. Francis was executive producer (through Zoetrope), Roman did second unit as he always would, and Eleanor shot the documentary. This had become a ritual, a way of having her reassuring presence close to hand.

Eleanor watched with pride as Coppola gave directions to actors, and light up when she saw a performance orientate toward her intentions. She watched too as her daughter dealt with a producer reminding her of the schedule or the budget, as if profligacy might be a family trait. And she saw the relief when a less than co-operative actor completed their allotted time.

Coppola was good with an old pro like Woods. Knowing when to apply the charm. "Less *jambon* for the next take, please," she would joke if he got a little broad. On his last day she presented the actor with a tin of canned ham mounted on a trophy base, and he laughed like a gutter.

She was born to this.

It was scrappy. She had a month to find the film in her head. The pressure never went away, but the images came.

That style arrived fully formed. She was mixing opposing forces: suburban malaise and teenage desire. The ordinary infused with the magical. Suburbia was a world she had never known, and her research took her to William Eggleston, Bill Owens, and what she termed, "the hazy, backlit style of 1970s *Playboy* photography." That specificity came from her training in art and photography. The movies offered the Spielbergian romanticism of sunsets and lawn sprinklers, and *Picnic at Hanging Rock*, *Badlands*, and *Rumble Fish* – elegies to doomed youth.

"When you direct," she said, "is the only time you get to have the world exactly as you want it."

Easy-going cinematographer Edward Lachman had worked on *Desperately Seeking Susan* and *Far From Heaven*, so he knew angst and yearning. Coppola told him she wanted to convey how strong that feeling was when you first fall in love, and he put the glint in Lux's blue eyes when she first sees Trip. They would leave the camera running on those languorous shots of the girls draped around their rooms like Pre-Raphaelite mean girls. Only when they got bored did the little, natural details come out. That was when they stopped acting. Finally, she called upon French pop stylists Air to extend the aura of detachment with their haunted synths, reminding us that the story is being recalled from a far-off present.

When Coppola put it before an audience for the first time it was in Cannes, as part of the debut strand Director's Fortnight. That was nerve-wracking. Her eyes were glued to the audience, until Faye Dunaway's cell phone went off. But the reviews were good. Venerated French critical journal *Cahiers du Cinéma*, nursery of Truffaut and Godard, even placed it in their top ten of the year.

The film was picked up and squandered by Paramount Classics (that studio never knew what they had with this family), making only $10 million on its release.

Coppola remained humble. "I have fond memories of it just not being a total disaster."

Far from it, with time, a cult has grown up around the raptures of *The Virgin Suicides* – new generations of teens drawn to it like a siren call.

By contrast, Roman Coppola made his directorial debut in 2001 with an in-jokey ode to the lunacy of filmmaking and eternal chic of France in the 1960s. The hero is a tense, ex-pat American editor turned director who might be a cypher for Roman Coppola. But it is really a film about his father.

With a first-time movie, he reasoned, "you make it about a world you are familiar with."

While fully immersed in the industry – as second-unit director, writer, producer, and special effects technician – Roman has only ever directed two feature films. Which comes as a shame, as he revealed an urge to explore and satirise the artform that consumes his family.

Though shot in Luxembourg in November 2000, *CQ* (Morse Code for "seek you") is set in Paris – the city of Roman's birth – in 1969. This is where we catch up with the calamitous production of *Codename: Dragonfly*, the latest in a series of science-fiction baubles, with icy-blonde model-turned-actress Angela Lindvall (his sister's suggestion) playing model-turned-actress Valentine, who plays Moon-bound secret agent Dragonfly.

Roman affectionately pulls back the curtain on a specific era of shag-carpet, sci-fi, impersonating the comic-book psychedelia of a semi-clad Jane Fonda cavorting about the galaxy in *Barbarella* and the clunky-cool secret-agent dash of *Danger: Diabolik*. A fact doubly underlined by the presence of John Philip Law, who starred in both, as Dragonfly's in-movie nemesis the Chairman.

"This movie is my 1960s movie," declared Roman, "the *Barbarella* kitsch-stuff on the one hand, and then Godard and Antonioni on the other, where filmmakers were making uncompromising, personal expressions."

With director Andrezej (Gerard Depardieu) fired for having artistic intentions, and his Polanski-like replacement (Jason Schwartzman) laid-up with a broken leg having failed to negotiate a Paris roundabout, the task of finishing the film falls to the editor Paul (Jeremy Davis). But Paul too is afflicted with aspirations toward meaningful, personal films in heavy-duty black and white. We are granted slivers of the first-person auto-documentary he is shooting in his bathroom, Roman's homage to *David Holzman's Diary,* Jim McBride's faux documentary from 1967 about a filmmaker caught in a creative crisis.

Is art really more worthwhile than spaceships? That is the question.

Roman's Paris demi-monde overflows with egotistical cineastes, revolutionaries, charlatans, models, and know-all producers, but he sees only this mad Shangri-La of filmmaking. Tribute is paid to Antonioni, Godard, and Fellini's self-conscious classic *8 ½.* Any resemblance between Giancarlo Giannini's swaggering Italian producer and *Barbarella* (and Fellini) producer Dino De Laurentiis is entirely deliberate. And if all this pretentious agonising over art and commerce has a familiar ring, that is because at heart *CQ* is a film about growing up in the shadow of Francis Ford Coppola.

Paul aspires to personal expression but has little choice but to do his best with studio trash. Andrezej is a visionary with radical ideas and a thunderous temper. He demands that his movie end, "not with a bang but with a whimper." The framed section of dented wall he displays is the actual segment of wall Francis put his fist through on *The Godfather.* The central joke is that no one can figure out an ending to this cheeseball sci-fi movie.

The irony spilled into life. *CQ* also premiered at Cannes, in 2001, where it gained appreciative reviews: though what, if anything, it all added up to no one was entirely sure. Wouldn't you know, 2001 was the year Francis returned to the scene of the crime with *Apocalypse Now Redux.* There was only one Coppola headline in town.

"It probably, in retrospect, didn't help my movie because people like to react and compare," reflected Roman with characteristic equanimity. With the release delayed to 2002 – as distributor United Artists dealt with financial woes dating back to the original release of *Apocalypse Now* – *CQ* disappeared at the box office.

To be a Coppola is to accept the name. Roman knew there would always be "extra scrutiny" on what he was doing. You couldn't just take a car chase movie or a horror sequel and think who gives a damn –

the magnifying glass would come. That made it doubly important to do things from the heart.

Still, you wonder why he hasn't directed more. The urge wouldn't take him again until 2012, with the 1970s-set break-up fable *A Glimpse Inside the Mind of Charles Swan III*. Was the seal set when he slipped without hesitation into Gio's place on *Gardens of Stone*? Was that then his designated role? To be reliably stationed at the side of his father or sister as they went about their superstar business? Was he the family consigliere?

That sells him short. Roman had the entrepreneurial urge. He diversified. Setting up his own production company in 1994 – The Director's Bureau. "It was sort of a romantic notion," he said, sounding not unlike his father, "like 1920s Paris, or the Beat era in the '50s. And even the name, The Director's Bureau, had a bit of intrigue to it that I liked, like the FBI or something…"

With The Director's Bureau you see the original Zoetrope spirit adapt to the times: commercials, music videos, marketing, and what he called "concepting". Roman moved into a future where the line between the purity of the filmmaker and the jack-of-all-media was blurring. He shot videos for The Strokes, Daft Punk, and Fatboy Slim; he designed and sold bespoke tote bags through the Pacific Tote Company.

In middle age, sporting designer suits and tinted lenses, his thick Coppola locks and beard tending to the unruly, he has cultivated the aura of a flamboyant Italian producer from the 1960s in search of genius. But he has less of his father's ringmaster bluster, and more of his mother's quiet obduracy.

By 2021, he had collaborated with Wes Anderson on five occasions, including joining the dapper director and cousin Jason Schwartzman to dash around India – without pampering – to map out a story for *The Darjeeling Limited*. Anderson nicknamed the dependable, versatile, unflappable Roman "Swiss Army knife".

And Roman was the first Coppola to venture into the heady world of modern television. In 2014, he developed (with cousin Jason) and directed four episodes of *Mozart in the Jungle* for Amazon Studios. Harkening to that other family legacy, the four-season show captured the behind-the-scenes intrigues of the New York Symphony Orchestra.

Surely most significantly, Francis handed over ownership of American Zoetrope to his two children, which Roman now oversees from those same offices in The Sentinel Building in San Francisco. Despite all the financial earthquakes, the company has endured. And it is Roman who is at the head of the family business (you've got to watch the quiet ones); all of his father's and sister's films fall under his purview.

There remains a special bond between brother and sister. They grew up on movie sets. Which was thrilling, but there were rarely other kids around. They learned to depend on each other. After Gio, it was the two of them. Roman will always be there on Coppola's sets, directing second unit, backing up her vision. "He knows what I like," she said, as if it was a sixth sense. Sofia named her first child Romy after her brother.

In its more chilled and less political (then so was America in the 1990s) way, history was repeating. Coppola and her brother were classified as members of a new breed of Brat – a generation raised on (and raised by) the Movie Brats of the 1970s. Rather than film schools, they came out of the world of commercials, music videos, fashion and photography, but with much the same aim as their predecessors – to fashion original movies. They shared their dreams at Sundance and Cannes. With one foot in the studio system and one in a buoyant indie scene (Miramax! New Line! October!) they challenged the orthodoxy to shape a decade or more of vivid expression.

The Coppolas' immediate peers were the hipster band of Jonze, Anderson, Cassavetes, Paul Thomas Anderson, Alexander Payne, and Noah Baumbach. But this minor key revolution included Quentin Tarantino, Todd Haynes, David Fincher, Steven Soderbergh, and David O. Russell. They had their own books, their own controversies, their own mythology: Peter Biskind's *Down and Dirty Pictures*, Sharon Waxman's *Rebels on the Backlot*.

These were the more self-conscious and less self-destructive (and sometimes literal) heirs to the Coppolas, Scorseses, and Spielbergs. But they had their own sensibility. The New Brats were whimsical and mischievous, playing their postmodern games with structure and style. They weren't grappling with Vietnam or Nixon, or their very souls. They grappled with genre. They had soundtracks not scores. Defining an era with the likes of *Pulp Fiction, Three Kings, Boogie Nights, Fight Club, Traffic, Rushmore,* and *Sideways.*

"People have to find these scenes to fit you into, really. It makes it easier to write about you, I guess," sighed Coppola, always happier to be out of the loop. She accepted there is a shared aesthetic with her peers, like Godard, Truffaut, and the French New Wave, but the only thing that mattered was the next film.

In June 1999, as Coppola edited *The Virgin Suicides* and Jonze finished *Being John Malkovich,* they tied the knot on the bucolic lawns of her parents' Napa Valley estate. With an unending supply of the finest wines, two generations of filmmaking rebels mixed. Francis and George Lucas sizing up Russell and Baumbach. The hippest filmmaking couple of their generation was serenaded by the gravelly tones of Tom Waits. It wouldn't last.

CHAPTER 11

TOKYO DRIFT

Lost in Translation (2003)

Ross Katz called from the airport. "The Eagle has landed," he said, and she felt a rush of elation and relief so pronounced she could have been high. Filmmaking could flow through your veins like a drug. But there was no time to savour the pleasure, she had a movie to make in less than a calendar month, and a movie star in the traffic headed for his hotel.

Sofia Coppola had gambled everything on Bill Murray. And even now, with preproduction underway in Tokyo, she had no way to be certain he would arrive. He didn't sign contracts. He looked you in the eye and made a promise. "He'll show up," Wes Anderson had assured her. He had learned to decipher his gnomic foibles on *Rushmore*, one of the many who had endeavoured to open a pipeline of communication with the elusive star.

Katz was a rising star on the independent scene, having produced *Happiness* and *In the Bedroom*. The former DJ had begun his career as a grip on *Reservoir Dogs*. He and Coppola had the same mix of unassuming and iron determination. At their first meeting, she put it in simple terms: "Bill Murray is my leading man." The movie was inconceivable without him. She pictured him in a tuxedo, and a kimono. If he turned them down, she would abandon the project.

The snag was there was no simple way of even getting a script to Murray. He had an agent but made it a point of pride to avoid his calls. For a year she gave chase. Letters, answerphone messages, notes passed through mutual acquaintances – it was like dealing with an ex. Associate Producer Mitch Glazer, who had fallen for *Lost in Translation* after reading the ten-page treatment with a cover page of Kate Moss shot from behind, had known Murray for twenty years. He sent the script then called. "This is going to change your life," he said. But Murray would only talk baseball.

Every phone call from Coppola's father began with the same question. "Have you heard from Bill?"

Did Murray comprehend that he was up against one of the most tenacious forces in film with the Coppola family?

Finally: serendipity. Glazer and his wife, the actress Kelly Lynch, meet Murray for dinner at Il Cantinori in New York. They have been at a funeral together, but Glazer has to tell him that Sofia is in town.

"Call her," says Murray.

Coppola is on her way to a play.

"Just get here," says Glazer.

She flew across New York and virtually landed in Murray's lap. This was her moment, and she gave it everything: flirtation, compliments, and jokes, while drip-feeding him descriptions of the film she wanted to make. It was another virtuoso display of Coppola persuasion, and Murray drank it in. They were instantly at ease in one another's company.

The group went on to an Austrian restaurant for dessert, where Coppola and Murray began swapping ideas. The actor pitched a scene where his character is bamboozled by a treadmill. Back walking the streets like lovebirds, she mentioned she had never driven in the city and he tossed her his car keys. She stored that up for *On the Rocks*, her second film with Murray.

Into her life came that moon-like face, gently cratered, a map of the soul you can never fully decipher. We are reminded of Brando, skirting the obvious, drawing us close. Murray, the runic marvel, was about to have his greatest moment. "Watching Bill Murray in Sofia Coppola's *Lost in Translation*," effused *Slate*'s David Edelstein, "I felt as if I were seeing his face for the first time... This is the Bill Murray performance we've been waiting for: *Saturday Night Live* meets Chekhov."

How do you explain Murray? Can you explain Murray? He was alien to this world from the very beginning. Or is it the other way around – the only sane man in an insane universe? As if *Ghostbusters* or *Groundhog Day*, the blockbuster comedies that had brought this actor from Evanston, Illinois unwanted adoration, were closer to reality than you think.

Coppola had adored him as the depressed tycoon in Anderson's bittersweet *Rushmore*. It was like a second coming – no more elephants or marshmallow ghosts or days on repeat, just him. She loved how you were never quite sure what was going on inside his head. Murray's gift is to always be somewhere else. That is why he was a perfect fit for Tokyo and Coppola, and her study in alienation. *Lost in Translation* was a film about lost souls. This was casting as narrative.

"I thought if you were going to put yourself on the line," he told her, "I would too."

Nevertheless, months later, when her producer headed to pick up her leading man from Narita International Airport, she held her breath. There were a lot of foreign distributors hanging on his arrival.

With *Lost in Translation*, both Murray and Coppola reached an apex in their careers. This was a very modern masterpiece, and a deeply personal mission. There was no source novel. It was one from the heart. "The film is a memory of something that only lasts a short time yet stays with you forever." This was the shorthand Coppola developed for talk shows and interviews – always faced with that most agonising of all questions: what is your film about?

To elaborate: it is about Murray's Bob Harris, an ageing actor on the downslope of his career and marriage, who has come to Tokyo to shoot a whisky commercial. And it is about Scarlett Johansson's Charlotte, a recently married Yale grad, neglected by her husband, a showbiz photographer in town to shoot a rock band.

"It's two characters going through a similar personal crisis, exacerbated by being in a foreign place," explained Coppola. "Trying to figure out your life in the midst of all that…"

It is about what happens when they meet, crossing paths in the midnight bar of the Park Hyatt Hotel.

A memory: of 1976, and returning to the Philippines for the family business, a Sisyphean struggle known to all as *Apocalypse Now*, the Coppolas take a brief stop in Hong Kong. They have a suite in the Peninsula Hotel. Up in the palatial eyrie are bouquets of roses, television sets, vast marble bathrooms, and a butler on call. They are insulated from the city. As night falls, it becomes a shimmering carpet of Christmas lights. Neon signs advertise Sony, Sanyo, and Gucci. Her father goes shopping for the latest gadgets. Her mother buys embroideries. Sofia is five and makes Santa beards out of cotton buds.

Lost in Translation has its deepest roots in Coppola's peripatetic childhood following her father's creative pursuits: city-by-city, country-by-country, suite-by-suite. She woke up in so many hotels and watched her lonely mother drift with her father's tides.

Another memory: of 1991 and driving through dense Tokyo traffic. Eleanor and Sofia are headed for what has been billed as the most expensive hotel in the city, the Park Hyatt. Sofia has come to Japan to publicise *The Godfather Part III* with her father. Their suite is on the top floor. The room is filled with bouquets, including one from Akira Kurosawa. By night, the living room is filled with a neon glow from the signs on the buildings opposite. "Fuji Bank, Kawai, Panasonic, Sogo, Dentsu," recalled Eleanor, "blinking in the cityscape."

She also remembered the melancholy that settled over her. "Once again I was tagging along in Francis's life and now also Sofia's."

By the late 1990s, Japan had become a frequent destination for Coppola. Flying in and out of Narita, the city a theme park. She had been invited to a fashion show, where she got talking to potential business partners, which led to the founding of the Milkfed brand: designer T-shirts and streetwear exclusive to Japan. She soon opened a Tokyo store.

Like the family wine business, fashion gave her a financial backbone. She didn't need to rely on filmmaking. That way, she could make whatever she wanted.

So she flew into Tokyo for business meetings. Including a promotional visit for *The Virgin Suicides*, she must have returned six or seven times in the space of two years. Once she could afford it, she stayed at the Park Hyatt, with its unlikely New York-themed jazz bar looking out over those *Blade Runner* skylines from forty storeys up. "This silent floating island in the middle of Tokyo," she said.

Coppola's local guide was fashion editor Fumihiro Hayashi, though he liked to go by the name "Charlie Brown". Through his eyes, she got to know the secret side of the city: basement bars, karaoke joints, places that were gone when she next returned. They would end up singing late into the night. Hayashi always picking "God Save the Queen", and the sight of him consumed by the punk anthem was planted in her brain: "That was one of the first images I wanted to make a movie around."

We find Hayashi in the movie emoting "God Save the Queen" in the glorious karaoke sequence. Coppola staged it as a party, letting the actors sing what they wanted. Though it was her idea for Murray to do Roxy Music's "More Than This" just to see how he would cope with that ridiculous high note on the opening line. His awkwardness is another human touch – half Murray, half Bob.

Back in those early trips, Coppola would return to the shimmering hotel and feel the loneliness and abstraction high above the city. Hotel rooms were like movie sets. They shared the same indeterminate space – a hyperreal yet finite experience. "A weird oasis where your life doesn't exist," said Coppola. Staged living. But they also had this way of bringing life into focus. They act as amplifiers of the heart. "Things are distorted, exaggerated," she said. "You're jet-lagged and contemplating your life in the middle of the night."

She would sit by the window and see her reflection gazing back at her. Images began to be stored up, twinned with songs on her iPod. She thought of two people, strangers in a strange land, who meet in a hotel and make a connection. A script began to take shape – a romance, possibly, between two very different, culturally alienated individuals adrift in the Park Hyatt.

"The camaraderie of foreigners," she called it. "They meet, they break up." A lifetime would go by in a week.

One, Sofia now knew, would be Murray.

The other character was still vague; maybe because it was her.

Returning home to Los Feliz, she began writing her unclassifiable movie. At first, she laboured, even with the support of Roman. After twenty unsatisfactory pages, she knew her environment was wrong. She couldn't write this script from home, and leapt on a flight for Tokyo, booked into the Hyatt, and let herself drift on the currents of the city, shooting video, taking photographs – assembling an image bank from which the script would spring.

She loved the way Western culture infiltrated Tokyo: you would see posters of Kevin Costner or Harrison Ford, or Brad Pitt's face on a vending machine, advertising coffee and beer, and find all these Western hits on the karaoke menus. There was this surreal fusion of worlds. "It was a little embarrassing," she knew, and would subtly poke fun at such juxtapositions. That's one of the film's themes – this insinuation of the West, just as Playboy Bunnies had invaded Vietnam in *Apocalypse Now*.

In 1979, her father agreed to join his hero Kurosawa (during the shooting of *Kagemusha*) in a Japanese commercial – for Suntory whisky. To which his daughter pays wry homage with Murray as Bob, bound into a tuxedo, shooting his $2-million whisky commercial. "For relaxing times," he says, raising a glass, "make it Suntory time." Barely able to contain her laughter, Coppola feeds names to the fictional director to throw at him – Dean Martin! Joey Bishop! – and Murray responds with pitch perfect impressions.

Coppola has that magpie tendency to pick from culture touchstones like a songbook in a karaoke joint. There are clear movie inspirations. David Lean's *Brief Encounter*, with Celia Johnson and Trevor Howard the passing strangers as fragile as a porcelain vase. She liked the dynamic between Humphrey Bogart and a much younger Lauren Bacall in *The Big Sleep*. The way their flirtation moved like a dance, but the explicit sexual element confused her – that didn't seem to fit, not exactly. She wanted the meandering sensation of Michelangelo Antonioni's neo-realist classic *L'Avventura*, which did away with plot, but never lost your interest. And the way Chinese director Wong Kar-wai's *In the Mood for Love*, "has the feeling of being on the verge of something happening."

Together, Bob and Charlotte, the sleepless couple, watch *La Dolce Vita* on a hotel room television: Federico Fellini's fabled derivé through the Roman night.

The slender budget of $4 million was financed through foreign distribution deals. Only once she had a first cut did Focus Features pick it up for the U.S.. She didn't want studio backing, because she wasn't willing to change a thing. She needed to be lean, but this way she got the final say. "Sofia is made of steel," said Murray, admiringly. But it wasn't about power so much as freedom.

When the script was finished it was barely seventy pages long, sending a ripple of concern among the financers. Was there a film there? There was, of course, but most of it was still in Coppola's head. What was half a page in the script – Charlotte walks alone in Kyoto – ended up as a four-minute sequence.

It's another treasure among many: Johansson's Charlotte numbly drifting between Buddhist temples and imperial palaces to an ethereal wash of synth and guitar provided by Air.

She worried that it was narcissistic, but she related to Charlotte. "It's her demeanour; she's understated, not extroverted and hyper," claimed Coppola. Indirectly, or not, she was putting herself on the screen, as she had with Lux in *The Virgin Suicides*. Johansson caught on straightaway: "Sofia bleeds through the characters."

Maybe a touch more movie star, but Johansson even looked like Coppola: plump-lipped, waif-like, and uneasily pretty, with a habit of letting her gaze drift into the distance. Solemnity suits them, but those rare smiles are like sunshine.

Coppola had remembered Johansson's poise from the indie drama *Manny & Lo*, when she was only eleven, and she had been coolly blasé in *Ghost World*, and amusingly worldly in the Coens's noir *The Man Who Wasn't There*. Not yet a superstar, she turned eighteen during the shoot, but uncannily self-possessed. That lovely, gravelled voice like Kathleen Turner really helps. Like Murray she is elusive.

Central to what makes the film work is how the two characters become intensely aware of what they mean to each other without daring to articulate it. Words like romance and love and sex don't apply. The two actors delighted in Coppola's openness: adding lines, glances, and gestures, improvising a private language.

Johansson arrived on set one day in her hotel slippers.

"Oh, you should keep those on," said Coppola – that tiny nuance of hotel life.

In interviews, the director hinted at meaningful relationships with older men that were always chaste. Charlotte's judgmental attitude was pure Coppola. As was her quick, ironic sense of humour. "It's a culmination of different stages of my life in that character," she accepted.

Coppola was a similar age to Charlotte after the mauling of *The Godfather Part III*, a time when she totally lost focus. Being a Coppola could be savage. Everything was so public. *Lost in Translation* is also taken as a Rosetta Stone for decrypting her faltering marriage to Spike Jonze, with Ribisi's self-absorbed John a cypher for her then husband. Had she felt the same desertion when he went off to make *Being John Malkovich*?

Pushed for answers from a gossip-hungry press, Coppola dissembled. "It's a compilation of a lot of people."

They were still together during production. Jonze shot a making-of documentary – he is introduced from behind the camera but never appears on screen. But there is little doubt Coppola was working through something. Charlotte can't see a way forward, abandoned in a marriage that is far from what she had expected. Bob is at the other end, wondering what his relationship amounts to as his wife faxes over renovation plans, her voice on autopilot. Is that her mother and father?

"I feel like every movie has something I'm trying to figure out, but I never really know until afterwards."

Coppola and Jonze would divorce in 2003. "I wasn't fully formed," was as much as she was willing to say.

She wanted snapshots like memories. Setting up elaborate, rigorously lit shots was both impractical and self-defeating. They would barely touch a tripod. Filming from September 29, 2002, out on the streets they would run-and-gun, slithering between permits, capturing the city with a documentary-like clarity. "Non-invasive," she demanded, and they scuttled onto the subway, cameraman and director following Johansson. That was forbidden. "We wanted to be able to throw away the map and go and do what we wanted."

Her father had once told George Lucas that one day there would be a camera small enough to let them tell their stories on the street, and that is exactly what she is doing.

"She knew the movie upside down and backward," said Katz. "She spilled it right from her head onto the screen."

This was a style to embody her themes – the way our memories work like montages. Spinning from location to location, they were on a city-bound picaresque, Truffaut and Fellini in its giddy freedom. The film is very European.

Cinematographer Lance Acord worked miracles amid the currents of Tokyo life; with no time or space to debate the issue he shot in only natural or practical light. With a tiny, mobile crew, he utilised a lightweight camera and high-speed film stock, operating himself, against the ambient glow of Tokyo's electric surfaces. It's ironic that the film it recalls from Francis's work is *One from the Heart*, a monument to artifice. Why build Tokyo on a soundstage when Acord could grab shots from the second-storey window of a Starbucks?

There are few close-ups. Coppola wanted to reveal her characters in relation to space, and people, jostled by life. They even stuck a ladder down amid the video-game chaos of Shibuya Crossing and got their shots.

They had news of rain and leapt for joy, ditching their planned interior, grabbing the equipment, and running to an intersection where there were digital screen cycled pictures of elephants and dinosaurs. Coppola wanted a shot of Charlotte in the midst of hundreds of umbrellas. There came news of a potential typhoon, the biggest since World War II (was the family cursed?), but it barely glanced the production.

She had one diktat toward tradition. It had to be shot on film. "Film gives a little bit of a distance, which feels more like a memory to me," she iterated. "Video is more present tense."

In other words, Coppola wanted nostalgia. It is as if the events of the film are being recalled. The soundtrack was equally crucial. Music was the undertow to everything, as characteristic to the world of the film as the voice-over in *Apocalypse Now*. Coppola teamed up with music producer Brian Reitzell, who had worked on *The Virgin Suicides*, to curate a collection of ambient pop that became its own success story.

Every nuance was clear to Coppola. How far it would lean into the humour of cultural misunderstanding, and when to draw back. We see the city through these dislocated characters, literally unable to translate what is being said around them. How funny and relaxed the film is, with Murray dialling down the comic gestures to hints and feints of his old persona.

While the film would thrive on improvisation and the kind of looseness that could change a location over lunch, the idea – the all-encompassing *mood* – was completely thought through. Coppola's generation revere preparation. They are control freaks, rather than out-of-control freaks.

"… A daughter growing up in war can become a great fighter," observed David Thomson in *The New Biographical Dictionary of Film*, "or someone who'd take any diversion to avoid the mad breath of conflict."

Eleanor flew out to Japan to visit her daughter, staying in the Park Hyatt. She marvelled at how much taller Murray was than any of his co-stars; he towered over the Japanese crew. But he exuded happiness. They were shooting the scene of Bob and Charlotte fleeing a bar, the furious owner pursuing them with a BB-gun. She marvelled too at how Sofia worked, "with a kind of excited ease." Roman was in position behind the second camera, her granddaughter Gia drafted in as an extra, and at the last moment Eleanor was handed a video camera for a documentary.

The entire situation amused her. "Moviemaking, which as I grew up seemed so exotic, was now a way my family spent an evening together."

Out on the street, there is a chaos that Eleanor knows well, but no desperation, no obsession. Production assistants and ADs, armed with crackling walkie-talkies, control the pedestrians, bicycles and occasional cars that filter down the lane where they are shooting. As the evening draws on, drunken businessmen wander into shots regardless.

The reviews bordered on the ecstatic. She would call her parents with updates, the publicity department already in the know. "Mom, we heard we're getting a good review from *The New York Times!*" she beamed, giddy as a child. "*Ebert and Roper* give it two thumbs up!"

Eleanor couldn't help but notice how often articles referred to the influence of the father, but she never got a mention. Even when they pointed out her daughter's "quiet strength." She remembered Italia, Francis's mother, once berating a journalist, "Don't forget, Francis got half his talent from me."

But she was thrilled when her daughter became only the third woman to be nominated for Best Director at the Oscars. She knew that a man could never have made *Lost in Translation*.

The box office followed suit. Nearly $120 million worldwide marked Coppola's arrival in that promised land of artistic and commercial success that her father gained with *The Godfather*, both at the age of thirty-two, though the two pictures, and their circumstances, couldn't be more different. In fact, the effect of *Lost in Translation* was to make Sofia *less* of a Coppola and more of her own person. Or maybe that is *more* of a Coppola. She was now the one you immediately thought of when you heard the name. Those inevitable comparisons were no longer inevitable.

Here are longueurs her father would never try. The opening shot of Johansson from behind in sheer pink panties, which caused a few prudish tongues to wag, suggested a sexual yearning in abandoned Charlotte. An erotic charge is present in her connection with Bob, but it will never heat up beyond flirtation. In their parting, there is that famous whisper that we never hear. Something so intimate even the audience is kept out.

Lost in Translation will be nominated for four Oscars in total: Best Original Screenplay, Best Director, Best Actor, and Best Picture. A familiar dance begins: the gala dinners, on-stage Q&As, interviews, ritzy ceremonies, and exhaustion. Coppola is given so many bouquets of flowers her room looks like a funeral parlour. It doesn't suit her – the parade.

On the night, she and her father present Best Adapted Screenplay together. "Welcome the only sixty-four-year-old man and thirty-two-year-old woman not dating each other," quips host Billy Crystal. Francis drops a lame joke in a lame Italian accent about always wanting his daughter to be part of the "family business." But it's an emphatic moment. The Coppola dynasty is on display. When she wins for Best Original Screenplay, her father is the first to spring to his feet. "Every writer needs a muse," she says, letting that smile free, "and mine was Bill Murray."

CHAPTER 12

FOUNTAINS OF YOUTH

Marie Antoinette (2006), Youth Without Youth (2007)

The story goes that she was booed at Cannes. Fists were raised, feet were stomped, angry whistles and vituperative comments filled the stuffy air. How they hated *Marie Antoinette*. Which wasn't quite true, but it made for a great headline. Sofia Coppola loses her head at the Cannes Film Festival. Her overblown, overpriced biopic of the notorious French queen was laughed out of court.

"It was very French," she recalled, her Zen poise unchecked, but the hint of a pout. "There was a standing ovation too. I think the booing was not really that loud."

It was also very Coppola.

Liberation called the film a scandal. "History is merely decor and Versailles a boutique hotel for the jet set, past and present," fumed Agnes Poirier, missing that this was the point.

Marie Antoinette is a smoothly seditious piece of work – a period film with Bow Wow Wow's spunky punk anthem "I want Candy" cheering on the crackpot decadence of French aristocracy. It was indeed another film about luxurious hotels (née palaces), and loneliness, and disconnection, with the added spice that it was set between the years 1770 to 1792.

"I set out to challenge myself with each movie and having to do a period film was a huge challenge," said Coppola. "How to do it in a fresh way, and from the point of view of a strange girl in a strange world. If you attempt something new, it's always a risk."

That sounds familiar.

She had been writing *Marie Antoinette* before *Lost in Translation*, taken with Lady Antonia Fraser's revisionist biography of the Dauphine, wife to the future King Louis XVI of France, trapped in a vice of pomp and ceremony while revolution stirred (here no more than a subplot). Coppola and Fraser became friends.

"Outwardly, she's very gracious and sweet," noted the British author. "What you see is this lovely, rippling stream, but inside I suspect it's a deep, raging torrent."

There were lunches in lovely restaurants.

"Would it matter if I leave out the politics?" asked Coppola.

"Marie Antoinette would have adored that," replied Fraser.

Coppola didn't need any another sources. What fascinated both filmmaker and writer was the reality that ran beneath the standard portrayal of the callous French queen who fell victim to the guillotine. Circumventing the sensationalist stuff – no heads roll – Coppola reached for a real person, whether historically accurate or not.

"It's a history of feelings rather than a history of facts," explained Kirsten Dunst, cast as the languorous queen with a chiselled grin and eggshell blue eyes. She is good with Coppola's oblique approach to emotion – we have to look closely to see the pain. The Austrian princess was no more than a bargaining chip to assure peace between nations, carted off to Versailles to provide an heir with Jason Schwartzman's nebbish Louis-Auguste, who can barely look her in the eye let alone deposit the royal seed. That gets tongues wagging.

The film flits across the years in a series of tableau-like episodes: Marie's arrival at court; her trials in the bedroom; her disaffected drift into hedonism; and the downfall of the crown.

The withdrawal of political detail, the grand clockwork of period drama, frees Coppola to dwell on the "insulation" of a life trapped in luxury. Marie and her social class were sealed off from the outside world in the gilded labyrinth of rooms and rules that was Versailles. "It is a self-governing architectural island, like Kane's Xanadu," wrote Roger Ebert of the *Chicago Sun-Times*, who loved the film.

Coppola was handling a big cast. There were thirty named parts, an entire court. The actors were as eclectic as the shoes. Rip Torn as a randy Louis XV; Judy Davis as the officious Comtesse de Noailles; Steve Coogan as the hard-pressed Austrian Ambassador Mercy; Asia Argento as the king's scurrilous mistress Madame du Barry; and a suave Danny Huston as Marie's worldly, older brother Joseph, parachuted in to give Louis advice on picking certain locks in the bedroom. There is even a piquant cameo as a huffish aristocrat for Aurore Clement, who once haunted the French Plantation of *Apocalypse Now*.

It is a film of great finesse, but very little plot. The angry mob cited *One from the Heart*, her father's prettified extravaganza – won't this family ever learn? But that wasn't quite true either. It may lack the immediate warmth of *Lost in Translation*, but *Marie Antoinette* is poignant and heartfelt, and an often very funny satire of social mores past and present.

In a comic routine worthy of Neil Simon or Elaine May, Dunst's Marie sits naked and shivering on the edge of her bed as the privilege of placing on her undergarments is passed up the social ranks. "This is ridiculous," she cracks with Californian exasperation. Is there a better film on curtseying?

Despite being so removed in time and place from its predecessors, *Marie Antoinette* is regarded as Part III in a coming-of-age trilogy. While never wholly conscious of connections, following her intuition, the flow of images through her imagination, even Coppola accepted that this was the third part of something. There was a thematic link, and that same melancholic current.

"I feel like this is sort of the final chapter of something I was working on," she mused as if it had only now occurred to her, "it's the next step of a girl's evolution from *Lost in Translation* [where] she's on the verge of trying to find her identity. I feel like this story is her going from a girl into a woman."

Which only reinforces the sense of an autobiographical sketch beneath the ruffles and four-poster beds.

Marie Antoinette is a film about celebrity: the queen's, the director's, and the royal courts in which each grew up. By the time she was promoting the film, Coppola was thirty-five, with a child on the way, and living between New York and Paris with her musician boyfriend Thomas Mars. But she had suffered her share of unwanted attention amid the sunburst of celebrity that followed *Lost in Translation* and the end of her marriage. "I was out of my mind for a minute," she confessed. The "It Girl" thing became absurd, cameras and lies followed her everywhere, and there was an inevitably publicised fling with Quentin Tarantino.

And maybe it is a film about actresses, so rarely wanted for anything but their pretty face, costumed frames, and great hair. Hairstyling in *Marie Antoinette* was treated like a special effect. Poufs tottering like whipped cream. On set, joked producer Ross Katz, "they weren't waiting on the lighting, they were waiting on the hair!"

Comparisons were made with the meteoric rise of Scarlett Johansson after *Lost in Translation*, or Princess Diana, consumed by privilege. Marie is a person required to be a symbol. She lives this cossetted life like an 18th-century Versailles *Entourage*, surrounded by stylists and gossips, toy dogs and Manolo Blahnik slippers, multi-coloured macarons and cream cakes that receive no more attention than a dipped forefinger. Unable to express herself, Marie sinks into hollow hedonism, gambling, partying and shopping.

Everyone puts on a costume and plays a part in the theatre of Versailles. Jonathan Romney, writing in *The Independent*, drew a likeness to Stanley Kubrick's *Barry Lyndon* and *The Devil Wears Prada*. Coppola created collage books to express the film's heightened aesthetic: sherbet-like colours and modish ad-like montages segueing into naturalism as Marie grows older. She let her cast keep their accents, as the actors did in *Amadeus* (an important touchstone). "They felt like real people to me," she remembered. She let the vernacular slip into modern idiom to make it relatable. "I *love* your hair," oozes the Duchess de Polignac, played by a gorgeously LA-bitchy Rose Byrne.

We should turn momentarily to Schwartzman. He's family. Coppola claimed she had wanted her cousin for the overwhelmed Louis because of his "vulnerable and sensitive side", and when you looked at the portraits, he did have something of the Bourbon about him.

Schwartzman is the younger son of Talia Shire, and the late producer Jack Schwartzman (*Being There*), brother of Robert, nephew of Francis, cousin to Sofia and Roman, and Nicolas Cage.

Born in Los Angeles in 1980, he'd never entertained being an actor. Oh, he had done the family picnics, the little plays they put on, usually with cousin Sofia directing. He had a leading role in *Bernice Bobs Her Hair*. He was seventeen and mostly played drums when she insisted he try out for the lead in Wes Anderson's *Rushmore*.

The role of love-struck Max Fischer, as described, was a willowy fifteen-year-old prep school student who looked like a young Mick Jagger. Anderson was pleased to see that the stocky, decidedly hirsute, more Ringo Starr-like Schwartzman had at least fashioned his own blazer and school badge. And they really liked one another's sneakers. And somewhere in all of that Schwartzman got the role, was quite brilliant in the film with a bratty-but-loveable Dustin Hoffman vibe, and became a muse for Anderson (when he wasn't otherwise focused on Bill Murray).

The path was set. The Coppola trade it was. For a while, Schwartzman specialised in slackers and oddballs: *Slackers*, *I Heart Huckabees*, and the vapid horror director in Roman's *CQ*. Then Coppola asked him to play a king. Albeit the plump, myopic, prudish ruler of France in the lead-up to revolution. In other words, he was to play a slacker king.

Schwartzman flew to Paris, gained twenty-five pounds (via Uncle Eddie's Cookies), learned to ride, and generally how to comport himself as the heir apparent of Versailles. He's very good at genial neurotics, and a quietly affecting love story grows between these political pawns.

The rest is history. Judd Apatow's serious *Funny People*, one of the evil ex's in Edgar Wright's *Scott Pilgrim vs. the World*, and a songwriter in Hollywood in-joke *Saving Mr. Banks*. As well as his continued presence in such Andersonian wonders of dysfunction as *The Darjeeling Limited* (which he helped write with Roman), *Moonrise Kingdom*, *The Grand Budapest Hotel*, and *The French Dispatch* (for which he and Roman helped conceive the story).

Of the extended family, he is perhaps the most blasé about the film business. Talia took the time to raise him and his brother Robert away from the industry. Away, he said, from the vultures. "I have no memories of being on film sets, I have memories of playing baseball."

Eleanor is there for the first day of shooting in Millemont, an eighteenth-century chateau a car ride from Paris. She has been asked to do a documentary. Her fifth. "Sofia looks so small and unprepossessing to be the director of a $40-million movie," she writes in her diary that night.

"Hi mom. Can you believe it?"

The first day always feels unreal.

They are shooting Marie entering her suite of rooms for the first time. Dunst's hair is still in rollers. Coppola often giggles in delight at her performers. Stifling the laugh with a hand while they are rolling.

A month later, Francis pays a visit. They are in Versailles, in the Hall of Mirrors, and he sits quietly to the side. They are rehearsing the scene where Argento's scowling Madame du Barry purposefully collides with the Dauphine.

"…This is where the haughtiness starts," explains Coppola. "She is not going to get out of your way. It's very high school, like the Socs and the Greasers. Du Barry is definitely a Greaser."

After the first take, Sofia is laughing.

"That looked like a mosh pit slam."

That Sony willingly paid a king's ransom for an arty film about a pretentious French queen said a lot about Coppola's reputation. But if she felt the pressure of a tenfold increase in spending, she never let it show.

They shot through the spring of 2005. She called on the mercurial European gods – Antonioni! Fellini! Godard! – editing in her head as she went, filling the gap between the bare bones of the script and a film billowing with thoughts and gestures and feelings. Her films have such a smooth edge it's never clear where director ends and celluloid begins.

Schwartzman joked that his cousin was like a horse whisperer for actors. "I've never been on a set like that, where you go there and it's as if a spell has been cast."

It also said much of Coppola's reputation (in her adopted home) that she was given free rein to roam the halls of Versailles. Is this what sparked such furies among local critics, that she danced in history's actual footprints? The crew were left in terror of breaking some irreplaceable vase from 1752.

Katz insisted they "were not making a chintzy museum piece." Yet here they were, shooting in the chintziest place in the world. They thrived on such contradictions. Through Marie's eyes, the palace is lyrical, dreamy, and almost haunted, with a constant whispering layered into the sound mix.

We take the veneer of pop as part of the Coppola stylebook. The soundtrack of post punk anthems (New Order, The Cure, Siouxsie and the Banshees serenading the masked ball) that swoon behind her vivid montages not as anachronism but invocation – the karaoke in Coppola's head and heart as she directed the scene. This has the paradoxical effect of making the film feel (that all-important word) more authentic. Marie would never be aware that she is living in the past. The music that overlays her emotions channels the "now" of her life.

Fraser loved the film. "I adore the look... I thought it was magically beautiful. It's something film can do that I could never do."

Naturally, Francis was another cheerleader. "You're aware moment to moment of everything [Marie Antoinette] is feeling... It has Sofia's personality throughout, which is what I hope as filmmakers my kids would do."

Released in October 2006, *Marie Antoinette* was nonetheless viewed as a disappointment after the highs of *Lost in Translation*. It divided critics right up to the end, and while $60 million might be viewed as a good return on such a hip proposition, it's not when you are carrying a heavy budget.

Whatever her disappointment – and it has matured into a distinctive vintage – Fraser's husband, the outspoken, often disparaging British playwright Harold Pinter, was so taken with her blasphemies he wrote her a letter of appreciation.

Coppola could laugh. "If it turns out that nobody else likes it, I can still say, 'Well, at least Harold Pinter did'."

It was the longest drought of his career. Ten years had passed since he had made a film. Gossips were beginning to wonder if he had retired to his vineyards, happy to bask in the reflected glories of his talented children. What did gossips know? That mad ambition still flowed in his veins. But Francis admitted he had been struggling with director's block.

"I had spent the last several years labouring over an ambitious original screenplay that was defying my efforts to complete it," he confessed, meaning the city-sized dream of *Megalopolis*. "The project was intended to be the crowning achievement of my career..."

Crowning achievements are tough to second guess. They need the grand themes, the big stuff. In his isolation, he had taken a turn for the philosophical. What was the sum total of his life's work? What did art even achieve? Questions he wanted his epic to answer.

Which is the point Wendy Doniger, an old friend from Great Neck High – one of the flotilla of schools he had attended in his youth – recommended a book. As Professor of Religions at the University of Chicago, and having a quite brilliant mind, she was a sounding board for *Megalopolis*. *Youth Without Youth* was a novella by the metaphysical Romanian writer Mircea Eliade, a former mentor of hers. Eliade liked to chew on the big stuff: time, consciousness, love, Nazis. She thought it might help.

Francis was enthralled with this strange and complex concoction, floating somewhere between dream and science fiction and historical thriller, "not unlike an episode of *The Twilight Zone*."

The year is 1938, and the city of Bucharest, to begin with. In a fit of creative despair, elderly linguistics professor Dominic Matei (Tim Roth, bald and wrinkled) heads out in his pyjamas to kill himself only he is struck by lightning and begins to grow younger. On the advice of his doppelganger, he returns to his life's work – to discover the origin of language. With his brain also supercharged by the bolt from the blue, he can learn languages in a thrice.

In adapting the book, Francis was making a film about his own artistic dilemma: "The lightning I was hit by was this story, and it's going to make me a young experimental filmmaker."

Youth Without Youth has the architecture of American fable – *The Wizard of Oz* or *Benjamin Button* – smothered in a cloak of Kafkaesque gloom and thematic overdrive. The story crosses World War II, as the Nazis give chase, determined to extract his unbound biology. It threatens to become an espionage movie, as Matt Damon cameos as a putative American agent. Then things get really complicated. Halfway up a Swiss mountain, Matei meets the spitting image of his lost love Laura (Romanian born actress Alexandra Maria Lara), who also ends up struck by lightning. There is talk of reincarnation. Babbling in Sumerian. Any grip on reality slips away.

"I loved the way one darn thing after another kept happening," said Francis. You're reminded – in its baroque way – of his line in quest movies:

You're a Big Boy Now (sexual), *The Rain People* (responsibility), *Apocalypse Now* (mythical), and *One from the Heart* (romantic).

He was sixty-eight and joked that he had finally got his career back on track. Was his daughter rubbing off on him? He woke up to the moment. The wines and hotels provided the collateral for a $17 million production. There was nothing to stop him. He felt like a painter, or a poet. "All I needed was myself and my enthusiasm."

The plan was to shoot in Romania, using locations Eliade referred to. He led the crew from a Dodge Sprinter, an up-to-date version of the vans in which he had ploughed across America for *The Rain People*. He brought along his granddaughter Gia, now eighteen, for the family connection (and that echo of Gio), and to channel her youthful perspective. Fred Roos joined as executive producer, for old times' sake. For 85 days he crisscrossed Romania, which filled in for Switzerland, India, and Malta as well.

Out of this jubilant experience was birthed Coppola's strangest film. He was calling on those sombre gods of film history – Bertolucci! Tarkovsky! Visconti! – who took on the big stuff in their autumnal visions. This is a mystical, yearning, rambling contemplation of existence, beautifully shot (by local cinematographer Mihai Malaimare Jr. in a blend of sepia and shadow not unlike *The Godfather*) and performed with great agility by Roth and Lara. How we had missed those glorious Coppola montages. But with so much arcane soliloquising – "…I am a mutant, like a character in a science-fiction novel," imagines Matei with a nudge of satire – it ends up disappearing down a philosophical well.

Think of it as a crossover between the existential crises of *The Conversation* and the time-travelling loopiness of *Peggy Sue Got Married*. "The film is stubbornly, almost insanely, itself, and the convoluted journey it makes – from age to youth, ignorance to omniscience, despair to bliss – can't help but evoke the filmmaker's long strange trip of a career," said Dana Stevens in *Slate*, and offered a simpler solution. Could it simply be a retelling of *A Christmas Carol*: "An embittered old man travels backward in time, revisits his lost loves and abandoned dreams, and comes back with his passion for life renewed."

CHAPTER 13

INSIDE STORIES

Tetro (2009), Somewhere (2010), The Bling Ring (2013),
The Beguiled (2017)

They finish rehearsal with a masquerade. Every actor is instructed to wear the costume his or her character would have chosen. Alden Ehrenreich decides Bennie would decide on Ernest Hemingway. Vincent Gallo goes as the title character's mother *and* father. That is a sight. It is a lively evening. Drinks, food, party games, and intimate conversation, but strictly in character, with Francis Ford Coppola watching patiently from the edge of festivities. He will rewrite the last third of his new film with what he sees.

"When people engage in an improv like that for three or four hours, they're exhausted," he explained. "It's a lot of work not to be yourself."

The character becomes the actor. The film becomes the director.

Let us take a look at him – the great director at seventy. The glasses are fashionably small; he no longer hides behind them. His thinning hair is brushed back from his lined forehead, his beard silver. On set he has been seen sporting a beret or panama, his shirts buttoned up to the collar. He has the bohemian air of a modernist painter in his dotage, full of thoughts, still a rogue, but the rage has subsided. Black-and-white portraits suit him.

More important is what is going on *inside* his noble head. We need to take stock of this new mindset. After the unencumbered pleasures of *Youth Without Youth*, Francis was still intent on going back to the beginning.

"I wanted to annihilate myself – and learn it all again."

He remembered Toshiro Mifune in Kurosawa's *Yojimbo*, beaten down and rebuilding his confidence. He was rebuilding the young filmmaker he once was, scrabbling for budget, and without the crutch of extraordinary collaborators like Vittorio Storaro or Gordon Willis, with their hotel bills and plane tickets.

"I am an amateur filmmaker now," he declared proudly. "They don't have to pay me to work on a film like *Tetro* because the payment is just to participate in cinema, which is a magical medium and one you can keep learning about."

This was his reward: not to make films for money or a career, but films whose true subject was the heart and mind of the filmmaker, like Fellini or Bergman. Where *Youth Without Youth* symbolised reigniting the spark of youth, plump with Oedipal strife, *Tetro* was an exploration of his family background – the youth that created the filmmaker.

Of course, this is a relative distinction. He had been baring his soul his entire career. But where movies used to drive him insane, now they were therapy.

There was no time to lose. He had begun writing *Tetro* while *Youth Without Youth* was still in the edit – his first original screenplay for thirty-four years. He sought a dream language in the way Kubrick and Bergman had done with *Eyes Wide Shut* and *Persona*. He saw it as a chance to get more personal, to portray things even he didn't know about himself.

"Personal filmmaking is a thrilling experience," he said, "it's like posing a question you don't know the answer to. When you've made the film and it's all over, then you begin to see what the answer is."

Shot in velvety black and white to chime with those classics of sibling love and rivalry Elia Kazan's *On the Waterfront* or Luchino Visconti's *Rocco and His Brothers*, or indeed Francis Ford Coppola's *Rumble Fish* – with muted colour scenes heavy with grain reserved for flashbacks – *Tetro* takes place in Buenos Aires. Here angelic Bennie (another discovery in the radiant Ehrenreich) disembarks the cruise ship where he works (with its cogent echo of Vito Corleone arriving in New York) in search of his lost brother Tetro (Vincent Gallo).

The Tetrochinis are as dysfunctional as the Corleones, or the Coppolas. An aspiring writer, Tetro had fled New York and their contemptuous, egotistical father, the great composer Carlo (Klaus Maria Brandauer), his washed-up twin Alfie (also Brandauer), and the death of his mother in a terrible accident.

He was back in the Hofstra library channelling Greek tragedy, Eugene O'Neill, and Tennessee Williams. But they were only guides, accepting the golden coin to take him across the river. He described the writing process as "trance-like". He may not have been adapting a book, but he was adapting his own psyche, writing on the flesh of his childhood.

Carlo rages that there is only room for one genius in the family. The antagonism between twins illuminates an intense rivalry that existed between Carmine and his more successful brother Anton. Can we take Bennie to be a young Francis? And that Tetro is a thinly disguised version of August?

"Nothing like this happened, and everything is true," the director announced cryptically when the film made its debut in Cannes.

As they shot through March 2008, like *Youth Without Youth* there was no Silverfish, with everyone hanging out on set; he used cheap local crews, and cut down on extras, which cut down on the lunches. "My way is you have a smaller lunch," he laughed, "But a better one." The budget was down to $5 million. Which gave him more leeway as he shot in the bohemian district of La Boca, where the Italian immigrants had arrived after the war. That atmosphere was one of the reasons he'd chosen Argentina.

Gallo was a handful. Though he wasn't the first to struggle with the constant rehearsal, the endless tweaking of a scene in the moment. He felt his spontaneity was being diluted and had to break through his fear. Francis was back among the family rivalries of the first two *Godfather* films: the dominating patriarch, the fitful brothers, the monochromatic imagery, and languid cultural nuance. "[The] movie is alive from beginning to end," thrilled Mick LaSalle in the *San Francisco Chronicle*.

"I feel like I'm an emotional guy and my films often don't show that," said Francis. Think of all those locked-up antiheroes: Michael Corleone, Harry Caul, Willard, and even Peggy Sue.

Creative rivalry passes down the generations. Bennie aspires to be an artist like his older brother, and tension flares in their tentative re-acquaintance. Tetro's patient girlfriend (the excellent Maribel Verdu) is required to act as peacekeeper. Then they share the same subconscious knot.

Tetro has written an autobiographical novel, but tore himself apart in search of an ending, swearing off art and the past. So Bennie takes it upon himself to find the answer, transforming his brother's palimpsest of mirror writing – the point being reflection: life and art – into a play. Coppola becomes increasingly dreamlike, heading off to Patagonia for a literary festival among the luminous mountains, and a confrontation with the past as the play is performed.

"Some have called *Tetro* a return to form," wrote Keith Uhlich in *Time Out*, "but it's more the work of a man who has gone over the proverbial edge and lived to tell about it."

Francis ended up as his own distributor in the U.S., deliberately (and perversely) launching his strange family drama into the summer of 2009 against the cacophony of blockbusters – the bombastic aftermath of New Hollywood. He figured there might be those out there who wanted to see something more personal.

"It's funny, when you [release] a movie it's like turning the shower on at a hotel you haven't stayed at before. The water either comes out with all the pressure or dribble, dribble, dribble."

His film may have dribbled, but it was a bold reminder of his artistic powers. And the fates weren't done with him. As a postscript, in October of the same year, his brother August died suddenly from a heart attack at seventy-five.

Francis had lost his role model.

"I'm sure I can't know the difficulties of having me as a father," admitted Francis, but he determined things would be different to how it was with his father. He was the benign patriarch, encouraging mutual support. He wanted everyone to have their day in the sun. Nevertheless, his legacy still cast a long shadow.

Sofia Coppola was having trouble escaping her own shadow. She had taken a three-year break, the early rush having given way to a hangover.

She couldn't face another six months of period precision. "After *Marie Antoinette* I was over movies," she said. The royal epic, loved and loathed in equal measure, had left her drained. It took a chance meeting with cinematographer Harris Savides to reinvigorate her muse. He spoke about how much he enjoyed simpler productions, less fuss. He encouraged her to think small again.

So Coppola would follow her startling, innovative opening trio with three succinct films, plying her themes and laconic mood to mixed results. The first was about things she knew well: fathers, daughters, movies, hotels, and celebrity.

Somewhere was a conscious reworking of *Lost in Translation*, but along the lines of a father-daughter relationship, and younger on both counts. Coppola was back in the alternative reality of high-end hotels, but instead of the nocturnal glow of Tokyo's Park Hyatt, this is sun-smeared, celebrity magnet the Chateau Marmont, perched over Sunset Boulevard like the haunted castle from a Roger Corman picture.

Within this hermetic Babylon, supine beside the cerulean pool or cocooned in snowy sheets, we meet bad boy superstar Johnny Marco (Stephen Dorff). Between films, his life is a waft of booze, cars, pills, parties, pole dancers, hangers-on, and creeping boredom. He has become detached from himself, symbolically breaking his arm falling down the hotel stairs. That is until his eleven-year-old daughter Cleo (Elle Fanning) is unexpectedly dumped on him by his ex-wife.

That was the age the idea that her father was somehow famous began to seep into Coppola's consciousness. They would walk into a restaurant and the *Godfather* theme would start to play. Fame became something to decipher or treat like a malady.

"I made *Somewhere* after I'd started noticing that everyone wanted to be famous," she explained. "I wondered: what happens when you get there? I guess growing up having a famous director father, I noticed a little that people found celebrity attractive."

There is so little plot the film borders on a meditation. The script was forty-three pages long, and there isn't a line of dialogue for fifteen minutes. It is the most European film ever made about the ennui of Hollywood extravagance. Fellini's *La Dolce Vita* by way of *Entourage*. Father and daughter will run the gamut from tentative communication to genuine connection – she is a circuit to the outside world, pumping reality into his anaesthetised existence. A few days in her company will change his life.

Coppola had known Dorff for years. He was a surprising choice, his career had never soared to the level of Johnny Marco, but she had him in mind as she wrote the script. Like Murray, there was something in his demeanour, a natural goodness in his body language. Beneath the fog of celebrity, Johnny has a decent soul. The film opens with a slow–slow zoom as he hurls a sports car round and round the same circuit, trapped in a thrill-seeking loop.

Producer Fred Roos had suggested Fanning, despite Coppola's wariness over-pampered Hollywood kids. She wanted the opposite feeling, a freshness that would wake the audience up. Meeting Fanning, she knew she had it – that natural vitality and wit, staring daggers across the breakfast table at her father's latest conquest, giving the film its heartbeat.

Throughout her interviews, Coppola maintained a careful distance between her and Cleo. She insisted the character was based on a friend's daughter. She merely sprinkled on a few of her own experiences, she said, "to make it real." Memories had welled up from her childhood during the writing. "I just remember going on trips as a kid," she said. "My dad was excited to let us be in worlds that kids don't usually go to." The indoor picnic in the Milan hotel suite where they sample every flavour of gelato on the menu, and the craps lesson at a Las Vegas table were delivered direct from life.

Coppola had stayed in the Chateau. She had seen her share of Johnny Marcos stultifying by the poolside, she knew the lazy Hollywood rhythms of press conferences and award shows. LA, she said, "is not like anywhere else, and the whole city revolves around show business."

Largely shot in and around the hotel from June 24, 2009, with excursions to Milan and Vegas, *Somewhere* was the apotheosis of Coppola's minimalist approach to production: six weeks, no screaming assistant directors, no moody grips, no loud noises, unless specifically called for by the script. Harmony was established on and off screen. It cost $7 million, which was more than she wanted.

Built in 1927, the Chateau was of course the third lead, creaking with Hollywood ghosts: the trail of passing celebrity goes back to Greta Garbo,

Jean Harlow, Clark Gable, and John Belushi breathing his last in one of the bungalows. There was something louche and strange about the place. Coppola remembered Romulo Laki, the famous singing waiter, serenading her with Elvis Presley's "Teddy Bear" in the lobby, when she was only Cleo's age – another memory repeated in the film. She called in a few favours to take over the fifth floor for three weeks, with Dorff living on site, directly above his fictional room.

She wanted it to feel out of time, almost like a period film, with her long dialogue-free takes running into minutes, using the exact same lenses her father used for *Rumble Fish*. She studied the soft glaze of 1970s and 1980s Hollywood parables like *Shampoo* and *American Gigolo*. "[It's] one of the great cinematic portraits of a city," sang *The New Yorker*.

The film possesses hypnotic wonder, but its alien spirit would keep it to the margins of the box office, where it made $14 million. *Lost in Translation* was beginning to look like the exception to Coppola's more rarefied appeal.

There were those critics who wondered if she was only ever going to concern herself with the trials of the over-pampered, but the rich have long been the focus of Hollywood's leery eye. And it was, above all, a film about observation. "Coppola is a fascinating director," wrote the critic Roger Ebert. "She sees, and we see exactly what she sees." There are those, including Quentin Tarantino, who consider it her best film. He was at the head of the jury when it was awarded the Golden Lion at the Venice Film Festival in 2010 – Coppola was only the fourth woman to win. Cynics were quick to point out that he was also her ex-boyfriend.

"Let's go shopping," chirps Rebecca (Katie Chang), one of *The Bling Ring*, her Valley Girl accent like milk on the turn. This it turns out is code for robbery. Coppola's fifth film is the cuckoo in the nest. It was based on the real life (or at least what serves for real life in the moneyed bubble of Los Angeles) case of a gaggle of self-winding teens whose crime spree took in the mega-mansions of out-of-town celebrities: Paris Hilton, Lindsay Lohan, Rachel Bilson, and Orlando Bloom. Once they got back to their none-too-shabby homes and airhead parents, they posted details of their swag online: a magpie clutter of designer clothes, handbags, jewellery, and watches. Then they went and did it again. Why?

Well, not for the stuff. Maybe it was to rub shoulders or at least the bathrobes of the rich and famous. As Marc (Israel Broussard), the sole boy of the quintet, whines, "they just want to be part of the *lifestyle*." It was an act of becoming. Maybe it was for the rush that comes with breaking and entering. Maybe, and this could be where Coppola's interest began to stir, out of sheer abject teenage boredom.

They were caught eventually. Suddenly thrust into the glare of their own overnight celebrity. For some it meant jail. All of it captured in a *Vanity Fair* article, *The Suspects Wore Louboutins*, written by Nancy Jo Sales in 2010.

At forty-one, Coppola was more fashionable than famous. She'd had her brief spell in the Los Angeles light in her twenties, but now lived beyond its borders: New York and Paris, a mother of two (her second daughter Cosima was born on May 18, 2010), married to a hip French musician, making her untroubled films in her untroubled way. She liked ballet, art, theatre, and collected photography (William Eggleston, Tina Barney, Helmut Newton), she read (Edith Wharton, Yukio Mishima), and tried to keep up with movies and music. Between films, she shot commercials for Miss Dior fragrances and designed bags for Louis Vuitton. The style magazines coveted her mix of European chic and Californian cool – it never looked as if she tried too hard.

"You have to go out of your way to show them you're not a jerk." That was her mother's advice and she stuck to it. In short, don't act like a celebrity. Coppola grew to be guarded but polite in interviews, more like her mother, her handshake featherlight – nothing like the confessional outpouring it awoke in her father. She was simply the Napa Valley Girl, where fame lived over the horizon. Even by 2011, she didn't have a Twitter account, or Facebook, and had never watched reality television. She was like her films: somewhere else.

So why did she make *The Bling Ring*? She hadn't planned to – too shrill, too fast paced, too acidic – only picking up the rights to the article thinking there was something in it for Zoetrope. But reading the interviews and police transcripts, talking to Sales, absorbing this teen hunger, something clicked.

"It seemed to say so much more about contemporary culture, and how trashy pop culture has become dominant," she said. These kids weren't dumb, they were misguided, the product of a really bad cultural diet. *The Bling Ring* was almost like a scientist examining an alien life form – what do they want? "It sounded like it had the elements for a fun pop movie," she insisted. "I also realised that what they did really took some ingenuity." By monitoring gossip sites, they worked out when their marks would be away filming or at a launch. They found unlocked doors or windows; Hilton's house key was under the doormat.

Backed by an $8-million budget from a consortium of production companies and distributors, Coppola filled out her cast with Emma Watson (the only real name, transmuting from the *Harry Potter* films with a drawl like a sick cat), Claire Julien, Taissa Farmiga, and Georgia Rock. She spoke with two of the real gang, Nick Prugo and Alexis Neiers, who later denounced the film as "trashy and inaccurate." Which sounded a lot like the reviews for *Marie Antoinette*. As was her wont, Coppola built up a book of references including angles on Hilton's Aladdin's Cave shoe closet, and pictures of the firefly LA skyline shimmering like a dream.

They shot in March 2011, locating Christmas Tree mansions in West Hollywood, Malibu, Lynwood, the Hollywood Hills, and Venice Beach. Hilton was game enough to offer them the use of her house, *that* shoe closet, and take a cameo. They had to sneak in at night (the irony!) with filming forbidden in the neighbourhood.

As is her forte, Coppola often kept the camera at one remove, as if avoiding the drama. Framing one of the Ring's Hollywood heists from outside the darkened mansion, we watch as each window lights up as they go room to room.

It is slick and clever – with strobes of heady montage – but a hard film to love. Trapped in a spin-cycle of repetition, these kids raid one deserving victim after another. *The Bling Ring* is a study in warped superficiality – truly rebels without a cause – but there is no enlightenment, no sign of souls willing to stir. Once they were caught and got their fifteen minutes, the kids were almost delusional. They talked about the number of Facebook friends they had gained – the burglary was a side effect. Coppola didn't identify with them. She simply reports that a monster had awakened, and her nihilistic young things fizzled to a box office total of $20 million.

"She may imply that the Bling Ring is the product of a culture staggering in its shallowness," complained *Vogue*, "but her approach is neither satirical (perhaps because her characters are self-satirizing) nor alarmist."

But it does connect. Haphazardly, *The Bling Ring* touches on themes that unify Coppola's films: the empty hedonism of *Marie Antoinette*, the unknowable currents of youth in *The Virgin Suicides*, and the nexus of Los Angeles and celebrity in *Somewhere* (which is almost a sister film). But after the silken hypnotism of her early films, it was a caffeinated buzz that wore off too quick.

Eager to cleanse herself of the tacky hysteria of *The Bling Ring*, Coppola was intent on making something more optimistic. And it speaks volumes to those hereditary Coppola contradictions that she would opt to remake a heated Civil War psychodrama in which Clint Eastwood gets his leg amputated. It's not a remake, she insisted, it's a reinterpretation.

"Remake is a bad word in our family."

It turns out, there's more to this.

Coppola had spent months working on a reinterpretation of *The Little Mermaid* for Universal. As blockbusters go, it seemed the perfect fit: the lonely, rich girl (a princess!) who washes up on alien shores. She had Maya Hawke in mind for Ariel and was shooting test footage. Growing as ambitious as her father, she was exploring the idea of shooting the underwater scenes in the open ocean. In hindsight, she did admit, "That would probably have been impossible."

Obviously, it would have marked a significant departure from her chosen path: a big budget, special effects, all the hype and expectation, and the studio's hot breath constantly on her collar. Naively, she admitted, she thought she could do it her "singular" way. Then came the meeting that broke her resolve – or brought her to her senses.

It was some executive, so anonymous compared to those long-gone players and playboys like Robert Evans or Charlie Bluhdorn, who nonchalantly raises the question.

"What's going to get a thirty-five-year-old man into this movie?"

"And I'm like, 'Into *The Little Mermaid*'?" The memory still stirred a mix of open-mouthed incredulity and desert-dry sarcasm. It was the last in a litany of reasons to abandon ship. So she walked. Which was hard, with all she had put into the film. But she couldn't be a director for hire. With these big projects, there are too many people to please. She only wanted to please herself.

Which still begs the question of how she replaced *The Little Mermaid* with *The Beguiled*?

"I wanted to do something beautiful, that's all I knew."

It was a friend and frequent collaborator, production designer Anne Ross, who told her about the original version of *The Beguiled*, directed by that bastion of machismo under fire Don Siegel in 1971, based on the 1966 novel by Thomas P. Cullinan, and starring not only Eastwood, but Geraldine Page and Elizabeth Hartman. Both of whom, by chance, had previously appeared in her father's second film, *You're a Big Boy Now*. Ross insisted it was ripe for reinterpretation.

Coppola duly watched the Siegel version, and was startled by its feverish swirl of libidinous manipulation and gender dynamics encamped in a heightened Southern setting. It stayed with her – this crazy premise. So she sought out the novel, which was out of print, and began to conceive of what she could do with it.

The plot has wounded Yankee soldier Corporal McBurney take refuge in Miss Martha Farnsworth's Seminary for Young Ladies, a dilapidated Confederate manse enshrouded in forest. His animal charms soon begin to wreak merry hell among what remains of the school body – all of them female. In particular, he will stir up tension between lovelorn teacher Edwina, wilful student Alicia, and the school's strident headmistress Miss Martha. As his charms and wounds begin to sour, the vengeful women will turn on their unwelcome guest. Things do not end well. It was big on castration symbolism.

Coppola began a thought experiment. What would happen if she reframed the story through the women's eyes? It would be a real departure. She had never done genre before, and this was the heady chamber of Southern Gothic. She had never had stuntmen on set, never dealt with gore. For the first time since *Marie Antoinette*, she would be returning to the exoticism of period. This was 1863 Virginia – a lost world.

And it still played to her strengths. The idea of an invasion of something, "so dirty and masculine into this lacy, soft world." She saw it as a spiritual sequel or prequel to *The Virgin Suicides*, with these women (mostly ghostly blondes) confined among the mangroves and willows of the plantation. She looked to Peter Weir's *Picnic at Hanging Rock* and Roman Polanski's *Tess* for a fittingly ethereal atmosphere.

Ironically, *The Beguiled* was owned by Universal, who made the original. So that was a fait accompli. "It was either talking to them, or not making it," she said, but channelled through their specialist arm Focus (who had backed *Somewhere*), a budget of $10.5 million was forthcoming.

Coppola immediately set about cutting away the more salacious elements of Siegel's film: flashbacks to incest and rape, hallucinated threesomes, and a general strain of B-movie horniness among the womenfolk. Worried she conformed to a stereotype, she also took out the black slave Hallie (Mae Mercer). That was a knowing risk. After that, she needed to get the original movie out of her head.

The script was far more intricate than anything she had done before. She pushed herself to write more dialogue, detail the specificity of scenes. Nicole Kidman sprang into her mind as the steel-magnolia Miss Martha. There had been discussions for *The Little Mermaid*, and Coppola had a clear image of the versatile Australian star holding a candelabrum over the house anatomy book as she prepared for amateur surgery. Staying in touch with former glories, she brought in Kirsten Dunst to play stifled Edwina, and Elle Fanning as the over-ripened Alicia.

McBurney was a mystery. This was a masculine figure who shape-shifts to relate to a twelve-year-old girl and attract a forty-year-old woman. In the book he was written as Irish, which led to a meeting with Colin Farrell, and the historically justifiable idea of him keeping his natural Dublin accent. He had a current of danger beneath the roguish charm, his good looks slipping easily into the swarthy (he was forbidden from using shampoo). She would keep the actor away from set until the last minute, disturbing the cosy communal feeling created by weeks of history lessons and etiquette classes.

"I wanted it to be this feminine, gauzy world that doesn't look threatening at all," said Coppola, "so that it's a real surprise when the story shifts." The pageant of the Southern lifestyle fascinated her. Despite the shattered world outside their gates, the school still runs through its roundelay of French lessons, music practice, and frivolous chatter.

Something she had taken from her father was a willingness to talk to the actor during the take. It was unorthodox, but effective. "The camera captures them thinking, which is always interesting," she said. She needed the varied inner lives. The different reactions these women have to the male catalyst.

"The South is always very exotic to me: I wanted the film to represent an exaggerated version of all the ways women were traditionally raised there just to be lovely and cater to men – the manners of that whole world, and how they change when the men go away."

The antebellum springs out of the tableaux of vérité and fantasy, big on fabric: taffeta gowns, corsets, diaphanous skirts, drapes, muslin veils, all the tremulous detail of civility holding out against the dark. The grounds outside were conceived almost as fairy tale, with smoke machines enveloping the drama in mists as mythical as *Apocalypse Now*. The war is reduced to distant cannon fire, and the occasional Confederate patrol sniffing at the gates. With its cutaways to battle, Siegel's film cut closer to the real world.

They shot at Madewood, an 1846 Greek-revival property at the centre of a sugarcane plantation at Napoleonville, Louisiana, for the exteriors. While a beautifully preserved town house, belonging to actress Jennifer Coolidge, in the Lower Garden District of New Orleans, provided the claustrophobic interiors. Moving miraculously fast for period, they were done in twenty-six days, with French cinematographer Philippe Le Sourd using natural light, with the gloomy interiors picked out by candlelight.

The Beguiled entered the world on June 23, 2017, instantly more provocative and topical as sexual harassment and the #MeToo movement came to the forefront of the culture discussion. Coppola put it plainly: "Our movie's about these women who are just fed up with that, and they turn on the guy." It was read as feminist, which made sense to her, but she had never written with categories in mind. Like her father, she was not an explicitly political filmmaker. It was a story that possessed a female perspective – flawed, contradictory, and powerful – and those were rare enough. Which led to an ironic objectification of the male body.

A larger controversy lay in wait. With the removal of the single African American character from the story, the one link to slavery, Coppola was accused of whitewashing – and it was getting complicated. Every interview was backing her into a corner. Was she or the film racist on some level?

"I was like, 'This is getting out of control'."

So she released a statement to put her case across. She had wanted her film to be this very specific thing – a story about this group of women. The casting of a single black slave would have been a dangerously token gesture and pushed the story in a different direction. That she didn't want to reinforce a cliché was fair. But she missed that Mae Mercer's Hallie is by far the most interesting and morally attuned character in the original.

Coppola had already returned home to New York when word came through that she had won Best Director at the Cannes Film Festival – only the second woman to do so in seventy years (these records were piling up). In fact, she was on her way to Coney Island with her daughters, where they bought extra hotdogs to celebrate.

Riding out the controversies, $27 million worldwide marked a decent return. *The Beguiled* may lack the wacky ferocity of the original, but it is an eerie, evocative account of the diabolical strains of human passion – the animal grunting beneath the etiquette. You suspect this is as close as she will ever come to a horror movie. This is as far upriver as she'll ever get.

Being six films into an award-winning career and fully established as an artist, did not prevent journalists from circling back to another infuriating issue. How did she feel about being referred to as the daughter of Francis Ford Coppola? QED: was it all down to him? Sofia Coppola would sigh, get that faraway look in her eyes, purse her plump limps, and set the record straight.

"It very much depends on the way it's said. I'm proud to be his daughter. I learned to have balls from him, and integrity. But I have a body of work now, and it has its own identity. He's a great master, but I'm happy to carve out my own way of working."

CHAPTER 14

A FAMILY BUSINESS

*Twixt (2011), Palo Alto (2013), A Glimpse Inside the Mind of Charles
Swan III (2012), Dreamland (2016), Paris Can Wait (2016),
The Unicorn (2019), The Argument (2020),
Love is Love is Love (2020), Mainstream (2021)*

By the second decade of the millennium, Francis Ford Coppola's dream
had, in its way, come true. He hadn't stormed the Hollywood citadel, he
didn't have the run of his own studio (though there was a fleeting and
frustrating spell on the MGM board), there was no filmmaking collective
gathered beneath the Zoetrope flag. Though to be fair, everyone talked
about "previz" these days.

The firebrand had mellowed into the wealthy vintner.

By 1990, the Niebaum-Coppola vineyard had finally become profitable.
By 1997, it was on a serious upswing. The best viticulturists were hired,
guided tours were initiated, and the Inglenook chateau was refurbished
by Dean Tavoularis to include a gallery devoted to memorabilia from fifty
years of filmmaking. Here was an original scarlet Tucker Torpedo (rotating
on a turntable as if it was the centrepiece of an automobile show), Vito
Corleone's antique desk, and Francis's five Oscars, long since repaired to
their former glory (as he had repaired his ragged heart). Did he ever pause
to consider that his great career was now sealed behind glass?

What of the wines? There was the Francis Coppola Reserve Director's
Cut, in a Cabernet Sauvignon or Chardonnay. The Cinema collection
included a fine Zinfandel. Sofia was a light sparkling Blanc des Blancs

bottled with pink cellophane – Tavoularis specially designed all the labels. Wines were produced in honour of his wife, his mother, and his long dead grandfathers, with the flagship a robust red named Rubicon. Millions poured in.

In 2004, he bought and renovated the stunning Palazzo Margherita, which overlooked Bernalda on the Gulf of Taranto, the town of his grandfather's birth, nestled in the hills where his ancestors had played out their bitter feuds. In 2018, including restaurants, hotels, pasta sauces, and returns from films like *The Godfather* and *Apocalypse Now* (long since in profit), his wealth was estimated at $300 million.

And under the mantle of the steadfast American Zoetrope, a stream of original and intensely personal films was being made outside of the studio system. If he had always hoped that his film company would have the complexion of a family, then that too had come true – it was his family who were doing the directing.

Including his daughter's period drama, *The Beguiled*, in the space of a decade Zoetrope had made ten films. And he had returned to the genre with which he had first made his mark over fifty years before – horror.

Twixt was a nightmare – quite literally, it had "grown out" of a terrible dream that had come to him one night in Istanbul. He had been drunk on Raki, the potent aniseed spirit favoured by locals. But even in the midst of his midnight hallucinations, part of his brain saw the promise of a new film. Pulling out his phone, he recorded everything he could remember. "I realised that it was a gothic romance setting," he said, "so in fact I'd be able to do it all around my home base."

Like the opening scene of *Apocalypse Now*, where Willard unbridles his soul, *Twixt* was the direct product of the director's unconscious. Which proved surprisingly derivative.

What did he have? A lot of scattered ideas thrust together under the cover of a ghost story. Val Kilmer is downwardly trending horror author Hall Baltimore – "the bargain basement Stephen King" – whose book tour has veered to Swan Valley, exactly the kind of under-populated, where-in-the-hell small town that crops up on the arboreal King circuit. Witch stories are Baltimore's beat; but he's tiring of toeing the commercial line. He has ghosts of his own to confront.

In an amusingly self-reverential montage, tormented by the blank page of a new novel and thickly oiled by booze, Baltimore descends into iffy Brando impressions from *Apocalypse Now* (during which the muse had danced out of Coppola's reach). A scene that smacks of Kilmer improvising laughs out of his director.

The only taker at the book signing is the town's sheriff, an old coot in the shape of Bruce Dern, who fancies himself a writer, and might be the source of fresh material – there is a local legacy of murder going back to the 1800s. Dern appears to be trying a riff on Dennis Hopper's freeform ramblings from *Apocalypse Now*.

The local hotel promises the sullen author that Edgar Allan Poe had once stayed there, and the references start piling up – Baltimore is the town where the gothic doyen lived and drank and died. When Baltimore falls asleep, and the film wakes up, he is visited by the moon-bright incarnation of a dead girl named V (Elle Fanning) who feeds him the mystery of her death, and a droll apparition of Poe himself (Ben Chaplin) to discuss the bind of writing. From here on the plot contorts itself into a garbled confrontation with sins past and present.

Self-financed, and largely shot in and around his front yard at Napa, as well as the nearby town of Kelseyville, Francis became even more aggressively experimental. Following the Freudian surrealism of *Tetro*, he was enjoying the possibilities of dream narrative – to be free from the vice of logic. That pull had always been there in his films, upriver toward dreams in *The Rain People*, *The Conversation*, *Peggy Sue Got Married*, and *Bram Stoker's Dracula* (that other florid horror). And indeed those swampy latter reaches of *Apocalypse Now* unbuttoned from reality.

There are split dioptres and Dutch angles in *Twixt* to match the genre fireworks of Movie Brat Brian De Palma. It looks unreal quite deliberately, claimed film website *The Spool*, admiring the film's "unapologetic sincerity". This was a return to the unironic visual abandon of *Rumble Fish* – and Alden Ehrenreich's vampire biker strikes a chord with Mickey Rourke's Motorcycle Boy – and *Dementia 13*, from his Corman days, working with nothing but his wits. Mihai Malaimare Jr. returned as cinematographer, bringing some deft advances. The digital look varies from a soft autumnal daylight to a nightly gothic weave that borders the synthetic noir of *Sin City*: red highlights smeared onto monochrome. There were two sections of 3D for cinemas.

Nurturing future plans to direct, Gia Coppola served as Francis's assistant and driver – enjoying the chance to spend time with her grandfather. It was a way of getting to know her lost father. No one had been closer to Gio. And this is where a gimmicky dance with genre gets personal.

That Baltimore's daughter died tragically in a boating accident leaves little wriggle room for interpretation – Francis was digging further than the soil of his childhood used in *Tetro*. What he was rooting out of his psyche was far more painful – a buried memory of the day when his son had died. "Was this where the nightmare was taking him?" he had worried. Follow this path and there was no retreat later on.

"It was something I had never looked at before," he confessed, his voice catching. "That Gio had asked me to go with him. I had thought he meant kids boats, little boats, and I had no idea it was speedboats. I should have been there. Had I been there…"

There were serious plans to take *Twixt* on a thirty-city tour as the latest experiment in Live Cinema. He would carry the film with him as a digital file, and gauging the audience response, rearrange his story accordingly. More of this, less of that, adjusting the uneasy mix of tones as easily as the house lights. He would be a conductor of story.

In 2016, Coppola would direct a "proof-of-concept" Live Cinema production of *Distant Voices*, or at least the 1920s tenement portion of his 500-page Italian-American family saga (the story of three generations whose history spans the development of television) utilising the facilities and students of UCLA. The script was performed in full, like theatre, with Coppola choosing the shots like a football game, vowing one day to complete the entire story by the same means.

With the tour proving untenable, having to "freeze" *Twixt* into a final cut traps the movie in a rictus full of creepy visual tricks but little narrative sense. "Easily his silliest work," said *The Hollywood Reporter*. "Tedious," grumbled *The Guardian*.

Coppola waved away the protests. He was free of the opinions of others.

It must have become wearisome. For every interview and every review to begin by triangulating her identity: "From the granddaughter of Francis Ford, and the niece of Sofia Coppola…" Inevitably, that's how it was for Gia Coppola when she made her film debut in 2013 with the piquant study in teenage ennui *Palo Alto*, based on the short stories of James Franco. Which myopic critics immediately grouped with the dreamy elixir of *The Virgin Suicides*.

So this is Gia's story. Graduating from Bard College in upper state New York – where she had studied but grown weary of photography – she had no inclination toward feature films. Besides the olive-dark eyes, natural wariness, and slightly birdlike voice, Gia shared her aunt's early resistance to being a Coppola. She tried all sorts, including a stint in bartending school. More by luck than ambition, making contacts through friends, she began directing short films for fashion labels. Hence she rediscovered photography, and gravity began to take hold.

Gia had grown up between Napa Valley and her mother, Jacqui de la Fontaine, in Los Angeles. Fontaine had married Gordon Getty, scion of the Getty dynasty, with Francis walking her down the aisle in Napa. So Gia marked a second generation raised on movie sets: *The Godfather Part III*, *Bram Stoker's Dracula*, *Jack*, and *The Rainmaker*.

"I do remember being on *Dracula*," she said. "But definitely seeing Sofia take on directing made it appealing. She did it in a way I could relate to."

Her true film education was at her aunt's side: *The Virgin Suicides*, *Lost in Translation*, *Marie Antoinette*. Admiring how Coppola always stayed "truthful to her own nature."

Gia had met polymath Franco through her mother. He acted, directed, produced, painted, wrote fiction, and evaded Hollywood definitions. She liked that. He encouraged her photography and sent her a copy of *Palo Alto*. Based on his memories of growing up in the affluent Silicon Valley suburb, and those he had gleaned from local high school kids, the twelve interconnected stories depict the lives of twelve disaffected teenagers hanging out, messing up, falling in love, and driving around a blissed-out netherworld of adolescence. Gia got it straightaway; it felt authentic. Franco made the suggestion.

"I think you should do it."

Depressed by endless *American Pies* treating kids as horny punchlines with perfect skin, she was longing for a movie about teenagers "that felt realistic." Where they smoked and cursed and fell to pieces without quite knowing why. She wanted to show the world through their eyes, she said, and how they "move in a way that you don't move when you get older."

Francis could have warned her that the Coppola name may open doors but that's when you hear the purse strings tighten. It took two-and-a-half years to get *Palo Alto* financed, falling apart and breaking her heart on too many occasions to mention. Resilience was the hardest lesson.

Franco would produce and take the complex role of the girls' soccer coach Mr. B with an unwholesome habit of snaring babysitters, while Gia slimmed the book down to a core of four intertwined stories. There is naïve, introverted April (an excellent Emma Roberts), drawn into Mr. B's predatory orbit, but yearning for Teddy (Jack Kilmer, Val's son). Teddy has artistic talent and a good heart but is swept into petty crime by the aggressions of stoner Fred (Nat Wolff). Fred's unresolved anger will lead him to exploit the hollow and available Emily (Zoe Levin). Any parenting is remote and clueless. The atmosphere has the woozy, inconclusive haze of weed, with long, patient cuts of cramped parties and empty streets.

Made through the winter of 2012 in Woodland Hills near Los Angeles – Palo Alto itself was beyond their $1 million budget – this was not simply *Virgin Suicides* territory, but a genre that recalled the listless delinquents of *The Outsiders* and *Rumble Fish*. But Gia isn't mythologising the young; she orientates closer to the films of Larry Clark. Observing her characters without judgement. Animals in their habitat: drugs, alcohol, sex, and skateboards.

On set, she had the same mellow frequency as Coppola. She was twenty-seven, and this wasn't new to her. Half her life had been a de facto film school. In fact, it was so low key the boys were staying with her mother, who would drive them home at the end of the day's shooting and cook dinner. Fontaine took a small role as April's mother, veiled in vape smoke, and Talia Shire briefly appears as a school counsellor. Robert Schwartzman, her second cousin (who we'll come to shortly), scored and curated a Sofia-esque playlist as mood enhancer. Making a boon of a low budget, it concentrates on edgy young artists like Blood Orange.

The reviews were mixed (welcome to the family!). She was remixing familiar angst, but most saw the promise. But after a run at the big festivals, the film fared poorly at the box office, too real for its own good.

It would take Gia seven years to find her next subject – a love triangle in the age of social media. Filmed in 2019, but only gaining a sporadic, pandemic-stilted release in 2021, the more hyperactive *Mainstream* stars Maya Hawke (from *Stranger Things*), Wolff, and Andrew Garfield as a trio of anti-establishment LA artists streaming self-made videos – until one of them hits big. Garfield's manic Link was modelled on Nicolas Cage. And perhaps a line can be drawn across the generations in the film's cautionary exploration of the megalomania that bubbles up with mainstream success. Of curious note, the film features Colleen Camp, who long ago starred as Miss May, one of the Playmates stirring frenzy in *Apocalypse Now*.

"I was trying to portray the sensation of going through a break-up with the way the film was composed – kind of chaotic, kaleidoscopic; there's a fractured quality." So said Roman Coppola discussing his second film, eleven years after his debut.

Set in a hellzapoppin' 1970s Los Angeles, *A Glimpse Inside the Mind of Charles Swan III* is the story of a wildly successful album cover designer (Charlie Sheen), whose whirl of drugs, booze, fame, and sex is abruptly curtailed when the love of his life (Katheryn Winnick) exits his life. He immediately goes into a tailspin. The idea is that we will come to see the real Swan through the prism of his break-up, with Roman channelling past heartaches. Evidentially, Sheen is channelling a lot of what it is to be Charlie Sheen as well.

He and Roman had been friends since they were twelve when their fathers were drowning in *Apocalypse Now*. "We're going to have to make a movie one of these days," Roman had repeatedly told his friend down the years. "Our parents did it, now we have to do it." But when you cast Sheen, you send a trailer for all the baggage.

Swan's singlehood elicits a rush of self-reflection, alongside his best friend, stand-up Kirby (Jason Schwartzman beneath a Lenny Bruce afro), and uptight manager Saul (Bill Murray, looking as if he is overdue somewhere else). Murray's distinctive presence not only recalls the delectable ennui of Sofia's *Lost in Translation*, but his character's vain protestations over Charles's spendthrift ways ring rather close to home.

Murray hadn't changed. "He gave me the inclination that my movie could be something he may be interested in," laughed Roman, who did at least now have a direct line. Eventually, he showed up on set.

Swann and the film tumble headlong into a procession of reveries that allow Roman to dabble in the genre-hopping games of *CQ*. We are served visually acute parodies of westerns, musicals, documentary-like samples of Kirby's stand-up, and a 1960s espionage thriller in which a secret organisation of sexy feminists plot retribution on incorrigible male behaviour.

Was Roman reacting to the grand visions of his immediate relatives – playing the wild child with that wildest of children Sheen as his muse? He offers a zany antidote to all the solemnity. There had been an inkling of the story as far back as 2003. "A buzz at the back of your brain like you feel something is brewing," he said – a buzz that seldom comes to Roman.

"I did feel that if I was going to spend my time making a feature film, I wanted it to be distinctive and something that's true to my sensibility."

Following *CQ*, that sensibility was making itself clear: a hyperreal, highly referential eye candy grooving on 1960s–1970s cinema, now with added flashes of Bob Fosse's confessional moves in *All That Jazz*. Swan's dayglo album covers suggest the celebrated pop art explosions of Robert Miles Runyan – a cartoon Californian wonderland that pervades Swan's entire world. In its wacky way, it's a break-up story about the artistic process – very Roman. The name Charles Swan doffs toward Proust, a mad crosscurrent of which his father would surely have approved.

More than a few critics saw the kinship with the made-to-measure colour charts of Wes Andersonland. Then Roman (as well as Murray and Schwartzman) had spent a fair portion of the intervening years residing there. The first read through had taken place at the Venice Film Festival, with Roman, Schwartzman, and Anderson playing all the parts between promotional duties on *The Darjeeling Limited*.

Of course it's exactly the kind of ribald eccentricity to set critics' teeth on edge. "[An] obnoxious vanity project," cried *AV Club*. While *Time* despaired of its "haphazard frivolity." Celebrating Sheen's lifestyle was considered beyond the pale. Did no one notice he was being sent up? With returns at the box office negligible it went in search of a cult following.

Roman was unrepentant. "It's a crazy movie and I'm proud of it."

We need to talk about Robert Schwartzman. Born in Los Angeles in 1982, he is Shire's son, Jason's younger brother, nephew of Francis, and cousin of Roman and Sofia Coppola, and Nicolas Cage.

Working beyond the borders of Zoetrope, he is more of a Coppola clan outlier, best known as lead singer of Rooney, the alt-rock band he formed at high school and named after the principal in *Ferris Bueller's Day Off*. Between terms at the Eugene Lang College – a Hofstra-like liberal arts establishment in Greenwich Village – they got serious enough to tour with Weezer and The Strokes, plying a laidback Californian take on the British Invasion of the 1960s.

With tousle-haired, model-good looks, he tried out acting, as we've seen, appearing in Sofia Coppola's short *Lick the Star* and her feature debut *The Virgin Suicides*. He was seventeen years old in the latter, as Paul Baldino hilariously attempting a come on with Kathleen Turner's Mrs. Lisbon over the punchbowl, locking eyes as he sucks on a slice of pineapple.

By 2021, the highly productive Schwartzman had directed three films satirising modern relationship hang-ups among stunted thirtysomethings. It's a tune played through the years by Woody Allen, Mike Nichols, and Noah Baumbach, and Schwartzman has a bite not seen elsewhere in the family.

Dreamland, from 2016, is an unabashed retake of *The Graduate* about a diffident piano teacher (Johnny Simmons) who becomes the kept man of a disenchanted married woman (Amy Landecker, known for the sultry neighbour in *A Serious Man*). It's a routine coming-of-age parable with the moribund upper middle classes in its jaundiced eye, and brother Jason as an oddball bank manager.

His best, *The Unicorn*, from 2018, joins a couple attempting to instigate a threesome to pep up their flagging engagement. Lauren Lapkus and Nick Rutherford, as the couple in question, are as self-aware as the audience about how absurd things are getting.

"I'm just really sensitive to wanting to tell stories with characters that you feel for or you fall into their world," said Schwartzman, treating his films in much the same way he wrote his songs.

The Argument, from 2020, attempts a sociological high-concept: after a party descends into argument, three LA couples, a mismatch of actors, screenwriters, and agents (including Dan Folger, Emma Bell, and Maggie Q), meet again to re-enact the evening to see what went wrong – only for things to get worse. It is not as tidy or funny as *The Unicorn*, but there are smart ideas here about the gravity of human nature.

None of Schwartzman's films received more than a cursory release, but he was quietly fulfilling Uncle Francis's diktat on aiming small and finding your own voice. Moreover, he was the one, in his own way, who had taken on his uncle's dreams of circumventing the studio system. Through his company, Utopia Media, Schwartzman pioneered a new means of distribution during the pandemic called Altavod, offering filmmakers an avenue to stream content, making money direct from the audience. He was cutting out the middleman.

Eleanor Coppola had spent a lifetime being introduced as the wife of Francis Ford, and the mother of Sofia. Of course it needled. It was also a lifetime spent wondering if she too had a story to tell. The idea had been planted back in 1976, shooting documentary footage amid the furies of *Apocalypse Now*. "I was just mesmerised, looking through the viewfinder," she remembered. A distinctive voice emerged in her writing – she published a second collection of diaries, *Notes on a Life*, in 2008 (a book haunted by the loss of Gio) – and in the triumphant release of *Hearts of Darkness: A Filmmaker's Apocalypse* in 2001. Those introductions were expanded to include "acclaimed documentary maker".

Did people forget that she had also been a conceptual artist, a gifted fabric designer, and helped build and run a wine business? That she had stood by Francis, maintained him, supported him, and raised his children?

Passing into her seventies, she awoke one day with an overwhelming sense of why not make a feature film? What did she have to lose? "Everyone kept saying I would never get it done so I took that as a challenge," she laughed. And she had found a story. Genial and unambitious, *Paris Can Wait* is the genuine roman-à-clef in this new generation of Coppola films. Eleanor had been in Cannes as the wife of Francis, and they were about fly to Paris. Stricken with a head cold she couldn't face it. So a business colleague of her husband offered to drive her, taking in the sights along the way. It was all completely chaste but liberating – this journey set outside of time.

A friend had teased her. "Oh, that's the movie I want to see."

That stayed with her too.

So she began writing a script. At first, simply to see where it led. The answer was *Paris Can Wait* and Anne Lockwood (Diane Lane), wife to eminent and inattentive movie producer Michael Lockwood (Alec Baldwin), who swerves a private jet to Paris with severe earache. Instead, she goes by car, the vintage sky-blue Peugeot convertible owned by Jacques Clement (Arnaud Viard), her husband's rather mysterious business associate. The detours to scenic delights and a gourmand's treasure map of restaurants (food and wine are a signature motif) gradually evolve into flirtation – and Anne is confronted by another temptation. Never get off the boat.

The character played on so many aspects of Eleanor: the love of textiles, the photography, the husband consumed by his work, and the children who had fled the nest, leaving her wondering who had been left behind. She swore to herself that it had to be financed by outside parties, and not from the Coppola coffers. She needed that validation, but it took six years to get the money. So much his father, Francis struggled to be encouraging.

"It's more difficult with a wife," he said, "because there becomes a job vacancy if your wife is going to go off and become an artist." They had been married for forty-six years and that particular issue had never been resolved. But there was concern as well.

"A lot of it had to do with the fact that he thought I'd never get it off the ground, that I'd be heartbroken," she knew. After all, she was hardly offering what investors wanted: "There are no robots, nobody dies, there's no gunshots, no train wrecks."

But on the second try she did have Lane. They were old friends: Eleanor had watched the actress grow up across three of her husband's films. Only seventeen on *The Outsiders* in 1983, then so uneasily beautiful in *Rumble Fish* and *The Cotton Club*. Entering her fifth decade as an actress, the New York born Lane had defied Hollywood gravity with winning performances in *Hollywoodland*, *Secretariat*, and *Trumbo*. She had an uncomplicated charm, a fine line in East Coast detachment, and a windblown beauty that only grew more luminous when she frowned.

If Eleanor followed up with a big name as the distracted husband, then a pudding of foreign distributors and Lifetime Movies would provide a budget of $5 million. Nephew-by-marriage Nicolas Cage came and went. Offering something saltier to the dish, you imagine. Then by chance, Baldwin called Francis after a favour.

"I'm sorry, I can't," replied Francis. "But would you do *me* a favour?" It was like a bad out-take from *The Godfather*.

He was hesitant. It took Lane to convince the actor to get this "woman's film made," and in his short bursts, Baldwin is excellent: bumptious but likeable, and growing increasingly ragged down the phone as the reliable veneer around his marriage begins to crack. As a sworn devotee of *The Godfather*, it must have amused him to be partially channelling its director.

Shooting on location (Cannes, Provence, rugged Vaucluse) through the summer of 2015, at eighty, Eleanor was the oldest American to make their feature film debut. But it proved the flipside of being a documentarian – telling stories asked so much more of you. She was in a constant state of anxiety. There was never enough money, never enough time, choices had to be made: which shots were vital, which could be discarded? It was like one of those body-swap movies where some tilt of the universe had made her the director and her husband the silent partner.

But it was also liberating. She was in her own bubble. Everyone was elsewhere, busy with his or her art. She could make her own mistakes; invest the film with her own quirks.

Was she making a twee *Apocalypse Now*? Thirty-seven days in the sun-dappled French countryside hardly compared to the rain-lashed weeks at Pagsanjan. But it was strangely built the same way. A road movie, rather than river journey, made up of a string of encounters, including Aurore Clement as a concierge. "It's a collage of incidents," explained Eleanor, within which she gradually plays up the romantic tension, themes from *One from the Heart*. Jacques stalls to extend the journey, filling the backseat with roses or the table with chocolate dessert. Soaking up photogenic stops like Vézelay Abbey or the Roman aqueducts in Vers-Pont-du-Gard.

But he has his secrets. Why is it her credit card that ends up paying for the next restaurant, with all the fetishistic close-ups of their dishes? The term "impeccably lit cheese" carries a double meaning.

Released on October 15, 2016 to relatively positive reviews – there were always those who waved their Marxist torches at the Gallic clichés, bistro porn, and watching the rich at play – *Paris Can Wait* had the distinction of earning far more than her husband's recent experiments, with $13.2 million worldwide. And as the film flitted along the promotional circuit, it was Eleanor answering the questions.

Would she direct again?

The answer was yes. Three short films would be collected under the title *Love is Love is Love* in 2020. *Sailing Lesson* had Kathy Baker and Marshall Bell as an ageing couple thrust into close-quarters on a boating trip. The bittersweet *Two for Dinner* featured Joanne Whalley and Chris Messina (note: a film director) as the working couple reduced to having a date night via video chat. And *Late Lunch*, in which a young woman invites the friends of her late mother to lunch in order to glean something about who she was, with Rita Wilson, Cybill Shepherd, and Maya Kazan – granddaughter of Elia. Shot in and around San Francisco, they formed a triptych of telling inflections on the themes of loyalty and commitment drawn from life.

CHAPTER 15

FATHERS AND DAUGHTERS

On The Rocks (2020)

A 1959 lipstick red Alfa Romeo Giulietta jumps the Manhattan lights with Bill Murray at the wheel. The June night air is warm and electrically bright, and the star effortlessly slaloms the convertible through the traffic, squealing into corners and flooring the straights. Murray is quite a driver. More than confident enough to do his own stunts for the wide shots of what Sofia Coppola likes to think of as her "car chase scene". Her brother, Roman, shooting second unit, can only raise his eyebrows – it's hardly *The French Connection*. The shoot is making its unruffled tour of New York through the summer of 2019, before finishing by the beach in Mexico.

With his tightly cropped grey hair and aura of louche serenity, Murray is a fine fit for Felix Keane, semi-retired art dealer, playboy, philosopher, pin-sharp dresser – the Battistoni suits and scarves picked out by the director! – and questionable father. "I just thought it was very Felix to pick the most indiscreet car," said Coppola, "… It's the embodiment of his spirit!"

To give some context, Felix is currently in hot pursuit of his daughter's husband Dean (Marlon Wayans), who he suspects is having an affair with a leggy work colleague. Philandering is a subject on which he is a past master.

257

For some further context, we should note that this is the exact model of vintage Italian sports car on which Francis Ford Coppola, the director's father, had squandered his screenwriting prize money back in 1963. To glide about Los Angeles, playing the big shot. "One of the most beautiful cars ever, I say," he reminisced, so many years later, grey-haired and unreformed. "Some day I am going to have to get one again."

Beside Murray's Felix sits a harried brunette not a million miles from Coppola. Rashida Jones is playing his theoretically cuckolded daughter Laura, reluctant accessory in her father's games.

For all the unexpected (and brief) zipping about in polished sports cars, the sublime presence of Murray, thinly veiled autobiography, and cityscape softened into urban paradise signal that Coppola's seventh film, *On The Rocks*, had returned her to the delicate companionship of *Lost in Translation*.

Only this was a film about a father and daughter.

"I just thought I'd love to see a father and daughter buddy story," she explained. "Because, of course, I have so many memories and quotes from my dad, and that relationship was really impactful on me... He was bigger than life to me growing up."

She was paying tribute to that relationship.

The plot has Laura's stifled writer and mother pick up on hints that her workaholic husband might be unfaithful. But is this only her paranoia, fuelled by a general fortysomething funk, whispering in her ear? When her intermittent father drops by in his Town Car, he whips her suspicions into a movie plot in which the duo are transformed into private eyes. Isn't that what Francis would do?

Coppola was at pains to make it clear that there is more to Felix than a cypher of her famous father. He was made up: a cocktail (a strong Martini) of her father's friends, her friend's fathers, and her father-in-law — by all accounts quite a character himself. She wanted to examine the generational divide. The contrasting attitudes her father's era had to women and the world when they were young, and haven't shaken even as values evolved around them. In a wider sense, Felix represents an entire generation of men, and Coppola lightly but tellingly engages with contemporary sexual politics.

"I wanted them to be a little bit of an odd couple, a modern young woman and this old-world guy with those attitudes."

With the madcap adventure that ensues, with Felix and Laura getting a firm grip on the wrong end of the stick, it is a daughter's feelings for her father that come into focus. This sparkling man who hurt people as easily as he won them over. That was Coppola's charismatic father, drawing people into the next adventure. That was Murray too, thrilling and aloof.

"The character of Felix is complicated," she insisted. It required a delicate balance: he needed to be someone who both enraged and inspired Laura. "I needed someone like Bill who's so loveable, but can bring both of those sides."

She had known it was only a matter of time before she and her phlegmatic muse were reunited. Every day she glanced at a photo on her bulletin board – the two of them at a film festival clinking Martinis. Of course she had worried. Having to live up to the past. But as she wrote and rewrote the script, she only ever saw that quizzical face from the photo as her leading man. With Murray she knew that the rogue's heart would come through.

Discussing the film in the endless promotional back-and-forth, Coppola hit upon an apt description for Felix, her face sphinx-like behind the pun.

"He's sort of a fairy godfather."

Technically speaking, this was Coppola's third film with Murray. In 2014, she directed the indulgent meta-whimsy of *A Very Murray Christmas* – an hour-long folderol mixing TV movie and seasonal special. Made for Netflix, the medium-sized concept parodied those old-time variety shows decked in celebrities murdering the classics. The opening scene promises a familiar mood: Murray back at the window of an expensive hotel gazing onto a snow-globe New York, his face an uncertain mix of resignation and mischief, novelty antlers on his brow. He's playing himself, but we only see Bob Harris – as if there were any difference.

And so we go behind the scenes as "Murray" is cajoled into hosting a Christmas telecast despite a blizzard bringing the city to a halt. It's a New York inversion of the standard model – let's *not* put on the show.

The tone is pure, avuncular Murray, but we soon realise how much Johansson gave to the mystical algorithm of *Lost in Translation*. When a power cut eventually kills off the broadcast, Murray retires to the bar, and a procession of singers, stars, and Coppola's inner circle waft in and out to do much the same thing. It is crowded with in-jokes: members of French rock-outfit Phoenix, including husband Thomas Mars, appear as waiters; cousin Jason Schwartzman and pal Jones play a discontented couple on their wedding night. We are left to wonder if this is what it is like to spend Christmas with the Coppolas?

But her sleek atmospherics and Murray's elegant doldrums find no purchase. Broader laughs are called for than George Clooney in a dream sequence.

The venue for this cosy jamboree is Bemelmans Bar in the Carlyle Hotel, a dyed-in-the-wool New York jazz joint enveloped in Marcel Vertès murals, which also happens to feature prominently in *On The Rocks* – and no doubt the social lives of Coppola and Murray. One of a number of distinctly old-school Manhattan venues where the would-be sleuths hold gin-smoothed summits.

With Laura spiralling into self-doubt and suspicion, and a middle age where life is not conducive to art, this is as much the story of daughter as father. Another directorial self-portrait, and the next chapter in what Coppola described as "my way of exploring the identity crisis of a woman in different phases of her life…"

It's a unifying theme. From the girls adrift in *New York Stories* (which she co-wrote) and *Somewhere*, through the teenage anomie of *The Virgin Suicides* and *The Bling Ring*, to the twentysomething disillusion of *Lost in Translation* and *Marie Antoinette*, with *The Beguiled* capturing four repressed generations beneath the roof of a Civil War mansion. On every count men act as a catalyst.

On The Rocks picked up Coppola's project with a woman in her forties, as she was. "For me, it's not so much about growing up, but about her finding her role outside of this big father character. And her role in her life." We can read an entire career into that.

The idea took shape in 2012, when Coppola's two small daughters clamoured for her attention like bijou celebrities. Being creative in what she termed that "transition" was difficult. Filmmaking had to adapt to motherhood where her childhood had adapted to filmmaking. There was a strain to not being your fullest self. When Laura finds the space to start her new book, her office an oasis of sunlit order that surely corresponds to the director's own, she gets nothing done.

"As a writer you need hours to daydream," said Coppola, stressing a widely divergent approach from her father's non-stop frenzies at the typewriter. Is this why at forty-nine she had made seven films and at the same age her father had made sixteen?

The spur was the story a friend told her about hiding in the bushes to spy on her playboy father. Coppola reconfigured that to make father and daughter the detectives with a dash of Myrna Loy and William Powell in *The Thin Man* solving crimes between Martinis. The object of their homespun espionage became her husband, spotted leaping into cars with beautiful women. In effect it was one genre masquerading as another, a relationship movie done up as a caper as told through the prism of a father and daughter re-establishing a frayed bond.

On The Rocks needed to be verbose in ways Coppola had never been before. This was the tradition of Raymond Chandler, Dashiell Hammett, and Nora Ephron. The long, dialogue-rich scenes between insecure daughter and unreliable father were the soul of the movie. It helped to think of it as a play. The first draft was solely comprised of rambling conversations in bars and restaurants. And naturally she drew on life. Which meant her father. The scene where Felix watches *Breaking Bad* with his grandchildren was a direct lift from Francis babysitting his five-year-old granddaughter.

"But it's a great show," he protested, confronted by a mother's frown.

You suspect much of Felix's cod philosophising on the male species comes direct from Francis. The reasonable tone, the easy comebacks, the domineering advice.

"He's not that character," she said again and again, only bits of him. She remembered being in her early twenties and having Martinis with her dad while hung up on some guy.

"Let me tell you what's really going on," he said. "Playboys are like air traffic control, and women are the planes…"

Jones was at a similar place in her life to Coppola. She was entering her forties in need of a starring role. Their friendship went back to *Lost in Translation*, when Jones had come close to playing Charlotte. "I was workshopping the script at an acting class, and she played the role that Scarlett Johansson ended up playing," recalled Coppola. They were both daughters striking out on creative paths while bearing the burden of a heavyweight dad. Jones's paterfamilias is legendary music producer Quincy Jones (the man behind late Sinatra, classic Michael Jackson, and over forty film scores).

Born in Los Angeles and brought up in 1970s Bel Air, where being the offspring of a mixed marriage still carried a stigma, Jones was prodigiously intelligent. She flew from high school to Harvard, where she studied religion and philosophy, but discovered theatre. Her screen debut came in *The Last Don*, a 1997 miniseries based on a book by Mario Puzo (from his late cycle of *Godfather* makeovers). She had a quirky, chatterbox vulnerability that offset her dusky leading-lady beauty and gravitated into comedy: *The Office, Angie Tribeca*, and a recurring role on hit sitcom *Parks and Recreation*. She diversified into documentaries, scripts (with a hand in *Toy Story 4*), songs, and modelling, but feature films had been scarce.

"I knew she could play the straight man with Bill," said Coppola. It was all about the reactions. The vexation.

"Jones – exasperated, bewildered, ultimately resigned – is at least the equal of her older co-star," observed *The Irish Times*, and that's just it. Murray thrives in a double-act. Between them the two contrasting stars – air and earth – are the essence of what makes it Coppola's most mature and subtle film.

Having made sensual sport of Tokyo, Los Angeles, and Paris (in an off-centre sort of way in *Marie Antoinette*), New York was now her canvas: the city of her family, her birth, and her current home. "You try to create a world for the audience to go to. I wanted to do a film in New York because I live here, and also for the glamour of this city and tradition of movies set in Manhattan."

But she did something very clever, and almost self-satirising. She divided the world in two.

On one side was the retro myth, an unattainable, gentleman's Manhattan that takes in Felix's favourite ports of call where he flirts with the young waitresses, and Laura gets mistaken for his floozy. As well as Bemelmans, with its *Cotton Club* charms, locations included miraculously available space in Raouls, Indochine, and the 21 Club, where they filmed at the table of Bogart and Bacall. It is a fantasy into which Felix will whisk his daughter by Alfa Romeo, swerving tail lights, giving chase like they do in the movies. His apartment is like a showroom, or a hotel.

Meanwhile, Laura's New York comes hemmed in by construction sites and schoolyards, and the scruffy second-hand chic of the Strand and Greenlight Books. Her loft-like apartment is hardly shabby – Coppola and production designer Anne Ross decided Felix must have helped out as a way of always being present. But it is lived in rather than decorated, maybe along the lines of the director's place in the West Village.

"As with all of Coppola's pictures," appreciated *Time* magazine, "it's the layering of details that counts, the accretion of sly but not minor observations that come to form the whole, like the stippled strokes of a Seurat painting."

Money and luxury are no guarantee against loneliness and confusion.

As a sign of the times, and something inconceivable in her father's heyday, Apple TV financed *On The Rocks*. Which took it straight to streaming in 2020. With the pandemic this looked like salvation (the lockdown also made a fable of the bustling restaurants it depicted), but it was also a glimpse into an unreadable future. Gone were the slings and arrows of box office reports, but a film's success became harder to judge. There were new and more flexible routes to market, but every danger that the director would become anonymous, film devalued to product. The myth of the Movie Brat was written into the grain of their box office fortunes. What stories will we tell of the effortless availability of video on demand?

That being said, Coppola had reached the enviable position of her name and style being the main selling point like a hallmark. And with Apple's backing, she set her compass to post-Civil War New York and an adaptation of Edith Wharton's *The Custom of the Country*, with all the spaciousness that a miniseries could provide. In its way a saga every bit as venal as *The Godfather*, as newcomer Undine Spragg schemes and marries her way to the upper reaches of Manhattan society.

How do we define Sofia Coppola, the Moon in this story to her father's Earth? She has glided as a filmmaker, conflict adverse, but sure of her course. Family helped and hindered. The squalls of her childhood on movie sets, up close to the tormented artist who happened to be her father, painting voodoo pictures to pin to the family gates in order to ward off the bailiffs: all of that may have turned her to a more reflective, subdued sensibility. The luxury of her life is up there on the screen too. Being a Coppola offered her the choice of filmmaking – it was the family trade, now moving into a third generation – but it has been a burden. How do you escape the inky shadows of a father's legend?

They share more than you think, father and daughter. Her films have been a quixotic, yearning quest for identity. They flow on emotional currents. You could say, her defining style is a search for definition. No wonder we relate. *The Virgin Suicides*, *Lost in Translation*, the neglected ironies of *Marie Antoinette*, and the pinwheeling tragicomedy of *On The Rocks*, are elegant, consistent, modern (but not conditioned by fashion), and deceptively moving. Coppola fulfilled the career Francis wanted: small, personal, original, and free from interference. It suited her better.

"[She is] better known and more beloved than I am," announced a delighted Francis. The estate launched a new Sofia Chardonnay. According to the website, "Light in spirit. Elegant in character."

What of Francis? At eighty-two he had cultivated a peaceful existence among his vineyards, but embers of that old ferocity were still aglow. New York was on his mind too. *Megalopolis* still danced ahead of him like a mirage. This was to be the last, great Coppola epic; his great white whale.

Between discussions of his renewed interest in personal films, and waxing wise on the past, Coppola would occasionally drop hints about his progress on *Megalopolis*. Which wouldn't come cheap – he still reserved the right to his old habits. It will be a heartbreaking love story, he promised, and a period extravaganza spanning from the 1920s to the 1930s, into the '50s, and '60s… Snatches of plot he let slip told of an upstart architect who yearns to transform New York into a utopia only to draw swords with a conservative mayor, who turns to organised crime to ruin his foe. Was he aware he was telling his own story?

"I am just a builder," Coppola once said, his head lost in his grand plans. "I would like to build a city. I would like to build a new society…"

He came close in 2001, opening up a branch of Zoetrope in New York, moving into preproduction, and testing the power of special effects to build a cityscape to rival *Metropolis* or *Blade Runner*, using Roman history as his foundation. But the events of 9/11 tore everything asunder, not simply his immediate plans to film in the now devastated city, but the entire reasoning behind the project. How could he fabricate a utopia now? What did the word even mean anymore?

In 2009, *Megalopolis* stirred from its cocoon, and he was determined to cast Jude Law as his idealistic architect. He would finance it with his own money, from the wine and hotels, once again putting the family's security at risk for art. "I have an imaginary box full of imaginary money," he joked, but the years ticked by with the film no nearer to fulfilment.

During one of the Zoom interviews that reduced the old combat to digital windows during the pandemic in 2020, he defiantly waved a shoebox-sized screenplay at the camera. "This is it, complete with a subtitle borrowed from H. G. Wells – '*The Shape of Things to Come*'," he said. But fate may well have had its final say. What form will a utopia take in a post-pandemic world? Indeed what form will cinema take?

The past called to Francis as loudly as the future.

He became preoccupied with fighting old battles, settling scores, re-editing the troubled pictures to his satisfaction, and having the last word over dead producers. Robert Evans hung on until 2019, his hunches occasionally stirring (*Sliver*, *How to Lose a Guy in Ten Days*), but diminished by ill health he became reclusive, confined to Woodland, working through the last of his seven marriages.

There now exists a suite of director's cuts and alternative versions like a parallel universe (or an extension of Francis's theories of Live Cinema). *Apocalypse Now* received its *Final Cut* in 2019. In the same year, *The Cotton Club Encore* let the musical numbers stretch their nimble limbs and subplots to take dramatic shape by adding twenty-five minutes and removing thirteen. He didn't unearth a masterpiece – Richard Gere was still a drudge – but it made for a sweeter cocktail.

Francis grew grandiose in his tinkering. Didn't Leonardo Da Vinci keep dabbing at the Mona Lisa for twenty years? "I'm not comparing myself to Leonardo, just as an example," he quickly added, but with cinema rooted by the pandemic, on its thirtieth anniversary he returned *The Godfather Part III* – to how he foresaw it being if twitchy Paramount executives hadn't harried it into cinemas. When he had written it with Puzo, between lengthy dalliances on the casino floor, he had wanted to call it *The Death of Michael Corleone*. "We thought it wasn't a third part, but more of a coda, an epilogue."

The film is repositioned outside of the trilogy as more of a postscript. A commentary on *The Godfather* saga in the cold light of day, said the sagacious critic David Ehrlich, "to see what it means for a Great Man to outlive the blinding power of his own myth." That idea carried resonance behind the camera. That all this retrofitting amounted to an artist self-reflexively poring over his career to see what became of Francis Ford Coppola.

As far back as 1977, decades before television took narrative to novelistic heights, Coppola orchestrated a seven-hour combination of the first two *Godfather* films as a miniseries entitled *The Godfather Saga*, broadcast over consecutive nights on NBC. It made for an ambitious refit, a chance to edit the story to run chronologically from a young Vito to Michael stewing in his sins by Lake Tahoe. New footage was liberally reinserted, but the individual virtuosity of each film was lost. The same trick was pulled in 1990 with *The Godfather Trilogy: 1901–1980*, which included the third film, and ran to nearly ten hours. But it was only made available on VHS and laserdisc.

Things come full circle. The turbulent saga that went on behind the scenes takes shape as a television drama. As these words are being written, Barry Levinson prepares an HBO miniseries entitled *Francis and the Godfather*, from a coveted script by Andrew Farotte, pivoting around the battle of wills between director and producers. The potential cast is impressive and flattering: Oscar Isaac as Francis, Jake Gyllenhaal as Evans, Elle Fanning as Ali MacGraw, and Elisabeth Moss as Eleanor Coppola.

His life is becoming fiction.

How do you attempt to summarise the great thunderstorm of his life and career? To account for the chaos and contradiction, the recklessness, the sheer self-destruction that have contributed to the dancing electricity of his genius. Has there ever been a filmmaker so nakedly himself? How do you bottle the legacy of the man who made *The Godfather*? How do you cap the story of a patriarch and artist, head of an ever-widening travelling circus of filmmakers, not least a daughter revealed as the worthy heir? How do you get to grips with Francis Ford Coppola?

We start (and end) with the films. The hallowed 1970s that gave us a quartet of ravishing masterworks. *The Godfather* and its first sequel, the Dostoevskyian depths of *The Conversation*, and the seething currents of *Apocalypse Now* have a vitality that remains unrivalled. That era is still uppermost in American cinema. Hell, in American art. They are like a museum tour of paintings swooning in shadow – the depiction of a tainted soul.

The irony is that as often and as loudly as he declared independence, he did his best work within the studio system scratching at the walls. Even *Apocalypse Now* still had one damp boot in the enemy camp. Hadn't Michelangelo raged as he painted the Sistine Chapel? And he only had to deal with Pope Julius II, not Robert Evans. The truth is the strain of studio patronage brought out the best in him.

The standard argument runs that he left much of himself behind in the jungles of *Apocalypse Now*, where he lost track of the line that divided life and art. And the flame would be finally extinguished with the death of a son. But that's too easy. Fitfully perhaps, the flame burned on in fascinating, enduring films like *Rumble Fish*, *Peggy Sue Got Married*, *Tucker: The Man and His Dream*, *The Rainmaker*, and *Tetro*.

We know the flaws. That he neglected women as his focus – leaving that space free for the reflective power of his daughter. That despite beginning his career with forays into the softest porn his films tend to lack a libidinous charge. Then you recall heavenly Apollonia in *The Godfather*, or Diane Lane's salty flapper Vera in *The Cotton Club*, or the vampire urges of *Bram Stoker's Dracula*. Who else would decide to paint an A-list horror epic with the antique brushstrokes of silent movie? He ventured into films waiting for the bolt that sometimes never struck.

Of all the Movie Brats he was the most inconsistent, but the most daring. He led the way. He fulfilled their promise. We can compare him to fellow Italian-American Martin Scorsese, so tightly bound to his morally uncertain worlds, fascinated by wickedness and guilt, the line between story and storyteller indistinct in the kick of his filmmaking, his style. But Scorsese never gave us the opera, the excess, the wild torment of creation. Francis raged at the limits of filmmaking, living his life and career in high drama. And that was heroic.

We can compare him to Steven Spielberg and erstwhile best friend and technocrat George Lucas, caught in the upswell of popular raptures. Is there not, secretly, a closer kinship between Coppola and Spielberg than any of his peers? Light and dark, they upheld the Hollywood myth.

"He is multitudes," said film historian David Thomson, who has pressed his case so often. And that multiplicity could be its own worst enemy – he could be distracted by power, and was Hollywood's direst bookkeeper. When you talk about Francis, you mean the auteur, director for hire, screenwriter, playwright, conductor of theatre and opera, producer, mogul, publisher, scientist, innovator, figurehead, impresario, revolutionary, megalomaniac, brother, husband, father, and winemaker in repose.

He blurs into intriguing ambiguity in close-up. At once the great immigrant showman, cooking pasta for family and crew, sat at the head of the table, and the reclusive artist. Often close to darkness, he was still that lonely boy trapped beneath his sheets. All his films are tied to a man figuring out his own identity. He was equal parts Michael, Sonny, and Fredo Corleone.

"My films make my life," he confessed. "If you are a serious artist, your work will be about you."

There is one more story. What you might consider a parable or a fairy tale that he liked to tell, about a thief sentenced to death by a king. "And the thief calls out, 'Sire, don't kill me! I know how much you love horses. Well, I can teach your horse to talk. All I ask is three months, and you'll have the only talking horse in the land.'"

The storyteller knows all there is to know about the dramatic pause, and the building of suspense. We see it in the sepia grace notes hard won from Gordon Willis's camera, or Vittorio Storaro's pulses of colour.

"The king agrees to spare the thief's life and sends him to the palace stables. A stable hand asks him why he's there, and he explains. 'That's crazy,' says the stable hand. 'What are you going to do at the end of the three months?'

"'A lot can happen in three months,' the thief shrugs. 'The king may die. The law may change. I may be pardoned. And, who knows, I may get the horse to talk.'"

Francis Ford Coppola got the horse to talk.

EPILOGUE

It always comes back to family; the genius that runs in the blood. As the pandemic took hold in early 2020, the entire Coppola clan took refuge at Napa Valley, staying for months: twenty-two in total – children, grandchildren, nieces, and nephews, an entire dynasty under one roof.

More than anything, he loved being surrounded by children, the tiny typhoons reaping havoc across his placid life. That took him even further back – to what he lost and gained as a small boy.

Once the pandemic lifted, he would resume the ritual he has instituted with his grandchildren. When they reach the age of nine, he takes them anywhere in the world they have always wanted to see. "I've done it with three of my grandchildren and I have six of them, so I have three to go," he said. Of course, he was nine years old when he was bedridden with polio, when he could only travel in his imagination.

Surrounded by children and artists, the happy patriarch, inaugurated bi-weekly screenings in his private cinema, every Wednesday and Saturday. It was a crash course in cinema history.

"There was no collaboration or discussion," he said. "It was my idea to do it, so I got to choose the films that I think are the greatest movies ever made." Afterwards they would settle down to discuss whatever silent or foreign or American masterpiece they had watched. With good wine lubricating opinion.

"My greatest pleasure is learning," he said. It was like being back at Hofstra, or the early days of Zoetrope.

There was one house rule – nothing made by a relative. So they didn't watch *The Godfather*, or *The Conversation*, or *Apocalypse Now*. There was no debate over the merits of *One from the Heart* or *Rumble Fish*. They didn't savour *The Virgin Suicides*, *Lost in Translation*, or *Marie Antoinette*. Or *CQ*, or *Paris Can Wait*. For the sake of harmony, the family business went wilfully ignored.

ACKNOWLEDGEMENTS

Where do you start, and finish, but with the Coppolas – father and daughter, Francis Ford and Sofia. In their divergent yet interlinked ways, they represent two pivotal figures in the landscape of American film. And what a story they present the biographer. To travel with Francis is to be swept up in a thrilling storm at once creative and self-destructive (and those two things are not mutually exclusive). Shattering convention, indeed stretching the very nature of the medium, he has wrought some of the greatest films ever made. Sofia offers the calm at the eye of the hurricane. She grew up amid her father's chaos, and has forged her own distinctive path, shattering her own boundaries. Entering a new millennium, she has become the Coppola whom we turn to first.

All books stand on the shoulders of other books. There are some very fine biographies on Francis already out there, but I would highlight the transfixing detail of Michael Schumacher's *Francis Ford Coppola: A Filmmaker's Life* and the ongoing work of Peter Cowie, who has given us not only the excellent *Coppola*, but specific studies of *The Godfather* films and *Apocalypse Now*.

This book owes much to the film libraries of London and California, and the wider work of those who have written so candidly about Hollywood in the 1970s and beyond (all mentioned below).

Special mention must also go to Eleanor Coppola, whose diaries provide such a vivid illumination of husband, daughter, and herself. By stealth, and she has striven to avoid the eye of publicity, this is a biography of Eleanor too: artist, writer, and filmmaker, and so often the rudder to steer the family right. And I have reached out further to touch on those other Coppola descendants, from Nicolas Cage to Jason Schwartzman and Gia Coppola. Is there truly something in the blood? Family is both theme and life.

So my thanks go to all Coppolas, in every guise.

I would like to give my heartfelt thanks to my editor Robert Nichols, for his intuitive thoughts, his appreciation, and his great patience – I may have been a trifle late, but nothing compared to *Apocalypse Now*. And to my copy editor Catriona Robb, who has plunged down my own particular rabbit hole. No book begins with the first page, years of discussion and argument and learning lie behind every word, including the invaluable thoughts and help of Mark Dining, Damon Wise, Dan Jolin, Ian Freer, Adam Smith, Angie Errigo, Kim Newman, Nick de Semlyen, and Lyndy Saville.

And my eternal love and thanks go to Kat, who has sustained me through my own dark nights of soul.

SELECTED BIBLIOGRAPHY

Bach, Steven. *Final Cut.* William Morrow, 1985

Bergan, Ronald. *Francis Ford Coppola Close Up: The Making of His Movies.* Thunder's Mouth Press, 1998

Biskind, Peter. *Down and Dirty Pictures: Miramax, Sundance, and the Rise of Independent Film.* Bloomsbury Publishing PLC, 2005

Biskind, Peter. *Easy Riders, Raging Bulls: How the Sex-Drugs-And-Rock'n'Roll Generation Saved Hollywood.* Bloomsbury, 1998

Biskind, Peter. *The Godfather Companion.* HarperCollins Publishers Ltd, 1991

Boorman, John & Donohue, Walter, editors. *Projections 6: Film-makers on Film-making.* Faber & Faber, 1996

Brando, Marlon, with Lindsey, Robert. *Songs My Mother Taught Me.* Century, 1994

Carey, Gary. *Marlon Brando: The Only Contender.* Hodder and Stoughton Ltd, 1986

Coppola, Eleanor. *Notes on a Life.* Nan A Telise, 2008

Coppola, Eleanor. *Notes on the Making of Apocalypse Now.* Limelight Editions, 1979

Coppola, Francis Ford. *Live Cinema and its Techniques.* Liverlight Publishing, 2017

Coppola, Francis Ford. *The Godfather Notebook.* Regan Arts, 2016

Corman, Roger, with Jerome, Jim. *How I made a Hundred Movies in Hollywood and Never Lost a Dime.* Da Capo Press, 1998

Cowie, Peter. *Coppola.* Andre Deutsch Ltd, 1989

Cowie, Peter. *The Apocalypse Now Book*. Da Capo Press, 2001

Cowie, Peter. *The Godfather Book*. Faber & Faber, 1997

Evans, Robert. *The Kid Stays in the Picture*. Faber, 2004

Evans, Robert. *The Fat Lady Sang*. It Books, 2013

Gelmis, Joseph. *The Film Director as Superstar*. Martin Secker and Warburg, 1971

Jacobs, Diane. *Hollywood Renaissance*. A.S. Barnes & Company, 1977

Johnson, Robert. *Francis Ford Coppola*. Twayne Publishers, 1978

Kael, Pauline. *The Age of Movies: Selected Writings of Pauline Kael*. The Library of America, 2011

LoBrutto, Vincent & Morrison, Harriet R.. *The Coppolas: A Family Business*. Praeger, 2012

Manso, Peter. *Brando: The Biography*. Hyperion, 1995

Medavoy, Mike. *You're Only as Good as Your Next One*. Atria Books, 2013

Nashawaty, Chris. *Crab Monsters, Teenage Cavemen, and Candy Stripe Nurses: Roger Corman: King of the B-movie*. Abrams, 2013

Ondaatje, Michael. *The Conversations: Walter Murch and the Art of Editing Film*. Bloomsbury Publishing, 2008

Phillips, Gene D. & Hill, Rodney, editors. *Francis Ford Coppola Interviews*. University Press of Mississippi, 2005

Pollack, Dale. *Skywalking: The Life and Films of George Lucas*. Da Capo Press, May 31, 1999 (updated edition)

Puzo, Mario. *The Godfather Papers and Other Confessions*. William Heinemann Ltd, 1972

Pye, Michael & Myles, Lynda. *The Movie Brats*. Faber & Faber, 1979

Randall, Stephen, editor. *The Playboy Interviews: The Directors*. M Press, 2006

Schumacher, Michael. *Francis Ford Coppola: A Filmmaker's Life*. Crown Pub, 1999

Thomson, David. *A Light in the Dark: A History of Movie Directors*. Weidenfeld & Nicholson, 2020

Thomson, David. *The Big Screen: The Story of the Movies and What They Did to Us*. Penguin, 2013

Thomson, David. *Have You Seen…?: A Personal Introduction to 1,000 Films*. Penguin, 2010

Thomson, David. *The New Biographical Dictionary of Film*. Little, Brown, 2003

Wasson, Sam. *The Big Goodbye: Chinatown and the Last Years of Hollywood.* Faber & Faber, 2020

Author interview: Francis Ford Coppola, 2009

SOURCES

BACK COVER

Ross, Lillian. *Some Figures on a Fantasy: Francis Coppola. The New Yorker,* November 8, 1982

EPIGRAMS

O'Brien, Edna. *James Joyce.* Weidenfeld & Nicolson, 2020
Radish, Christina. *Bill Murray Gets Candid on 'Ghostbusters' Sequels, Groundhog Day, Working With Wes Anderson & Sofia Coppola and More.* Collider, April 5, 2021

PROLOGUE

Coppola, Eleanor. *Notes on the Making of Apocalypse Now.* Limelight Editions, 1979

CHAPTER 1 – WILL POWER

Academy of Achievement, Golden Plate Awardees: Francis Ford Coppola interview. Achievement.org, June 17, 1994
Biography of Francis Ford Coppola, unattributed, University of California, Berkley Art Museum & Pacific Film Archive, July 17, 1968
Boorman, John & Donohue, Walter, editors. *Projections 4 1/2: Film makers on Film-making.* John Boorman and Walter Donohue, Fabe & Faber, 1996
Braudy, Susan. *Francis Ford Coppola: A Profile. The Atlantic Monthly,* August 1976
Breskin, David. *The Rolling Stone Interview: Francis Ford Coppola. Rolling Stone,* February 7, 1991

Bulgakowa, Oksana. *Sergei Eisenstein: A Biography*. Potemkin Press, 2002

Cabanatuan, Michael. *Italia Coppola – Mother of Filmmaker. San Francisco Chronicle*, January 29, 2012

Coppola, Eleanor. *Notes on a Life*. Nan A. Talise, 2008

Coppola, Eleanor. *Notes on the Making of Apocalypse Now*. Limelight Editions, 1979

Coppola, Francis Ford. *Live Cinema and its Techniques*. Liverlight Publishing, 2017

Coppola, Francis Ford. *What's it All Really Mean.? Video Review*, January 1985

Corman, Roger, with Jerome, Jim. *How I made a Hundred Movies in Hollywood and Never Lost a Dime*. Da Capo Press, 1998

Cowie, Peter. *Coppola*. Andrew Deutsch Ltd, 1989

Cutts, John. *The Dangerous Age. Films and Filming*, May 1969

Fabricant, Florence. *For the Love of Pasta, a Director Movies Into Macaroni. The New York Times*, June 13, 2001

Francis Ford Coppola profile, BBC TV, April 6, 1985

Gelmis, Joseph. *The Film Director as Superstar*. Martin Secker & Warburg, 1971

Ginnane, Anthony I.. *Francis Ford Coppola. Cinema Papers*, November-December 1975

Insdorf, Annette. *Francis Ford Coppola on the Future of Cinema, Marlon Brando and Regrets*. 92Y, July 27, 2015

Nashawaty, Chris. *Crab Monsters, Teenage Cavemen, and Candy Stripe Nurses: Roger Corman: King of the B-movie*. Abrams, 2013

Phillips, Gene D.. *Francis Ford Coppola Interviewed. Film in Review Vol. 40, No. 3*, March 1989

Rodriguez, Robert. *Francis Ford Coppola Interview*. Director's Chair Ep. 5, June 23, 2019

Rose, Charlie. *Francis Ford Coppola interview. Charlie Rose*, January 28, 1994

Ross, Lillian. *Some Figures on a Fantasy: Francis Coppola. The New Yorker*, November 8, 1982

Rubin Harriet. *The Art of Darkness. Fast Company*, September 30, 1998

Savage, Andrew. *Francis Ford Coppola Interview*. The Commonwealth Club of California, November 18, 2016

Schumacher, Michael. *Francis Ford Coppola: A Filmmaker's Life*. Crown Pub, 1999

Talese, Gay. *Francis Ford Coppola Interview*. Esquire, July 1981

Thompson, Howard. *Dementia 13*. The New York Times, October 24, 1963

Thomson, David & Gray, Lucy. *Idols of the King*. Film Comment, September–October 1988

CHAPTER 2 – MOVIE BRAT

Biskind, Peter. *Easy Riders, Raging Bulls: How the Sex-Drugs-And-Rock'n'Roll Generation Saved Hollywood*. Bloomsbury, 1998

Coppola, Eleanor. *Notes: The Making of Apocalypse Now*. Eleanor Coppola, 1979

Cowie, Peter. *Coppola*. Crown Pub, 1999

Cowie, Peter. *The Apocalypse Now Book*. Da Capo Press, 2001

Cowie, Peter. *The Godfather Book*. Faber & Faber, 1997

Gelmis, Joseph. *The Film Director as Superstar*. Martin Secker & Warburg, 1971

Gilmore, Geoffrey. *Interview with Francis Ford Coppola and Martin Scorsese, Hollywood Insiders*, 1977

A Legacy of Filmmakers: The Early Years of American Zoetrope. Warner Bros., 2004

Murray, William. *Playboy interview: Francis Ford Coppola*. Playboy, July 1975

Nathan, Ian. *The Less Expensive a Film is, the More Ambitious it Can Be....* Empire, June 2009

Phillips, Gene D.. *Francis Ford Coppola Interviewed*. Film in Review Vol. 40, No. 3, March 1989

Rodriguez, Robert. *Francis Ford Coppola Interview*. Director's Chair Ep. 5, June 23, 2019

Schumacher, Michael. *Francis Ford Coppola: A Filmmaker's Life*. Crown Pub, 1999

Sragow, Michael. *Godfatherhood*. The New Yorker, March 24, 1997

Thomson, David & Gray, Lucy. *Idols of the King*. Film Comment, September–October 1988

CHAPTER 3 – LEAVE THE GUN. TAKE THE CANNOLI

The 45th Academy Awards. *Oscars.org*, 1973

Biskind, Peter. *Easy Riders, Raging Bulls: How the Sex-Drugs-And-Rock'n'Roll Generation Saved Hollywood*. Bloomsbury, 1998

Biskind, Peter. *The Godfather Companion*. HarperCollins Publishers Ltd, 1991

Coppola, Eleanor. *Notes on a Life*. Nan A. Talese, 2008

Coppola, Francis Ford. *The Godfather Notebook*. Regan Arts, 2016

Cowie, Peter. *Coppola*. De Capo Press, 1994

Cowie, Peter. *The Godfather Book*. Faber & Faber, 1997

Evans, Robert. *The Kid Stays in the Picture*. Faber, 2004

Farber, Stephen & Green, Marc. *Dynasty, Italian Style. California Magazine*, April 1984

Freedland, Jonathan. *The Godfather: How the Mafia Blockbuster Became a Political Handbook. The Guardian*, October 31, 2020

Hatch, Robert. *The Godfather. The Nation*, April 3, 1972

Insdorf, Annette. *Francis Ford Coppola on the Future of Cinema, Marlon Brando and Regrets*. 92Y, July 27, 2015

Jones, Jenny M. *The Annotated Godfather: The Complete Screenplay*. Black Dog & Leventhal, August 20, 2009 edition

Kael, Pauline. *Alchemy. The New Yorker*, March 18, 1972

Kael, Pauline. *Fathers and Sons. The New Yorker*, December 23, 1973

Klmesrud, Judy. *Talia Shire: No Longer the Kid Sister. The New York Times*, November 22, 1976

Manso, Peter. *Brando: The Biography*. Hyperion, 1995

Murray, William. *Playboy interview: Francis Ford Coppola. Playboy*, July 1975

Ondaatje, Michael. *The Conversations: Walter Murch and the Art of Editing Film*. Bloomsbury Publishing, 2008

Paglia, Camille. *It All Comes Back To Family. The New York Times*, May 8, 1997

Puzo, Mario. *The Godfather Papers and Other Confessions*. William Heinemann Ltd, 1972

Rubin, Harriet. *The Art of Darkness. Fast Company*, September 30, 1998

Savage, Andrew. *Francis Ford Coppola Interview*. The Commonwealth Club of California, November 18, 2016

Schumacher, Michael. *Francis Ford Coppola: A Filmmaker's Life*. Crown Pub, 1999

Seal, Mark. *The Godfather Wars. Vanity Fair*, February 28, 2009

Simon, Alex & Keefe, Terry. *The Hollywood Interview: Talia Shire. The Hollywood Interview.com*, November 23, 2012

Sragow, Michael. *Godfatherhood. The New Yorker*, March 24, 1997

Thomson, David. *Have You Seen...?: A Personal Introduction to 1,000 Films*. Penguin, 2010

Wasson, Sam. *The Big Goodbye: Chinatown and the Last Years of Hollywood*. Faber & Faber, 2020

Zimmerman, Paul D.. *The Godfather: Triumph for Brando. Newsweek*, March 13, 1972

CHAPTER 4 – CONTROL FREAKS

The 47th Academy Awards. *Oscars.org*, 1975

Babitz, Eve. *All This and The Godfather Too. Coast*, April 1975

De Palma, Brian. *The Making of The Conversation: An Interview With Francis Ford Coppola. Filmmakers Newsletter*, May 1974

Biskind, Peter. *Easy Riders, Raging Bulls: How the Sex-Drugs-And-Rock'n'Roll Generation Saved Hollywood*. Bloomsbury, 1998

Francis Ford Coppola Interview on The Conversation, TCM Classic Film Festival, 2016

Biskind, Peter. *The Godfather Companion*. HarperCollins Publishers Ltd, 1991

The Conversation Collector's Edition Blu-ray, Studio Canal, October 31, 2011

Canby, Vincent. *The Godfather Part II is Hard to Define. The New York Times*, December 13, 1974

Coppola, Eleanor. *Notes on a Life*. Nan A. Talese, 2008

Cowie, Peter. *Coppola*. De Capo Press, 1994

Cowie, Peter. *The Godfather Book*. Faber & Faber, 1997

Farber, Stephen & Green, Marc. *Dynasty, Italian Style. California Magazine*, April 1984

Gelmis, Joseph. *The Film Director as Superstar*. Martin Secker & Warburg, 1971

The Godfather Trilogy Corleone Legacy Edition Blu-ray, Paramount, August 12, 2019

Kael, Pauline. *Fathers and Sons. The New Yorker*, December 23, 1973

Lindsey, Robert. *Promises to Keep. The New York Times*, July 24, 1988

Murray, William. *Playboy interview: Francis Ford Coppola. Playboy*, July 1975

Ondaatje, Michael. *The Conversations: Walter Murch and the Art of Editing Film*. Bloomsbury Publishing, 2008

Phillips, Gene D.. *Francis Ford Coppola Interviewed. Film in Review Vol. 40, No. 3*, March 1989

Rodriguez, Robert. *Francis Ford Coppola Interview*. Director's Chair Ep. 5, June 23, 2019

Rosen, Marjorie. *Francis Ford Coppola Interview, Film Comment, Vol. 10, No. 4*, July–August, 1974

Ross, Lillian. *Some Figures on a Fantasy: Francis Coppola. The New Yorker*, November 8, 1982

Schumacher, Michael. *Francis Ford Coppola: A Filmmaker's Life*. Crown Pub, 1999

Sragow, Michael. *Godfatherhood. The New Yorker*, March 24, 1997

Wasson, Sam. *The Big Goodbye: Chinatown and the Last Years of Hollywood*. Faber & Faber, 2020

CHAPTER 5 – NEVER GET OFF THE BOAT

The 51st Academy Awards. *Oscars.org*, 1979

Bach, Steven. *Final Cut*. William Morrow, 1985

Biskind, Peter. *Easy Riders, Raging Bulls: How the Sex-Drugs-And-Rock'n'Roll Generation Saved Hollywood*. Bloomsbury, 1998

Conrad, Joseph. *Heart of Darkness*. Legend Press, 2020.

Coppola, Eleanor. *Notes on the Making of Apocalypse Now*. Limelight Editions, 1979

Coppola, Francis Ford. Cannes Press Conference, May 19, 2019

Cowie, Peter. *Coppola*. De Capo Press, 1994

Cowie, Peter. *The Apocalypse Now Book*. Da Capo Press, 2001

Ebert, Roger. *Apocalypse Now. Chicago Sun-Times*, November 28, 1999

Ebert, Roger. *Apocalypse Now Redux. Chicago Sun-Times*, August 10, 2001

Francis Ford Coppola profile, BBC TV, April 6, 1985

Geng, Veronica, *Mistah Kurtz – He Dead, The New Yorker*, August 26, 1979

Hearts of Darkness: A Filmmaker's Apocalypse, ZM Productions, 1991

Hitchens, Gordon. *Orson Welles's Prior Interest in Conrad's Heart of Darkness. Variety*. June 13, 1979

Hiu, Tony, *Coppola's Cinematic Apocalypse Is Finally at Hand. The New York Times*, August 12, 1979

Kauffman, Stanley. *Coppola's War. New Republic*, September 15, 1979

Lane, Anthony. *Darkness Revisited. The New Yorker*, July 29, 2001

Milius, John & Coppola, Francis Ford. *Apocalypse now Redux: An Original Screenplay*. Faber & Faber, 2001

Ondaatje, Michael. *The Conversations: Walter Murch and the Art of Editing Film*. Bloomsbury Publishing, 2008

Phillips, Gene D.. *Francis Ford Coppola Interviewed. Film in Review Vol. 40, No. 3*, March 1989

Pollack, Dale. *Skywalking: The Life and Films of George Lucas*. Da Capo Press, May 31, 1999 (updated edition)

Rich, Frank. *Apocalypse Now. Time*, August 1979

Rodriguez, Robert. *Francis Ford Coppola Interview*. Director's Chair Ep. 5, June 23, 2019

Rose, Charlie. *Francis Ford Coppola interview. Charlie Rose*, January 28, 1994

Savage, Andrew. *Francis Ford Coppola Interview*. The Commonwealth Club of California, November 18, 2016

Schumacher, Michael. *Francis Ford Coppola: A Filmmaker's Life*. Crown Pub 1999

Sragow, Michael, *The Conversation, The New Yorker*, August 15, 2016

Suid, Lawrence. *Apocalypse Now: Francis Ford Coppola Stages His Own Vietnam War. Cineaste*, Winter 1977-1978

Thompson, Richard. *Stoked. Film Comment*, July-August 1976

Unattributed. *Apocalypse Now Press Kit*. United Artists Corporation, 1979

Unattributed. *Heavy Typhoon Damage to Sets of Apocalypse Now. Variety*, May 28, 1976

Unattributed. *L'Histoire D' Apocalypse Now. Cannes Film Festival Program Note*, May 19, 1979

CHAPTER 6 – THREE FROM THE HEART

Biskind, Peter. *Easy Riders, Raging Bulls: How the Sex-Drugs-And-Rock'n'Roll Generation Saved Hollywood*. Bloomsbury, 1998

Coppola, Eleanor. *Notes on a Life*. Nan A. Telese, 2008

Coppola, Francis Ford. One From the Heart Press Conference, New York, January 15, 1981

Cowie, Peter. *Coppola*. De Capo Press, 1994

Haller, Scott. *Francis Ford Coppola's Biggest Gamble: One From the Heart. Saturday Review*, July 1981

Francis Ford Coppola profile, BBC TV, April 6, 1985

Hill, Logan. *The Wild, Wild Ways of Nicolas Cage. New York*, November 16, 2009

Italie, Hillel. *40 Years Later Hinton's The Outsiders Still Strikes a Chord Among Readers. The San Diego Union-Tribune*, October 3, 2007

King, Susan. *The Outsiders Stays Gold at 35: Inside Coppola's Crafty Methods and Stars' Crazy Pranks. Variety*, March 23, 2018

Lindsey, Robert. *Coppola Returns to The Vietnam Era, Minus Apocalypse. The New York Times*, May 3, 1987

Marchese, David. *Nicolas Cage on his Legacy, His Philosophy of Acting and His Metaphorical – and Literal – Search for the Holy Grail. The New York Times Magazine*, August 7, 2019

Osbourne, Robert. *The Outsiders. The Hollywood Reporter*, March 25, 1983

Phillips, Gene D.. *Francis Ford Coppola Interviewed. Film in Review Vol. 40, No. 3*, March 1989

Rodriguez, Robert. *Francis Ford Coppola Interview*. Director's Chair Ep. 5, June 23, 2019

Ross, Lillian. *Some Figures on a Fantasy: Francis Coppola. The New Yorker*, November 8, 1982

Rumble Fish – Masters of Cinema Edition Blu-ray. Eureka Entertainment Ltd., August 27, 2012

Schumacher, Michael. *Francis Ford Coppola: A Filmmaker's Life*. Crown Pub, 1999

Thomson, David & Gray, Lucy. *Idols of the King. Film Comment*, September–October 1988

CHAPTER 7 – HISTORY REPEATING

Attanasio, Paul. *Cotton Club: Coppola's Triumph. The Washington Post*, December 14, 1984

Corliss, Richard. *Let's Go to the Feelies. Time*, September 22, 1986

Cowie, Peter. *Coppola.* De Capo Press, 1994

Daly, Michael. *The Making of the Cotton Club: A True Tale of Hollywood. New York*, May 7, 1984

Evans, Robert. *The Kid Stays in the Picture.* Faber, 2004

Green, Jesse. *Kathleen Turner Meets Her Monster. The New York Times*, March 20, 2005

Greenburg, James. *Coppola-Cronenweth Union Rolling with Stone. Variety*, February 10, 1987

Gussow, Mel. *Parting Film Shots: Coppola and Dutch. The New York Times*, March 22, 1984

Hill, Logan. *The Wild, Wild Ways of Nicolas Cage. New York*, November 16, 2009

Kael, Pauline. *The Cotton Club. The New Yorker*, January 7, 1985

Kroll, Jack. *Harlem on My Mind. Newsweek*, December 24, 1984

Lindsey, Robert. *Coppola Returns to The Vietnam Era, Minus Apocalypse. The New York Times*, May 3, 1987

LoBrutto, Vincent & Morrison, Harriet R.. *The Coppolas: A Family Business.* Praeger, 2012

Marchese, David. *Nicolas Cage on his Legacy, His Philosophy of Acting and His Metaphorical – and Literal – Search for the Holy Grail. The New York Times Magazine*, August 7, 2019

Phillips, Gene D.. *Francis Ford Coppola Interviewed. Film in Review Vol. 40, No. 3*, March 1989

Ricky, Carrie. *Coppola Wants It Both Ways With "Cotton." San Francisco Sunday Examiner & Chronicle*, December 16, 1984

Ross, Lillian. *Some Figures on a Fantasy: Francis Coppola. The New Yorker*, November 8, 1982

Schruers, Fred. *Turner. Premiere*, August 1991

Schumacher, Michael. *Francis Ford Coppola: A Filmmaker's Life*. Crown Pub, 1999

Siskel, Gene. *Caring Coppola Brings Out the Best in Kathleen Turner*. Chicago *Tribune*, October 5, 1986

Siskel, Gene. *Celluloid Godfather*. Chicago *Tribune*, October 5, 1986

Thomson, David & Gray, Lucy. *Idols of the King*. *Film Comment*, September–October 1988

CHAPTER 8 – FATHERS AND SONS

Colburn, Marcia Froelke. *Preston Tucker Sets Chicago Dreaming – Until the Wheels Came Off*. *Chicago Tribune*, August 7, 1988

Coppola, Eleanor. *Notes on a Life*. Nan A. Telese, 2008

Cowie, Peter. *Coppola*. De Capo Press, 1994

Francis Ford Coppola Q&A, Sundance Kabuki Cinema, San Francisco, 10 August 2012

Gardens of Stone Limited Edition Blu-ray. Powerhouse Films. January 21, 2019

Guthmann, Edward. *Tucker Tells a Director's Kind of Tale*. San Francisco *Chronicle*, August 7, 1988

Kael, Pauline. *Two-Base Hit*. *The New Yorker*, March 20, 1989

Kehr, David. *Coppola's Garden too Solemn to Grow on You*. *Chicago Tribune*, May 6, 1987

Kempley, Rita. *Tucker: The Man and His Dream*. *The Washington Post*, August 12, 1988

Keough, Peter. *Coppola Carves a Cinematic Elegy: Gardens of Stone*. *Chicago Sun-Times*, May 10, 1987

Lindsey, Robert. *Coppola Returns to The Vietnam Era, Minus Apocalypse*. *The New York Times*, May 3, 1987

Lindsey, Robert. *Promises to Keep*. *The New York Times*, July 24, 1988

McGilligan, Patrick. *Arnold Schulman: Nothing But Regrets – Backstory 3*, Berkeley: University of California Press, 1997

Murray, William. *Playboy interview: Francis Ford Coppola*. *Playboy*, July 1975

Nerab, Jack R.. *From the Desk of Francis Ford Coppola*. *The Hollywood Reporter*, August 19, 1988

Phillips, Gene D.. *Francis Ford Coppola Interviewed*. *Film in Review Vol. 40, No. 3*, March 1989

Rafferty, Terrence. *Tucker: The Man and His Dream. The New Yorker*, August 22, 1988

Rubin, Harriet. *The Art of Darkness. Fast Company*, September 30, 1998

Schumacher, Michael. *Francis Ford Coppola: A Filmmaker's Life*. Crown Pub, 1999

CHAPTER 9 – THE DEVIL YOU KNOW

Biskind, Peter. *Francis Ford Coppola. Premiere*, September 1996

Boorman, John & Donohue, Walter, editors. *Projections 4 1/2 Film-makers on Film-making*. John Boorman & Walter Donohue, Faber & Faber, 1996

Campbell, Duncan. *Coppola Loses $20 million in Compensation for Lost Pinocchio. The Guardian*, March 22, 2001

Collin, Robbie. *Francis Ford Coppola on The Godfather Part III Backlash: "The Bullets That Went for Sofia Were Meant for Me." The Telegraph*, December 5, 2020

Coppola, Eleanor. *Notes on a Life*. Nan A. Telese, 2008

Coppola, Francis Ford. *Live Cinema and its Techniques*. Liverlight Publishing, 2017

Cornwell, Rupert. *God's Banker*. HarperCollins Publishers Ltd, 1984

Cowie, Peter. *Coppola*. De Capo Press, 1994

Cowie, Peter. *The Godfather Book*. Faber & Faber, 1997

The Godfather Family: A Look Inside. Paramount. 1990

Dworkin, Susan. *Coppola and Eiko on Bram Stoker's Dracula*. HarperCollins 1992

Gleiberman, Owen. *Jack. Entertainment Weekly*, September 7, 2011

Hearts of Darkness: A Filmmaker's Apocalypse, ZM Productions, 1991

Kroll, Jack. *The Corleones Return. Newsweek*, December 24, 1990

Lammers, Tim. *Talia Shire Talks The Godfather Coda, Rocky, More – Exclusive Interview. Looper.com*, January 5, 2021

Mars-Jones, Adam. *The Beautiful and the Damned. The Independent*, January 29, 1993

Maslin, Janet. *Hearts of Darkness: A Filmmaker's Apocalypse. The New York Times*, May 20, 2003

Mottram, James. *Sofia Coppola: "It's Hard For Me to Watch My 18-Year-Old Self."* The Independent, October 22, 2020

Ondaatje, Michael. *The Conversations: Walter Murch and the Art of Editing Film.* Bloomsbury Publishing, 2008

Parker, Ryan. *Francis Ford Coppola Says "Godfather: Part III" Recut Vindicates Film, Daughter Sofia.* The Hollywood Reporter, December 3, 2020

Robins, Cynthia. *Coppola Larger than Life.* San Francisco Examiner. November 16, 1997

Rubin Harriet. *The Art of Darkness.* Fast Company, September 30, 1998

Schumacher, Michael. *Francis Ford Coppola: A Filmmaker's Life.* Crown Pub, 1999

Seal, Mark. *The Godfather Wars.* Vanity Fair, February 28, 2009

Stein, Ruth. *Sofia and the Sequel.* San Francisco Chronicle. October 25, 1990

Turner, George. *Bram Stoker's Dracula: A Happening Vampire.* American Cinematographer, November 1992

Weintraub, Bernie. *Grisham's Law Attracts Coppola.* The New York Times, November 7, 1997

Whitty, Stephen. *Child's Play: Francis Ford Coppola Survey's his Career, His Future, and His Craft.* San Jose Mercury News, August 8, 1996

CHAPTER 10 – THE NEW BRATS

Biskind, Peter. *Down and Dirty Pictures: Miramax, Sundance, and the Rise of Independent Film.* Bloomsbury Paperbacks, 2016

Bradshaw, Peter. *Youth Without Youth.* The Guardian, December 14, 2007

Barcella, Laura. *Roman Coppola.* The Travel Almanac, April 25, 2013

Beal, Keaton. *Sofia Coppola on the 20th Anniversary of The Virgin Suicides: "It Means a Lot to Me That it Has a Life Now."* Vogue, April 21, 2020

Boorman, John & Donohue, Walter, editors. *Projections 4 1/2 Film-makers on Film-making.* John Boorman & Walter Donohue, Faber & Faber, 1996

Brown, Emma & Krueger, Lisa. *Legends: Sofia Coppola.* Interview, March 6, 2012

Coppola, Eleanor. *Notes on a Life.* Nan A. Telese, 2008

Hartlaub, Peter. *Coppola Reconnects With His Inner Auteur.* San Francisco Chronicle, December 10, 2007

LoBrutto, Vincent & Morrison, Harriet R.. *The Coppolas: A Family Business*. Praeger, 2012

Mottram, James. *Roman Coppola Interview. BBC.com*, October 28, 2014 (archived)

Singer, Leigh. *Roman Coppola: How to Make Films and Influence People. Dazed*, July 17, 2014

Thompson, Anne. *Isle of Dogs Co-Writer Roman Coppola on Becoming Wes Anderson's Collaborative Secret Weapon. IndieWire*, March 21, 2018

Unattributed. *Sofia Coppola: "Film is Our Family Business." The Talks*, June 22, 2011

Waxman, Sharon. *Rebels on the Backlot: Six Maverick Directors and How They Conquered the Hollywood System*. William Morrow, March 2, 2006

CHAPTER 11 – TOKYO DRIFT

The 75th Academy Awards, 2003. Oscars.org

Coppola, Eleanor. *Notes on a Life*. Nan A. Telese, 2008

Coppola, Eleanor. *Notes on the Making of Apocalypse Now*. Limelight Editions, 1979

Edelstein David. *Prisoner of Japan. Slate*, September 11, 2003

Haslem, Wendy. *Neon Gothic: Lost in Translation. Senses of Cinema*, April 2004

Hirschberg, Lynn. *The Coppola Smart Mob. The New York Times*, August 31, 2003

LoBrutto, Vincent & Morrison, Harriet R.. *The Coppolas: A Family Business*. Praeger, 2012

Lodge, Guy. *Sofia Coppola: "I Never Felt I Had to Fit into the Majority View." The Guardian*, July 2, 2017

Mottram, James. *Sofia Coppola: "It's Hard For Me to Watch My 18-Year-Old Self." The Independent*, October 22, 2020

Peretz, Evgenia. *Something About Sofia. Vanity Fair*, September 2006

Pillet, Line. *Lost in Translation Behind the Scenes. Nowness*, September 15, 2020

Sharf, Zack. *Lost in Translation, 15 Years Later: Sofia Coppola on Ending the Films on Her Terms and the Year it Took to Cast Bill Murray. IndieWire*, August 27, 2018

Thompson, Anne. *Tokyo Story. Filmmaker Magazine*, Fall 2003

Thomson, David. *The New Biographical Dictionary of Film*. Alfred A. Knopf Inc, 2002

Unattributed. *Let's Get Lost: Translation Talk with Sofia Coppola and Ross Katz*. Focus Features, 2003

CHAPTER 12 – FOUNTAINS OF YOUTH

Coppola, Eleanor. *Notes on a Life*. Nan A. Telese, 2008

Coppola, Francis Ford, Foreword, & Eliade, Mircea. *Youth Without Youth*. University of Chicago, 2007

Dunst, Kirsten & Schwartzman, Jason. *Jason + Kirsten Forever. Nylon Magazine*, October 2006

LoBrutto, Vincent & Morrison, Harriet R.. *The Coppolas: A Family Business*. Praeger, 2012

O'Hagan, Sean. *Sofia Coppola. The Guardian*, October 8, 2006

Peretz, Evgenia. *Something About Sofia. Vanity Fair*, September 2006

Poirier, Agnes. *An Empty Hall of Mirrors. Libération, via The Guardian,* May 27, 2006

Romney, Jonathan. *Marie Antoinette. The Independent*, April 1, 2009

Simon, Alex. *Francis Ford Coppola Interview. The Hollywood Interview*, January 7, 2008

Stevens, Dana. *Youth Without Youth. Slate*, December 14, 2007

Unattributed. *Kirsten Dunst Interview. World Entertainment News Network*, October 2, 2006

CHAPTER 13 – INSIDE STORIES

Barcella, Laura. *Roman Coppola. The Travel Almanac*, April 25, 2013

The Bling Ring DVD. Studio Canal, October 28, 2013

Brody, Richard. *A Place For Somewhere. The New Yorker*, December 15, 2010

Collin, Robbie. *Sofia Coppola Interview: The Beguiled, Slavery, and How Her Little Mermaid Got Lost at Sea. The Telegraph*, July 8, 2017

Coyle, Jake. *The Bling Ring at Cannes Film Festival 2013: Sofia Coppola's Movie About Celebrity Starring Emma Watson Opens. The Independent*, May 17, 2013

Ebert, Roger. *Lone Wolf of the Chateau*. *Chicago Sun-Times*, December 21, 2010

Galloway, Stephen. *Sofia Coppola: The Trials, Tears and Talent*. *The Hollywood Reporter*, May 8, 2013

Gilbey, Ryan. *Sofia Coppola on The Bling Ring: "What These Kids Did Took Ingenuity."* *The Telegraph*, July 4, 2013

Hills, Aaron. *The Conversation*. *LA Weekly*, June 5, 2009

Johnston, Shelia. *Francis Ford Coppola Interview*. *The Telegraph*, June 13, 2010

Kohn, Eric. *Sofia Coppola: How She Survived The Beguiled Backlash, Why She Won't Do TV, and Why Her Dad is Over Film*. *IndieWire*, November 27, 2017

LaSalle, Mike. *Tetro a Major New Step for "New" Coppola*. *San Francisco Chronicle*, February 9, 2012

LoBrutto, Vincent & Morrison, Harriet R.. *The Coppolas: A Family Business*. Praeger, 2012

Nathan, Ian. *The Less Expensive a Film is, the More Ambitious it Can Be....* *Empire*, June 2009

Powers, John. *Absolute Powers: Ten Stolen Thoughts on The Bling Ring*. *Vogue*, June 13, 2013

Uhlich, Keith. *Tetro*. *Time Out New York*, June 11, 2009

Unattributed. *The Beguiled Interview with Sofia Coppola, Kirsten Dunst, and Elle Fanning*. *Californiaunpublished.com*, March 12, 2019

Wilner, Norman. *Interview: Francis Ford Coppola*. *Now Magazine*, August 13, 2009

CHAPTER 14 – A FAMILY BUSINESS

Arabian, Alex. *Interview with Robert Schwartzman, Writer & Director of The Unicorn*. *Film Inquiry*, January 31, 2019

Barnard, Linda. *Interview: Sofia Coppola*. *Toronto Star*, January 8, 2011

Coppola, Francis Ford. *Live Cinema and its Techniques*. Liverlight Publishing, 2017

Douglas, Edward. *Interview: A Glimpse Inside the Minds of Jason Schwartzman & Roman Coppola*. *Comingsoon.net*, February 5, 2013

Earnshaw, Helen. *Roman Coppola Exclusive Interview*. *Female First,* October 21, 2013

Harkness, Alistair. *Interview: Gia Coppola on Her Film Palo Alto. The Scotsman*, October 13, 2014

Itzkoff, Dave. *A Man and His Bad Dreams: Coppola Turns a Nightmare into a New Movie. The New York Times*, November 5, 2010

LoBrutto, Vincent & Morrison, Harriet R.. *The Coppolas: A Family Business*. Praeger, 2012

Lodge, Guy. *Sofia Coppola: "I Never Felt I Had to Fit into the Majority View." The Guardian*, July 2, 2017

Nika, Colleen. *Gia Coppola's Suburban Fantasy. Dazed*, October 17, 2014

Steinmetz, Kary. *This is what it is Like to Be the Newest Coppola Director. Time*, May 9, 2014

Tabrys, Jason. *Interview: Roman Coppola on Working with Charlie Sheen, the Family Legacy, and a Glimpse Inside the Mind of Charles Swann III. Screen Invasion*, October 2, 2013

Utichi, Joe. *Eleanor Coppola on the Fundamental Truth of Movie Direction: "It's Never Easy." Deadline*, May 17, 2017

Unattributed. *LA Confidential: Sofia Coppola Interview. The Telegraph*, December 6, 2010

CHAPTER 15 – FATHERS AND DAUGHTERS

Aspden, Peter. *Breakfast with the FT: Francis Ford Coppola. Financial Times*, February 13, 2015

Bell, Keaton. *Sofia Coppola on Dressing Her Characters, Working with Her Husband, And Why We Need a Love Letter to New York Right Now. Vogue*, October 31, 2020

Biskind, Peter. *Easy Riders, Raging Bulls: How the Sex-Drugs-And-Rock'n'Roll Generation Saved Hollywood*. Bloomsbury, 1998

Brody, Richard. *On The Rocks, Reviewed: Sofia Coppola's Self-questioning Film About a Father's Destructive Dazzle. The New Yorker,* October 22, 2020

Collin, Robbie. *Francis Ford Coppola on The Godfather Part III Backlash: "The Bullets That Went for Sofia Were Meant for Me." The Telegraph*, December 5, 2020

Coppola, Francis Ford. *Live Cinema and its Techniques*. Liverlight Publishing, 2017

Dean, Jonathan. *Sofia Coppola Interview with Her New Film, On the Rocks, the Director Pulls Her Father, Francis Ford Coppola, Into the Frame. The Sunday Times*, September 20, 2020

Fisher, Kieran. *The Frustrating Story Behind Francis Ford Coppola's Megalopolis. Film School Rejects.com*, April 9, 2019

Francis Ford Coppola Q&A, Sundance Kabuki Cinema, San Francisco, 10 August 2012

Hattersley, Giles. *"We Didn't Know We Were Making a Period Movie": Behind the Scenes of On the Rocks with Sofia Coppola. Vogue*, October 11, 2020

Nolfi, Joey. *Meet Your Maker: How Drag, Dads, and NYC Icons Inspired Sofia Coppola. Entertainment Weekly*, October 21, 2020

Nolfi, Joey. *On the Rocks Star Bill Murray Says Bond with Sofia Coppola "Just Keeps Getting Better." Entertainment Weekly*, October 19, 2020

Nolfi, Joey. *Sofia Coppola Reveals Rashida Jones' Sweet Connection to Lost in Translation. Entertainment Weekly*, August 13, 2020

Parker, Ryan. *Francis Ford Coppola Says "Godfather: Part III" Recut Vindicates Film, Daughter Sofia. The Hollywood Reporter*, December 3, 2020

Rubin Harriet. *The Art of Darkness. Fast Company*, September 30, 1998

Schreffler, Laura. *Francis Ford Coppola: Protecting His Legacy During the Pandemic. Haute Living*, October 15, 2020

Travis, Ben. *On the Rocks: Sofia Coppola Took Inspiration From Her Director Dad For Family Comedy — Exclusive image. Empireonline.com*, October 30, 2020

Twixt VOD. Metrodome, 2013

Wallace, Rachel. *Sofia Coppola on Finally Making a New York City Movie With On the Rocks. Architectural Digest*, November 6, 2020

Zacharek, Stephanie. *Bill Murray and Rashida Jones Match Each Other Beat for Beat in Sofia Coppola's Wistful On the Rocks. Time*, October 23, 2020

EPILOGUE

Schreffler, Laura. *Francis Ford Coppola: Protecting His Legacy During the Pandemic. Haute Living*, October 15, 2020